Capital Budgeting and Investment Analysis

Capital Budgeting and Investment Analysis

Wilfred Harding

Larsen & Keller
www.larsen-keller.com

Capital Budgeting and Investment Analysis
Wilfred Harding
ISBN: 978-1-64172-095-3 (Hardback)

Larsen & Keller
Published by Larsen and Keller Education,
5 Penn Plaza,
19th Floor,
New York, NY 10001, USA

Cataloging-in-Publication Data

Capital budgeting and investment analysis / Wilfred Harding.
p. cm.
Includes bibliographical references and index.
ISBN 978-1-64172-095-3
1. Capital budget. 2. Investment analysis. 3. Capital investments--Evaluation. I. Harding, Wilfred.
HG4028.C4 C37 2019
658.152--dc23

Table of Contents

Preface

Capital budgeting is a planning process that determines the worth of long-term investments from a firm's capitalization structure. Some investments that an organization makes can include new and old machinery installation and maintenance, new products and services, new research and development projects, etc. The primary objective of capital budgeting and investment analysis is to enhance the capital benefit and value for shareholders. Some of the methods used in capital budgeting include accounting rate of return, payback period, profitability index, etc. An important technique in capital budgeting is real options valuation or investment analysis, which involves the determination of the present value of options. This textbook elucidates the concepts and innovative models around prospective developments with respect to capital budgeting and investment analysis. The topics included herein are of utmost significance and bound to provide incredible insights to readers. This textbook is an essential guide for business professionals and financial planners, as well as students.

A detailed account of the significant topics covered in this book is provided below:

Chapter 1, Capital budgeting is a process of planning, which determines whether the long term investments of an organization, including machinery installation, replacement, new product initiation, etc. are viable to the company's finances and capitalization structure. This is an introductory chapter, which will provide a brief overview of capital budgeting through an analysis of the fundamental concepts of payback period, capital asset, capital good, cost of capital, etc. **Chapter 2**, Cash flow refers to the virtual or real movement of money. The total cash flow of a company is a combination of the operating cash flow, investment cash flow and financing cash flow. This chapter has been carefully written to provide an easy understanding of the varied facets of cash flow and cash management, such as free cash flow, cash flow statement, valuation using discounted cash flows, burn rate and discounted payback period. **Chapter 3**, Capital budgeting involves allocating resources for capital, expenditures or investments. There is a certain degree of risk associated with investments. Any benefit accrued from an investment is known as a return. High risk investments generally have higher returns if successful. The topics elaborated in this chapter on financial risk, credit risk, liquidity risk, time-weighted return, holding period return, expected return, etc. will help in developing a better understanding of risks and returns in capital budgeting and Investment. **Chapter 4**, Investment is the allotment of money to a particular venture with the expectation of some return in the future. Capital investment may be done through durable goods, real estate, manufacturing processes, product development, etc. All the diverse facts of investment strategy, traditional investments, impact investing, alternative investment and portfolio investment have been carefully analyzed in this chapter. **Chapter 5**, Real options valuation is the application of the techniques of option valuation to capital budgeting decisions. This chapter discusses in detail the central aspects of real options valuation, such as option, expiration, exercise, valuation of options and real options valuation for a better understanding of the subject. **Chapter 6**, The theory of the time value of money proposes that there is a preferential profit in receiving money at the moment of transaction rather than later. It is based on the economic concept of time preference. The fundamental concepts of time value of money such as present value, net present value, adjusted present value and future value have been elaborately discussed in this chapter.

It gives me an immense pleasure to thank our entire team for their efforts. Finally in the end, I would like to thank my family and colleagues who have been a great source of inspiration and support.

Wilfred Harding

1

Introduction to Capital Budgeting

Capital budgeting is a process of planning, which determines whether the long term investments of an organization, including machinery installation, replacement, new product initiation, etc. are viable to the company's finances and capitalization structure. This is an introductory chapter, which will provide a brief overview of capital budgeting through an analysis of the fundamental concepts of payback period, capital asset, capital good, cost of capital, etc.

Capital budgeting is a company's formal process used for evaluating potential expenditures or investments that are significant in amount. It involves the decision to invest the current funds for addition, disposition, modification or replacement of fixed assets. The large expenditures include the purchase of fixed assets like land and building, new equipments, rebuilding or replacing existing equipments, research and development, etc. The large amounts spent for these types of projects are known as capital expenditures. Capital budgeting is a tool for maximizing a company's future profits since most companies are able to manage only a limited number of large projects at any one time.

Capital budgeting usually involves calculation of each project's future accounting profit by period, the cash flow by period, the present value of cash flows after considering time value of money, the number of years it takes for a project's cash flow to pay back the initial cash investment, an assessment of risk, and various other factors.

Capital is the total investment of the company and budgeting is the art of building budgets.

Features of Capital Budgeting

1) It involves high risk
2) Large profits are estimated
3) Long time period between the initial investments and estimated returns

Capital Budgeting Process

A) Project identification and generation

The first step towards capital budgeting is to generate a proposal for investments. There could be various reasons for taking up investments in a business. It could be addition of a new product line or expanding the existing one. It could be a proposal to either increase the production or reduce the costs of outputs.

B) Project Screening and Evaluation:

This step mainly involves selecting all correct criteria's to judge the desirability of a proposal. This has to match the objective of the firm to maximize its market value. The tool of time value of money comes handy in this step.

Also the estimation of the benefits and the costs needs to be done. The total cash inflow and outflow along with the uncertainties and risks associated with the proposal has to be analysed thoroughly and appropriate provisioning has to be done for the same.

C) Project Selection:

There is no such defined method for the selection of a proposal for investments as different businesses have different requirements. That is why, the approval of an investment proposal is done based on the selection criteria and screening process which is defined for every firm keeping in mind the objectives of the investment being undertaken.

Once the proposal has been finalized, the different alternatives for raising or acquiring funds have to be explored by the finance team. This is called preparing the capital budget. The average cost of funds has to be reduced. A detailed procedure for periodical reports and tracking the project for the lifetime needs to be streamlined in the initial phase itself. The final approvals are based on profitability, Economic constituents, viability and market conditions.

D) Implementation:

Money is spent and thus proposal is implemented. The different responsibilities like implementing the proposals, completion of the project within the requisite time period and reduction of cost are allotted. The management then takes up the task of monitoring and containing the implementation of the proposals.

E) Performance review:

The final stage of capital budgeting involves comparison of actual results with the standard ones. The unfavourable results are identified and removing the various difficulties of the projects helps for future selection and execution of the proposals.

Techniques

Capital budgeting consists of various techniques used by managers such as:

1. Payback Period
2. Discounted Payback Period
3. Net Present Value
4. Accounting Rate of Return
5. Internal Rate of Return
6. Profitability Index

All of the above techniques are based on the comparison of cash inflows and outflow of a project however they are substantially different in their approach.

A brief introduction to the above methods is given below:

- Payback period measures the time in which the initial cash flow is returned by the project. Cash flows are not discounted. Lower payback period is preferred.
- Net present value (NPV) is equal to initial cash outflow less sum of discounted cash inflows. Higher NPV is preferred and an investment is only viable if its NPV is positive.
- Accounting rate of return (ARR) is the profitability of the project calculated as projected total net income divided by initial or average investment. Net income is not discounted.
- Internal rate of return (IRR) is the discount rate at which net present value of the project becomes zero. Higher IRR should be preferred.
- Profitability index (PI) is the ratio of present value of future cash flows of a project to initial investment required for the project.

Factors affecting capital budgeting:

1. Availability of Funds
2. Working Capital
3. Structure of Capital
4. Capital Return
5. Management decisions
6. Need of the project
7. Accounting methods
8. Government policy
9. Taxation policy
10. Earnings
11. Lending terms of financial institutions
12. Economic value of the project

Capital Budgeting Decisions

The crux of capital budgeting is profit maximization. There are two ways to it; either increase the revenues or reduce the costs. The increase in revenues can be achieved by expansion of operations by adding a new product line. Reducing costs means representing obsolete return on assets.

Accept/Reject decision: If a proposal is accepted, the firm invests in it and if rejected the firm does not invest. Generally, proposals that yield a rate of return greater than a certain required rate of return or cost of capital are accepted and the others are rejected. All independent projects are accepted.

Independent projects are projects that do not compete with one another in such a way that acceptance gives a fair possibility of acceptance of another.

Mutually exclusive project decision: Mutually exclusive projects compete with other projects in such a way that the acceptance of one will exclude the acceptance of the other projects. Only one may be chosen. Mutually exclusive investment decisions gain importance when more than one proposal is acceptable under the accept/reject decision. The acceptance of the best alternative eliminates the other alternatives.

Capital rationing decision: In a situation where the firm has unlimited funds, capital budgeting becomes a very simple process. In that, independent investment proposals yielding a return greater than some predetermined level are accepted. But actual business has a different picture. They have fixed capital budget with large number of investment proposals competing for it. Capital rationing refers to the situation where the firm has more acceptable investments requiring a greater amount of finance than that is available with the firm. Ranking of the investment project is employed on the basis of some predetermined criterion such as the rate of return. The project with highest return is ranked first and the acceptable projects are ranked thereafter.

Importance of Capital Budgeting in Financial Management

The selection of the most profitable assortment of capital investment can be considered a key function of financial management. In addition, it is the most important area of decision-making for the financial manager. Actions taken by management in this area affect the operations of the firm for many years to come.

The importance of Capital Budgeting can be illustrated well on the following grounds:

(1) Heavy Investment: Almost all the capital expenditure projects involve heavy investment of fund. And these funds are accumulated by the firm from various external and internal sources. So their proper planning is becomes inevitable.

(2) Permanent Commitment of Funds: The funds involved in capital expenditure are not only large but more or less permanently blocked also. Therefore, these are long-term investment decisions. The longer the time, the greater the risks involved. Hence, a careful planning is essential.

(3) Long-term Impact on Profitability: Capital expenditure projects exercise a great impact on the profitability of the firm for a very long time. If properly planned they can increase not only the size, scale and volume and sales but its growth potentiality also.

(4) Complications of Investment Decisions: The long-term investment decisions are more complicated in nature. They entail more risk and uncertainty. Further, the acquisition of capital assets is a continuous process. So the management must be gifted ample prophetic skill to keep into future.

(5) Worth Maximization of Shareholders: Capital budgeting decisions are very important as their impact on the well-being and economic health of the enterprise is far reaching. The main aim of this process is to avoid over investment and under investment in fixed assets.

By selecting the most profitable capital project, the management can maximize the worth of equity shareholders' investment.

Thus, the significance of capital budgeting decisions becomes obvious. The other facts for its significance can be enumerated as follows:

Other Importance of Capital Budgeting

(1) Management loses his flexibility and liquidity of funds in making investment decisions so it must consider each proposal very thoroughly.

(2) Asset expansion is fundamentally related to further sales and future profitability of the firm and assets acquisition decisions are based on capital budgeting.

(3) The funds available of a firm are always in scarcity so they must be properly planned. Modern industrial organizations are characterized by large scale production and intensive mechanization. This all requires balanced and properly planned allocation of scarce capital resources to the most profitable investment proposal Hence, the process of capital budgeting has become very significant nowadays. The financial executive must plan capital budgets often years in advance. Some of the large companies in the U.S.A., for example, have ten year capital budgeting programmes.

Payback Period

Payback method is an investment project that is accepted or rejected on the basis of payback period. Payback period means the period of time that a project requires to recover the money invested in it. It is mostly expressed in years.

Unlike net present value and internal rate of return method, payback method does not take into account the time value of money.

According to payback method, the project that promises a quick recovery of initial investment is considered desirable. If the payback period of a project is shorter than or equal to the management's maximum desired payback period, the project is accepted, otherwise rejected. For example, if a company wants to recoup the cost of a machine within 5 years of purchase, the maximum desired payback period of the company would be 5 years. The purchase of machine would be desirable if it promises a payback period of 5 years or less.

Payback Period Formula – Even Cash Flow

When net annual cash inflow is even (i.e., same cash flow every period), the payback period of the project can be computed by applying the simple formula given below:

$$\text{Payback period} = \frac{\text{Investment required}}{\text{Net annual cash inflow}^*}$$

*The denominator of the formula becomes incremental cash flow if an old asset (e.g., machine or equipment) is replaced by a new one.

Example:

The Delta Company is planning to purchase a machine known as machine X. Machine X would cost $25,000 and would have a useful life of 10 years with zero salvage value. The expected annual cash inflow of the machine is $10,000.

Required: Compute payback period of machine X and conclude whether or not the machine would be purchased if the maximum desired payback period of Delta company is 3 years.

Solution:

Since the annual cash inflow is even in this project, we can simply divide the initial investment by the annual cash inflow to compute the payback period. It is shown below:

Payback period = $25,000/$10,000

= 2.5 years

According to payback period analysis, the purchase of machine X is desirable because its payback period is 2.5 years which is shorter than the maximum payback period of the company.

Example:

Due to increased demand, the management of Rani Beverage Company is considering to purchase a new equipment to increase the production and revenues. The useful life of the equipment is 10 years and the company's maximum desired payback period is 4 years. The inflow and outflow of cash associated with the new equipment is given below:

Initial cost of equipment: $37,500

Annual cash inflows:

Sales: $75,000

Annual cash Outflows:

Cost of ingredients: $45,000

Salaries expenses: $13,500

Maintenance expenses: $1,500

Non-cash expenses:

Depreciation expense: $5,000

Required: Should Rani Beverage Company purchase the new equipment? Use payback method for your answer.

Solution:

Step 1: In order to compute the payback period of the equipment, we need to work out the net annual cash inflow by deducting the total of cash outflow from the total of cash inflow associated with the equipment.

Computation of net annual cash inflow:

$75,000 – ($45,000 + $13,500 + $1,500)

= $15,000

Step 2: Now, the amount of investment required to purchase the equipment would be divided by the amount of net annual cash inflow (computed in step 1) to find the payback period of the equipment.

= $37,500/$15,000

=2.5 years

Depreciation is a non-cash expense and has therefore been ignored while calculating the payback period of the project.

According to payback method, the equipment should be purchased because the payback period of the equipment is 2.5 years which is shorter than the maximum desired payback period of 4 years.

Comparison of two or more alternatives – choosing from several alternative projects

Where funds are limited and several alternative projects are being considered, the project with the shortest payback period is preferred. It is explained with the help of the following example:

Example:

The management of Health Supplement Inc. wants to reduce its labor cost by installing a new machine. Two types of machines are available in the market – machine X and machine Y. Machine X would cost $18,000 where as machine Y would cost $15,000. Both the machines can reduce annual labor cost by $3,000.

Required: Which is the best machine to purchase according to payback method?

Solution:

Payback period of machine X: $18,000/$3,000 = 6 years

Payback period of machine y: $15,000/$3,000 = 5 years

According to payback method, machine Y is more desirable than machine X because it has a shorter payback period than machine X.

Payback method with uneven cash flow:

In the above examples we have assumed that the projects generate even cash inflow but many projects usually generate uneven cash flow. When projects generate inconsistent or uneven cash inflow (different cash inflow in different periods), the simple formula given above cannot be used to compute payback period. In such situations, we need to compute the cumulative cash inflow and then apply the following formula:

$$\text{Payback period} = \frac{\text{Years before}}{\text{full recovery}} + \frac{\text{Unrecovered cost at start of the year}}{\text{Cash flow during the year}}$$

Example:

An investment of $200,000 is expected to generate the following cash inflows in six years:

Year 1: $70,000

Year 2: $60,000

Year 3: $55,000

Year 4: $40,000

Year 5: $30,000

Year 6: $25,000

Required: Compute payback period of the investment. Should the investment be made if management wants to recover the initial investment in 3 years or less?

Solution:

(1). Because the cash inflow is uneven, the payback period formula cannot be used to compute the payback period. We can compute the payback period by computing the cumulative net cash flow as follows:

Initial investment: $200, 000		
Year	**Cash in flow**	**Cumulative cash in flow**
1	$ 70,000	$ 70,000
2	60,000	130,000
3	55,000	185,000
4	40,000	225,000
5	30,000	255,000
6	25,000	280,000

Payback period = 3 + (15,000*/40,000)

= 3 + 0.375

= 3.375 Years

*Unrecovered investment at start of 4th year:

= Initial cost – Cumulative cash inflow at the end of 3rd year

= $200,000 – $185,000

= $15,000

The payback period for this project is 3.375 years which is longer than the maximum desired payback period of the management (3 years). The investment in this project is therefore not desirable.

Advantages and Disadvantages

The payback period is useful from a risk analysis perspective, since it gives a quick picture of the amount of time that the initial investment will be at risk. If you were to analyze a prospective investment using the payback method, you would tend to accept those investments having rapid payback periods and reject those having longer ones. It tends to be more useful in industries where investments become obsolete very quickly, and where a full return of the initial investment is therefore a serious concern. Though the payback method is widely used due to its simplicity, it suffers from the following problems:

1. Asset life span. If an asset's useful life expires immediately after it pays back the initial investment, then there is no opportunity to generate additional cash flows. The payback method does not incorporate any assumption regarding asset life span.
2. Additional cash flows: The concept does not consider the presence of any additional cash flows that may arise from an investment in the periods after full payback has been achieved.
3. Cash flow complexity: The formula is too simplistic to account for the multitude of cash flows that actually arise with a capital investment. For example, cash investments may be required at several stages, such as cash outlays for periodic upgrades. Also, cash outflows may change significantly over time, varying with customer demand and the amount of competition.
4. Profitability: The payback method focuses solely upon the time required to pay back the initial investment; it does not track the ultimate profitability of a project at all. Thus, the method may indicate that a project having a short payback but with no overall profitability is a better investment than a project requiring a long-term payback but having substantial long-term profitability.
5. Time value of money: The method does not take into account the time value of money, where cash generated in later periods is worth less than cash earned in the current period. A variation on the payback period formula, known as the discounted payback formula, eliminates this concern by incorporating the time value of money into the calculation. Other capital budgeting analysis methods that include the time value of money are the net present value method and the internal rate of return.
6. Individual asset orientation: Many fixed asset purchases are designed to improve the efficiency of a single operation, which is completely useless if there is a process bottleneck located downstream from that operation that restricts the ability of the business to generate more output. The payback period formula does not account for the output of the entire system, only a specific operation. Thus, its use is more at the tactical level than at the strategic level.
7. Incorrect averaging: The denominator of the calculation is based on the average cash flows

from the project over several years - but if the forecasted cash flows are mostly in the part of the forecast furthest in the future, the calculation will incorrectly yield a payback period that is too soon.

Capital Asset

A capital asset is an asset that will be useful to your business over a long period of time (usually more than two years) and costs more than your usual day-to-day running costs. A capital asset could be a piece of equipment, or an investment.

Capital assets are also called 'fixed assets'.

Capital assets can be either "tangible" or "intangible", depending on whether you can see and touch them.

Examples of Capital Assets

- A computer for most businesses (tangible)
- A camera for a professional photographer (tangible)
- A patent for a software company (intangible)
- A high-value domain name (intangible)

Capital Assets and Depreciation

The capital asset's value is spread across the time it's going to be used in your business, which is called its "useful life". A proportion of the asset's value is shown as a day-to-day running cost, reducing your business's profit, for each year it'll be useful to the business. This is called "depreciation" for a tangible asset, or "amortisation" for an intangible asset.

There are two types of capital assets:

1. Long Term Capital Asset
2. Short Term Capital Asset

Long Term Capital Asset

"Long term capital asset" means a capital asset held by an assessee for more than 36 months. Long term capital gain arises on transfer of long term capital asset.

Short Term Capital Asset

"Short Term Capital Asset" means a capital asset held by an assessee for not more than 36 months, immediately prior to its date of transfer.

However, in the following cases, an asset, held for not more than 12 months, is treated as short-term capital asset:

- Equity or preference shares in a company listed in recognised stock exchange.
- Securities like debentures, bonds, Government securities, derivatives etc. listed in a recognised stock exchange.
- Units of UTI whether quoted or not.
- Units of an equity oriented fund whether quoted or not.
- Zero coupon bonds whether quoted or not.

Determine Period of Holding

In order to classify an asset as long term capital asset or short term capital asset, we need to determine the period for which the asset is held by the tax-payer before transferring the same.

The general principle applicable for determining the period of holding is to calculate the period from the date the asset is purchased by the tax-payer till the date when the same is transferred/ sold by him. But this general principle cannot be applied under all circumstances. There are few situations, where the method of calculating the period of holding is different.

Following are few such situations along with the method to calculate the period of holding:

1) Shares held in a company in liquidation: The period subsequent to the date on which the company goes in to liquidation shall be excluded.
2) When asset is acquired by will, succession or at the time of partition of H.U.F. or under amalgamation etc.: The period for which the asset was held by the previous owner should be included.
3) Allotment of shares in amalgamated Indian Company against shares held in amalgamating company: The period of holding shall be counted from the date of acquisition of shares in the amalgamating company (and not in the amalgamated company).
4) Allotment of Right Shares: The period of holding shall be counted from the date of allotment of right shares.
5) Right Entitlement: The period of holding shall be calculated from the date of offer to subscribe to shares to the date when such right entitlement is renounced by the person.
6) Bonus Shares: The period of holding shall be counted from the date of allotment of bonus shares.
7) Allotment of shares by the resulting company in the scheme of demerger: The period of holding of such shares shall be counted from the date of acquisition of shares in the demerged company (and not in the resulting company).
8) Flat in a co-operative society: The period of holding shall be counted from the date of allotment of shares in the society.

9) Sweat Equity shares allotted by the employer: The period of holding shall be counted from the date of allotment of such equity shares.

10) Shares/securities purchased through stock exchanges: The period will commence from the date of purchase by broker on behalf of the investor.

11) Shares/securities transferred through stock exchange: The period of holding shall be counted up to the date of broker's note provided such transactions are followed by delivery of shares and transfer deeds.

12) Shares/ securities purchased/ transferred directly between parties and not through stock exchanges: The period shall be counted up to the date of contract of sale as declared by parties provided it is followed up by actual delivery of shares and transfer deeds.

13) Transfer of a security by a depository (i.e. demat account): The period of holding shall be determined on the basis of first–in-first–out method (FIFO method).

Points to Ponder:

1) Shares in a company entitling right of occupancy in a flat

Where the assessee held certain shares in a company by virtue of which a right of occupancy in a flat is conferred on him, these shares cannot be treated as shares and securities mentioned above and hence where such shares are sold after being held for a period less than 36 months, gain arising therefrom is to be treated as short-term capital gain.

2) Transfer of depreciable assets

Any capital gain arising on transfer of depreciable asset is treated as short-term capital gain irrespective of period of holding.

3) Transfer of land after construction of building

Land is an independent and identifiable capital asset and it continues to remain so even after construction of the building. Hence period of holding for land would be separately determined from that of building, if the building was constructed after few years of acquisition of the land.

4) Conversion of stock-in-trade in to capital asset

When stock-in-trade is converted in to capital asset, and then the capital asset is transferred, the holding period of such asset would commence from the date when stock-in-trade was acquired by the assessee and not from the date when the same was converted in to capital asset.

5) Allotment of flat/plot by a housing board

In the case of allotment of a flat/plot by a housing board, the period of allotment will be determined from the date of allotment and not from the date when possession is given.

Reason for Division of Capital Assets

The tax incidence under the head "Capital Gains" depends upon whether the capital gain is short-term or long-term. If the asset transferred is short-term, capital gain would be short-term capital gain. Conversely, if the asset transferred is long-term, the capital gain would be long-term capital gain.

Long term capital gain is generally taxable at a lower rate. The benefit of indexation is also available for calculating long-term capital gain.

Capital Good

Capital goods are tangible assets that a business uses to produce goods or services that are used as inputs for other businesses to produce consumer goods. Said another way, capital goods are tangible assets, such as buildings, machinery, equipment, vehicles and tools that one organization uses to produce goods or services as an input to produce consumer goods and goods for other businesses. Manufacturers of automobiles, aircraft, and machinery fall within the capital goods sector because their products are used by companies involved in manufacturing, shipping and providing other services.

Capital good qualify as tangible assets that an organization uses to produce goods or services such as office buildings, equipment and machinery. Consumer goods are the end result of this production process. The industrials sector of the economy includes capital-goods-producing businesses such as Boeing, Caterpillar and Lockheed Martin.

Capital goods that a business does not consume within a single year of production cannot be entirely deducted as business expenses for the year of their purchase. Instead, they must be depreciated over the course of their useful lives, with the business taking partial tax deductions spread over the years that the capital goods are in use. This is done through use of such accounting techniques as depreciation, amortization and depletion.

Capital Goods as Tax Deductions

Depreciation accounts for the annual loss of the tangible asset's value during the course of its useful life. Amortization aligns an asset's annual expense with the revenue it generates throughout the course of its useful life. Depletion is an accounting technique utilized for spreading out the cost of natural resources as they are used by a business.

Depletion can be calculated by using either cost depletion or percentage depletion. For deducting the cost of standing timber, taxpayers must use the cost depletion technique, based on the total number of recoverable units and the number of units sold during the tax year. Percentage depletion assesses the cost of the materials as a percentage of the company's gross income during a given year.

Types of Capital Goods

Capital goods are not necessarily fixed assets, such as machinery and manufacturing equipment. The industrial electronics industry produces a wide variety of devices which are capital goods. These range from small wire harness assemblies to air purifying respirators and high-resolution digital imaging systems.

Capital goods are also produced for service businesses. Hair clippers used by hair stylists, paint used by painters, and musical instruments played by musicians are among the many types of capital goods purchased by service providers.

Core capital goods are a class of capital goods which excludes aircraft and goods produced for the Defence Department, such as automatic rifles and military uniforms. The Census Bureau's monthly Advance Report on Durable Goods Orders includes data on purchases of core capital goods, also known as core capex. This information is closely followed as a forward-looking indicator on the degree to which businesses plan to expand. Durable goods are products with an expected useful life of at least three years.

Examples of Capital Goods

The following are illustrative examples of a capital good.

Vehicles

Vehicles owned by a business are a capital good. Vehicles owned by an individual for their personal use are considered a durable consumer good.

Production Technology

Machines such as industrial robots, kitchen appliances in a restaurant or farm equipment that are directly used in production of products and services.

Computing Technology

Computing equipment and infrastructure such as networking equipment.

Electronics

Electronics such as a camera used by a film crew.

Software

Software used by businesses such as accounting software.

Power Technology

Power technology such as solar panels and batteries.

Infrastructure

Infrastructure such as private roads. Land is considered a separate factor of production.

Facilities

Facilities such as office buildings and data centres.

Furniture and Fixtures

Furniture and office equipment used by a business.

Tools

Tools such as construction tools or a kitchen utensils in a restaurant.

Instruments

Instruments such as a musical instrument used by a musician.

Financial Capital

Financial capital is the money, credit, and other forms of funding that build wealth. Individuals use it to invest. They can make a down payment on a home, or create a portfolio for retirement.

It should not be confused with the capital that's one of the four factors of production that drive supply. That's capital goods, such as machinery, equipment, and tools. The other three factors are natural resources (the raw materials), labour (the number of employees), and entrepreneurship (the drive to profit from innovation). A market economy automatically provides these components of supply to meet demand from consumers.

Sometimes financial capital is called the fifth factor of production. That's not accurate. It facilitates production by providing income to the owners of production. But it is not itself a factor of production.

In business accounting, capital is how companies invest in their businesses. That means they can't use it now to give themselves raises, increase dividends, or lower prices. They must use it to produce greater gains in the future. A business uses capital to transform itself into something more profitable.

Types of Financial Capital

Equity Capital

Otherwise known as "net worth" or "book value", this figure represents assets minus liabilities. There are some businesses that are funded entirely with equity capital, which is cash invested by the shareholders or owners into the company that has no offsetting liabilities.

Although it is the favoured form of capital for most businesses because they don't have to pay it back, it can be extraordinarily expensive. In addition, it could require massive amounts of work to grow their enterprises if they are funded this way. Microsoft is an example of such an operation because it generates high enough returns to justify a pure equity capital structure.

Debt Capital

This type of capital is infused into a business with the understanding that it must be paid back at a predetermined date. In the meantime, the owner of the capital (typically a bank, bondholders, or a wealthy individual), agree to accept interest in exchange for you using their money. Think of interest expense as the cost of "renting" the capital to expand your business; it is often known as the cost of capital.

For many young businesses, debt can be the easiest way to expand because it is relatively easy to access and is understood by the average American worker thanks to widespread home ownership and the community-based nature of banks.

The profits for the owners is the difference between the return on capital and the cost of capital; for example, if you borrow $100,000 and pay 10% interest yet earn 15% after taxes, the profit of 5%, or $5,000, would not have existed without the debt capital infused into the business.

Specialty Capital

This is the gold standard, and something you would do well to find. There are a few sources of capital that have almost no economic cost and can take the limits off of growth. They include things such as a negative cash conversion cycle (vendor financing), insurance float, etc. Let me explain.

Negative cash conversion (vendor financing): Imagine you own a retail store. To expand your business, you need $1 million in capital to open a new location. Most of the capital will be spent on buying or renting the property, product displays, cash registers, and equipment, purchasing inventory to stock your shelves, and hiring new employees. You wait and hope that one day customers come in and pay you. In the meantime, you have capital (either debt or equity capital) tied up in the business in the form of inventory. Now, imagine if you could get your customers to pay you before you had to pay for your merchandise. This would allow you to carry far more merchandise than your capitalization structure would otherwise allow. AutoZone is a great example; it has convinced its vendors to put their products on its shelves and retain ownership until the moment a customer walks up to the front of one of AutoZone's stores and pays for the goods. At that precise second, the vendor sells it to AutoZone which in turn sells it to the customer. This allows them to expand far more rapidly and return more money to the owners of the business in the form of share repurchases (cash dividends would also be an option) because they don't have to tie up hundreds of millions of dollars in inventory. In the meantime, the increased cash in the business as a result of more favorable vendor terms and/or getting your customers to pay you sooner allows you to generate more income than your equity or debt alone would permit. Typically, vendor financing can be measured in part by looking at the percentage of inventories to accounts payable (the higher the percentage, the better), and analysing the cash conversion cycle; the more days "negative", the better. Dell Computer was famous for its nearly two or three-week negative cash conversion cycle which allowed it to grow from a college dorm room to the largest computer company in the world with little or no debt in less than a single generation. Sam Walton built Wal-Mart on this principle and look where that got him - the Walton family is worth over $100 billion.

Float: Insurance companies that collect money and can generate income by investing the funds before paying them out to policyholders when a car is damaged, when a home is destroyed by a tornado, or when a business is flooded are in a very good place. As Buffett describes it, float is money that a company holds but does not own. It has all of the benefits of debt but none of the drawbacks; the most important consideration is the cost of capital – that is, how much money it costs the owners of a business to generate float. In exceptional cases, the cost can actually be negative; that is, you are paid to invest other people's money plus you get to keep the income from the investments. Other businesses can develop forms of float but it can be very difficult.

Sweat Equity

There is also a form of capital known as sweat equity, which is when an owner bootstraps operations by putting in long hours at a low rate of pay per hour. This makes up for the lack of capital necessary to hire sufficient employees to do the job well and let them work an ordinary forty-hour workweek.

Although it is largely intangible and does not count as financial capital, it can be estimated as the cost of payroll saved as a result of excess hours worked by the owners. The hope is that the business will grow fast enough to compensate the owner for the low-pay, long-hour sweat equity he or she infused into the enterprise.

Working Capital

Working capital is basically an indicator of the short-term financial position of an organization and is also a measure of its overall efficiency. Working capital is obtained by subtracting the current liabilities from the current assets. This ratio indicates whether the company possesses sufficient assets to cover its short-term debt.

Working capital indicates the liquidity levels of companies for managing day-to-day expenses and covers inventory, cash, accounts payable, accounts receivable and short-term debt that is due. Working capital is derived from several company operations such as debt and inventory management, supplier payments and collection of revenues.

Working Capital Formula

The formula for working capital is the following:

Working Capital = Current Assets - Current Liabilities

The working capital ratio is the indicator of whether ample short-term assets are possessed by an organization for taking care of short-term debt. A ratio lower than 1 is an indicator of negative working capital while positive/sufficient working capital is usually indicated by a ratio between 1.2 and 2.0. Anything exceeding 2 usually indicates there are excess assets that are not being invested by the company and therefore represents missed opportunity.

Sources of Working Capital

The sources for working capital can either be long term, short term or even spontaneous. Spontaneous working capital are majorly derived from trade credit including notes payable and bills payable while short term working capital sources include dividend or tax provisions, cash credit, public deposits, trade deposits, short-term loans, bills discounting, inter-corporate loans and also commercial paper.

For the long-term, working capital sources include long-term loans, provision for depreciation, retained profits, debentures and share capital. These are major working capital sources for organizations based on their requirements.

Types of Working Capital

There are several types of working capital based on the balance sheet or operating cycle view. The balance sheet view classifies working capital into net (current liabilities subtracted from current assets featuring in the company's balance sheet) and gross working capital (current assets in the balance sheet).

On the other hand, operating cycle view classifies working capital into temporary (difference between net working capital & permanent working capital) and permanent (fixed assets) working capital. Temporary working capital can be further broken down into reserve and regular working capital as well. These are the types of working capital depending on the view that is chosen.

Variable and Constant Capital

Constant capital is the value of goods and materials required to produce a commodity, while variable capital is the wages paid for the production of a commodity. Marx introduced this distinction because it is only labour-power which creates new value.

The constant capital includes that proportion of capital invested in the materials and components purchased but then embodied in the product when it is sold, as well as the materials, tools, machinery etc., which are used up, bit by bit in the course of production. If a million dollar machine, for example, is used in the production of 10,000 cars in the course of a year, before being worn out and replaced, then effectively every car has $100 worth of that machine in it. Thus constant capital includes both fixed and unit costs. The point is that no matter how much materials and components and machines are bought and sold, they do not create any new value. Whether they are stored in a warehouse before being sold, or used in factory, it makes no difference. Whatever value they had when a capitalist buys them for use in production, they still have the same value afterwards.

Variable capital means that proportion of capital which is invested in wages, in the purchase of labour-power. Marx called this capital "variable" because it is this proportion of capital which, if it is used wisely may produce a new, surplus value in the course of the labour process, over and above the "necessary labour time" which the worker needs to live and is paid in the form of wages. This investment is the only one which creates new value, because the worker is able to produce more than he needs in order to live.

So for example, let us suppose a worker earns $100 and consumes $1000 worth of materials and components to produce a product which is sold for $1300. This value could be represented as constant capital ($1000) + variable capital ($100) + surplus value ($200). That $200 of surplus value was added to the product solely by the activity of the worker. That is, of the capitalist's investment of $1100, only the variable capital, $100, expanded.

Marx represented this relation symbolically:

$$c + v \rightarrow c + v + s$$

The ratio of constant to variable capital, (c/v), he called the "organic composition of capital"; the ratio of surplus value to wages, (s/v), he called the rate of surplus value, or the rate of exploitation of labour, and s/(c + v) the rate of profit.

The contradiction brought out by this analysis is this. Every capitalist works might and main to reduce the wages bill, and turn over as much material as he can, investing in expensive machinery and increasing c to cut labour costs, v; this produces a general increase in the "organic composition of capital", c/v. However, since it is only the variable capital that produces profit, the result is a falling rate of profit.

Capital Accumulation

Capital accumulation is the process of acquiring additional capital stock which is used in the productive process. Capital accumulation can involve:

1. Investment in physical fixed capital (e.g. factories, machines);
2. Portfolio investment – purchase of bonds, shares and cryptocurrencies;
3. Investment in assets, such as housing.

Measuring Capital Accumulation

Capital accumulation can be calculated by measuring:

- Change in wealth/value of assets in an economy.
- Level of gross fixed capital formation – depreciation.

Ways of Capital Accumulation

1. Profit from business can be reinvested.
2. Foreign direct investment (important for developing economies with low capital basis).
3. Technological innovation which increases the productivity of capital.
4. Increase in human capital – e.g. better educated workforce enables an increase in production possibility frontier.
5. Discovering new sources of raw materials, e.g. oil reserves.
6. Increased level of savings. In the Harod-Domar model of economic growth, a higher proportion of income that is saved – enables more investment and higher rates of economic growth.

Corporate Capital Accumulation

Companies seek to accumulate capital primarily through profits from products and services they produce. A company's capital structure and capital health can be identified from their financial statements. Generally, the balance sheet provides a snapshot of a company's capital expressed as equity which represents a company's assets minus its liabilities. The cash flow statement also shows components of capital accumulation. The cash flow statement is usually broken down into three parts: cash flows from operating activities, investing activities and from financing activities. All three aspects of the cash flow statement can show capital accumulation from positive cash flows. The income statement also provides a comprehensive report on profits which can contribute to capital accumulation.

Investment Capital Accumulation

Investment capital accumulation occurs from regular savings, capital gains, interest or other positive capital flows that result from an investment. Investment capital accumulation can be achieved through various types of investments. Some common investments that offer potential for capital gains and capital accumulation include publicly traded stocks, bonds, exchange-traded funds and mutual funds. Regular contributions to these investments can help to provide for greater capital accumulation.

Various types of investors seek capital gains and greater capital accumulation. To generate greater capital accumulation an individual investor can acquire more shares of a particular stock or mutual fund over an extended period of time. Investors can manage capital in various types of accounts for comprehensive capital accumulation. 401k plans, brokerage accounts, money market accounts, savings accounts and checking accounts can all be used for capital accumulation.

Institutional investors manage portfolios with the goal of capital accumulation. They deploy an investment strategy or manage an investment program to accumulate capital for investors. They may choose to increase their holdings in a targeted position to accumulate greater capital. Retirement funds and pension funds rely on capital accumulation over a period of time to provide for income in retirement.

Capital Accumulation and Inequality

Capital accumulation often occurs from the profit or dividends from previous investment. Therefore capital accumulation can become a self-reinforcing cycle – with the wealthy able to increase their capital assets, enabling more profit/rent/dividends to finance further capital accumulation.

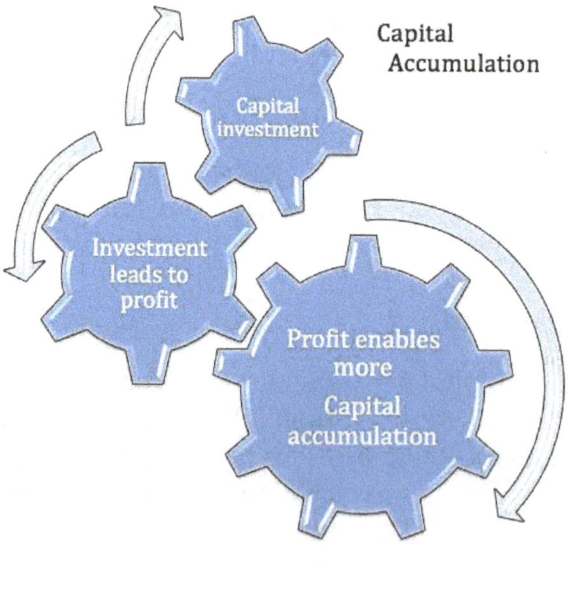

Capital involves man-made made equipment that is used to make other goods such as machines and factories.

Capital accumulation will need to exceed the amount of capital necessary to overcome depreciation. i.e. some capital wears out, so capital investment is necessary to overcome this. Capital accumulation involves additional purchases of capital.

Marxist views of Capital Accumulation

The Marxist view of capital accumulation concentrates on how profit from business is reinvested in more capital. This enables capitalist to increase their wealth and dominance of society. However, Marx also believed that capitalism was prone to crisis as there would be times when profit was greater than projects capitalist could invest in.

The modern-day economist Thomas Piketty argues that, unchecked, the process of capital accumulation can lead to rising inequality in society. Piketty notes capital doesn't have to be invested in business but can be invested in other assets, such as housing, shares, bonds.

As a general rule, Picketty argues wealth grows faster than economic output. He uses expression $r > g$ (where r is the rate of return to wealth and g is the economic growth rate. This is mainly due to the process of capital accumulation and the fact assets give a rate of return which can be re-invested.

Ricardo and Capital Accumulation

Ricardo's model of economic growth placed a high value on capital accumulation. To Ricardo, capital accumulation came from profit and the willingness and ability of owners to invest in more capital.

Capital Accumulation and Diminishing Returns

Growth models based on Solow's models argue that increasing the capital stock can soon lead to diminishing returns. They argue that economic growth is fundamentally determined by population growth and technological innovation.

Capital Accumulation and Endogenous Growth Models

Endogenous growth models hold that capital accumulation can increase the long run trend rate of economic growth. However, to permit capital accumulation it is necessary to increase the savings ratios.

Capital Accumulation Plans

Capital accumulation is often suggested as a means for developing countries to increase their long term growth rates. To increase capital accumulation it is necessary to:

- Increase savings ratios
- Maintain good banking system and system of loans.

- Avoid corruption
- Good infrastructure to make investment more worthwhile

Capital Expenditure

A capital expenditure (CAPEX) is an expense that a company makes towards the purchase of new equipment or the improvement of its long-term assets, namely property, plant, and equipment.

CAPEX usually pertains to maintenance expenditures that seek to extend the useful life of the company's assets through repair or upgrade or to expansion expenditures that the company makes when seeking expansion of its product line, entry in a new market or acquisition of a new business.

Long-term assets are a company's land, buildings, machinery, vehicles, furniture, computers, office equipment, software as well as patents, trademarks, and licenses. Companies report CAPEX on the cash flow statement and are amortized over the life of the related asset because, usually, the asset's useful life is longer than the taxable year and, therefore, CAPEX cannot be reported as an expense.

Example

Alexander works as an accountant in a manufacturing company. The company has made several capital expenditures over the past three years, and Alexander wants to construct a straight-line depreciation schedule to amortize CAPEX accordingly. In 2014, the company spent $500,000 for equipment upgrade and $350,000 for a software upgrade. In 2015, it acquired new vehicles for $200,000 and spent $800,000 for new machinery to increase capacity. On February 2016, the company acquired a new building for $1.35 million.

Capital Expenditure (CAPEX) Example

Straight-Line Depreciation	20%	5 Years							
			2014	**2015**	**2016**	**2017**	**2018**	**2019**	**2020**
Opening Balance	**Expense**	$	850	1,000	1,350				
CapEx									
2014	Equiment upgrade	500	(100)	(100)	(100)	(100)	(100)		
2014	Software upgrade	350	(70)	(70)	(70)	(70)	(70)		
2015	New machinery	800		(160)	(160)	(160)	(160)	(160)	
2015	New vehicles	200		(40)	(40)	(40)	(40)	(40)	
2016	New building	1,350			(270)	(270)	(270)	(270)	(270)
Total Depreciation			-170	-370	-640	-640	-640	-470	-270
Closing Balance			**680**	**630**	**710**	**(640)**	**(640)**	**(470)**	**(270)**

Alexander records the expenses that the company has made between 2014 and 2016 and uses the straight-line depreciation method to assess the impact of the depreciation expenses on the company's net income.

Capital expenditures affect the income statement indirectly. For example, in the above case, the net income will be lowered by the depreciation amount over the useful life of each asset. Yet, as the investment in the new machinery is likely to increase the company's sales, the net income may actually increase, even after deducting depreciation. Alternatively, the utility expense may rise, thereby lowering the net income. So, at the end of the day, CAPEX affects net income in different ways.

Calculating Capital Expenditures

When analysing the financial statements of a third party, it may be necessary to calculate the entity's capital expenditures. This is needed to see if the organization is spending a sufficient amount on fixed assets to maintain its operations. The best approach to calculating capital expenditures is the capital expenditure formula. The steps are:

- Obtain the financial statements of the target company as of the end of the year for the past two years.
- Subtract the net amount of fixed assets listed on the financial statements for the preceding year from the net amount of fixed assets listed for the year just ended. The result is the net change in fixed assets. However, it must be adjusted further with these additional steps:
    - Strip out of the calculation all intangible assets. We are assuming that you are only interested in the expenditures for tangible assets, so intangibles are not needed. Besides, most intangible assets were obtained through acquisitions, not through a capital expenditure program.
    - Strip out all assets obtained through acquisitions during the reporting period. This information should be listed in the notes accompanying the financial statements.
- Subtract the total amount of accumulated depreciation listed on the financial statements for the preceding year from the total amount of accumulated depreciation listed for the year just ended. The result is the total amount of depreciation for the year just ended. An alternative source is the depreciation expense listed in the income statement for the year just ended. This figure should not include any amortization, nor any depreciation associated with acquired assets.
- Add the total depreciation for the year to the change in the net amount of fixed assets. This is the total amount that the company spent on capital expenditures during the measurement period.

Alternatively, you may be interested in the amount that a company is expending on software development projects. This can be a critical item, if the expenditure is being capitalized instead of being charged to expense as incurred. This information may be disclosed within the fixed assets line item on the balance sheet, or in the accompanying footnotes. In either case, compare the information for the last two years to determine the change in expenditures on capitalized software projects.

An additional question involving capital expenditure analysis is to determine how many of the expenditures are related to the replacement of existing assets, versus expenditures targeted at the expansion of the business. There are three ways to estimate this information:

- Track capital expenditures on a trend line. If expenditures are relatively flat, the bulk of all expenditures are probably of the maintenance variety.

- Compare capital expenditures to sales. There is not a direct relationship with capital expenditures and sales. However, if you compare the two over multiple years, and the proportion of expenditures to sales is rising, it is likely that the company is investing in more than just maintenance capital expenditures.
- Match capital expenditures to business units. If the target company is experiencing rapid growth in a particular business unit, look in the footnotes for the amount of capital expenditures associated with that business unit.

Cost of Capital

Cost of capital is the minimum rate of return that a business must earn before generating value. Before a business can turn a profit, it must at least generate sufficient income to cover the cost of the capital it uses to fund its operations. Cost of capital consists of both the cost of debt and the cost of equity used for financing a business. A company's cost of capital depends to a large extent on the type of financing the company chooses to rely on. The company may rely solely on equity or debt, or use a combination of the two.

The choice of financing makes the cost of capital a crucial variable for every company, as it will determine the company's capital structure. Companies look for the optimal mix of financing that provides adequate funding and that minimizes the cost of capital.

In addition, investors use cost of capital as one of the financial metrics they consider in evaluating companies as potential investments. The cost of capital figure is also important because it is used as the discount rate for the company's free cash flows in the DCF analysis model.

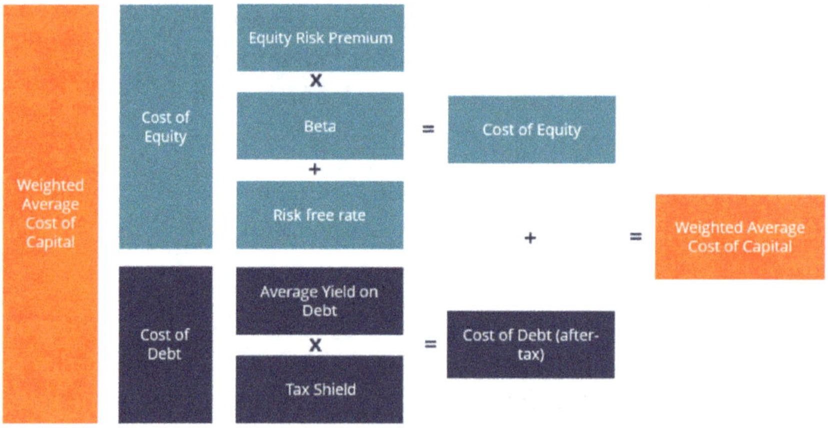

Cost of capital depends upon:

a) Demand and supply of capital,

b) Expected rate of inflation,

c) Various risk involved, and

d) Debt-equity ratio of the firm etc.

Significance of Cost of Capital

The concept of cost of capital plays a vital role in decision-making process of financial management. The financial leverage, capital structure, dividend policy, working capital management, financial decision, appraisal of financial performance of top management etc. are greatly influenced by the cost of capital.

The significance or importance of cost of capital may be stated in the following ways:

1. Maximisation of the Value of the Firm:

For the purpose of maximisation of value of the firm, a firm tries to minimise the average cost of capital. There should be judicious mix of debt and equity in the capital structure of a firm so that the business does not to bear undue financial risk.

2. Capital Budgeting Decisions:

Proper estimate of cost of capital is important for a firm in taking capital budgeting decisions. Generally cost of capital is the discount rate used in evaluating the desirability of the investment project. In the internal rate of return method, the project will be accepted if it has a rate of return greater than the cost of capital.

In calculating the net present value of the expected future cash flows from the project, the cost of capital is used as the rate of discounting. Therefore, cost of capital acts as a standard for allocating the firm's investible funds in the most optimum manner. For this reason, cost of capital is also referred to as cut-off rate, target rate, hurdle rate, minimum required rate of return etc.

3. Decisions Regarding Leasing:

Estimation of cost of capital is necessary in taking leasing decisions of business concern.

4. Management of Working Capital:

In management of working capital the cost of capital may be used to calculate the cost of carrying investment in receivables and to evaluate alternative policies regarding receivables. It is also used in inventory management also.

5. Dividend Decisions:

Cost of capital is significant factor in taking dividend decisions. The dividend policy of a firm should be formulated according to the nature of the firm— whether it is a growth firm, normal firm or declining firm. However, the nature of the firm is determined by comparing the internal rate of return (r) and the cost of capital (k) i.e., $r > k$, $r = k$, or $r < k$ which indicate growth firm, normal firm and decline firm, respectively.

6. Determination of Capital Structure:

Cost of capital influences the capital structure of a firm. In designing optimum capital structure that is the proportion of debt and equity, due importance is given to the overall or weighted average cost of capital of the firm. The objective of the firm should be to choose such a mix of debt and equity so that the overall cost of capital is minimised.

7. Evaluation of Financial Performance:

The concept of cost of capital can be used to evaluate the financial performance of top management. This can be done by comparing the actual profitability of the investment project undertaken by the firm with the overall cost of capital.

Measurement of Cost of Capital

Cost of capital is measured for different sources of capital structure of a firm. It includes cost of debenture, cost of loan capital, cost of equity share capital, cost of preference share capital, cost of retained earnings etc.

The measurement of cost of capital of different sources of capital structure is discussed:

A. Cost of Debentures:

The capital structure of a firm normally includes the debt capital. Debt may be in the form of debentures bonds, term loans from financial institutions and banks etc. The amount of interest payable for issuing debenture is considered to be the cost of debenture or debt capital (Kd). Cost of debt capital is much cheaper than the cost of capital raised from other sources, because interest paid on debt capital is tax deductible.

The cost of debenture is calculated in the following ways

(i) When the debentures are issued and redeemable at par: $K_d = r(1-t)$

where K_d = Cost of debenture

r = Fixed interest rate

t = Tax rate

(ii) When the debentures are issued at a premium or discount but redeemable at par

$$K_d = I/NP(1-t)$$

where, K_d = Cost of debenture

I = Annual interest payment

t = Tax rate

Np = Net proceeds from the issue of debenture.

(iii) When the debentures are redeemable at a premium or discount and are redeemable after 'n' period:

$$K_d = I(1-t) + 1/N(R_v - NP) / ½(R_V - NP)$$

where K_d = Cost of debenture .

I = Annual interest payment

t = Tax rate

NP = Net proceeds from the issue of debentures

Ry = Redeemable value of debenture at the time of maturity

Example:

(a) A company issues Rs. 1,00,000, 15% Debentures of Rs. 100 each. The company is in 40% tax bracket. You are required to compute the cost of debt after tax, if debentures are issued at (i) Par, (ii) 10% discount, and (iii) 10% premium.

(b) If brokerage is paid at 5%, what will be the cost of debentures if issue is at par?

Solution:

(a) We know, Cost of Debenture $K_d = \frac{I}{NP}(1-t)$

(i) Issued at per: $K_d = \frac{Rs.\,15,000}{Rs.\,1,00,000}(1-0.4) = 0.09$ or 9%.

(ii) Issued at discount of 10%

$$K_d = \frac{Rs.\,15,000}{Rs.\,90,000}(1-0.4) = 0.10 \text{ or } 10\%.$$

(iii) Issued at 10% premium

$$K_d = \frac{Rs.\,15,000}{Rs.\,1,10,000}(1-0.4) = 0.0818 \text{ or } 8.18\%.$$

(b) If brokerage is paid @5% and debentures are issued at par

$$K_d = \frac{Rs.\,15,000}{Rs.\,95,000\ (i.e., Rs.\,1,00,000 - Rs.\,5,000)}(1-0.4) = 0.0947 \text{ or } 9.47\%.$$

B. Cost of Preference Share Capital:

For preference shares, the dividend rate can be considered as its cost, since it is this amount which the company wants to pay against the preference shares. Like debentures, the issue expenses or the discount/premium on issue/redemption are also to be taken into account.

(i) The cost of preference shares (K_p) = D_p/NP

Where, D_p = Preference dividend per share

NP = Net proceeds from the issue of preference shares.

(ii) If the preference shares are redeemable after a period of 'n', the cost of preference shares (K_p) will be:

$$K_P = \frac{D_P + \frac{1}{n}(R_V - NP)}{\frac{1}{2}(R_V + NP)}$$

where NP = Net proceeds from the issue of preference shares

R_V = Net amount required for redemption of preference shares

D_P = Annual dividend amount.

There is no tax advantage for cost of preference shares, as its dividend is not allowed deduction from income for income tax purposes. Both in the case of debt and preference shares, the cost of capital is computed with reference to the obligations incurred and proceeds received. The net proceeds received must be taken into account while computing cost of capital.

Example:

A company issues 10% Preference shares of the face value of Rs. 100 each. Floatation costs are estimated at 5% of the expected sale price.

What will be the cost of preference share capital (KP), if preference shares are issued (i) at par, (ii) at 10% premium and (iii) at 5% discount? Ignore dividend tax.

Solution:

We know, cost of preference share capital (K_P) = D_P/P

(i) When preference shares are issued at par i.e., at Rs. 100 per share,

$(K_P) = \frac{Rs. 10}{Rs. 95}$ = 0.1052 or 10.52%, where, D_P=10% of Rs. 10, P=Rs. 100-5% of Rs. 100=Rs. 95.

(ii) When preference shares are issued at 10% premium (i.e., at Rs. 110 Per share)

$$K_P = \frac{Rs. 10}{Rs. 104.50} = 0.0956 \text{ or } 9.56\%,$$

Where D_P=10% of Rs. 100=Rs. 10. P=Rs. 110-5% of Rs. 110=Rs. 104.50.

When preference share are issued at 5% discount (i.e., at Rs 95 per share)

$$K_P = \frac{Rs. 10}{Rs. 90.25} = 0.1108 \text{ or } 11.08\%,$$

Where D_P=10% of Rs. 100 = Rs. 10, P= Rs. 95-5% of Rs.=Rs.90.25.

C. Cost of Equity or Ordinary Shares:

The funds required for a project may be raised by the issue of equity shares which are of permanent nature. These funds need not be repayable during the lifetime of the organisation. Calculation of the cost of equity shares is complicated because, unlike debt and preference shares, there is no fixed rate of interest or dividend payment.

Cost of equity share is calculated by considering the earnings of the company, market value of the shares, dividend per share and the growth rate of dividend or earnings.

(i) Dividend/Price Ratio Method:

An investors buys equity shares of a particular company as he expects a certain return (i.e. dividend). The expected rate of dividend per share on the current market price per share is the cost of equity share capital. Thus the cost of equity share capital is computed on the basis of the present value of the expected future stream of dividends.

Thus, the cost of equity share capital (K_e) is measured by:

$K_e = \frac{D}{P}$ where D = Dividend per share

P = Current market price per share.

If dividends are expected to grow at a constant rate of 'g' then cost of equity share capital

(K_e) will be $K_e = D/P + g$.

This method is suitable for those entities where growth rate in dividend is relatively stable. But this method ignores the capital appreciation in the value of shares. A company which declares a higher amount of dividend out of given quantum of earnings will be placed at a premium as compared to a company which earns the same amount of profits but utilizes a major part of it in financing its expansion programme.

Example:

XY Company's share is currently quoted in market at Rs. 60. It pays a dividend of Rs. 3 per share and investors expect a growth rate of 10% per year.

You are required to calculate:

i) The company's cost of equity capital.

ii) The indicated market price per share, if anticipated growth rate is 12%.

iii) The market price, if the company's cost of equity capital is 12%, anticipated growth rate is 10% p.a., and dividend of Rs. 3 per share is to be maintained.

Solution:

We know, cost of Equity $(K_e) = \frac{D}{P} + g.$

$$(i)\ K_e = \frac{Rs.\ 3}{Rs.\ 60} + 0.10 = 0.05 + 0.10 = 0.15\ or\ 15\%$$

$$(ii)\ \text{Market Price}\ (P) = \frac{Dividend\ (D)}{Cost\ of\ equity\ (K_e) - Growth\ rate\ (g)}$$

$$= \frac{Rs.\ 3}{15\% - 12\%} = \frac{Rs.\ 3}{3\%} = Rs.100.$$

$$(iii)\ \text{Market Price}\ (P) == \frac{Rs.\ 3}{12\% - 10\%} = \frac{Rs.\ 3}{2\%} = Rs.150.$$

Example:

Green Diesel Ltd. has its equity shares of Rs. 10 each quoted in a stock exchange at a market price of Rs. 28. A constant expected annual growth rate of 6% and a dividend of Rs. 1.80 per share has been paid for the current year.

Calculate the cost of equity share capital.

Solution:

$D_0 (1 + g)/ P_0 + g = 1.80 (1 + .06)/ 28 + 0.06$

$= 0.0681 + 0.06 = 12.81\%$

(ii) Earnings/Price Ratio Method:

This method takes into consideration the earnings per share (EPS) and the market price of share. Thus, the cost of equity share capital will be based upon the expected rate of earnings of a company. The argument is that each investor expects a certain amount of earnings whether distributed or not, from the company in whose shares he invests.

If the earnings are not distributed as dividends, it is kept in the retained earnings and it causes future growth in the earnings of the company as well as the increase in market price of the share.

Thus, the cost of equity capital (K_e) is measured by:

$K_e = E/P$ where E = Current earnings per share

P = Market price per share.

If the future earnings per share will grow at a constant rate 'g' then cost of equity share capital (K_e) will be:

$$K_e = E/P + g.$$

This method is similar to dividend/price method. But it ignores the factor of capital appreciation or depreciation in the market value of shares. Adjustment of Floatation Cost There are costs of floating shares in market and include brokerage, underwriting commission etc. paid to brokers, underwriters etc.

These costs are to be adjusted with the current market price of the share at the time of computing cost of equity share capital since the full market value per share cannot be realised. So the market price per share will be adjusted by (1 – f) where 'f' stands for the rate of floatation cost.

Thus, using the Earnings growth model the cost of equity share capital will be:

$$K_e = E/ P(1 - f) + g$$

Example:

The share capital of a company is represented by 10,000 Equity Shares of Rs. 10 each, fully paid.

The current market price of the share is Rs. 40. Earnings available to the equity shareholders amount to Rs. 60,000 at the end of a period.

Calculate the cost of equity share capital using Earning/Price ratio.

Solution:

We know, cost of equity capital $= \frac{E}{P}$

$$E = \text{Earnings per share} = \frac{Rs.60,000}{10,000} = Rs.\ 6.$$

$$P = \text{Current market price} = Rs.\ 40.$$

Cost of equity capital (K_e) $= \frac{Rs.\ 6}{Rs.\ 40} = 0.15\%$ or 15%

D. Cost of Retained Earnings:

The profits retained by a company for using in the expansion of the business also entail cost. When earnings are retained in the business, shareholders are forced to forego dividends. The dividends forgone by the equity shareholders are, in fact, an opportunity cost. Thus retained earnings involve opportunity cost.

If earnings are not retained they are passed on to the equity shareholders who, in turn, invest the same in new equity shares and earn a return on it. In such a case, the cost of retained earnings (K_r) would be adjusted by the personal tax rate and applicable brokerage, commission etc. if any.

Therefore,

$$K_r = K_e(1-t)(1-f),$$

Where,

$$K_e = \frac{D}{P} + g$$

t= Shareholders personal tax rate.

f= rate of floatation cost.

Many accountants consider the cost of retained earnings as the same as that of the cost of equity share capital. However, if the cost of equity share capital is computed on the basis of dividend growth model (i.e., D/P + g), a separate cost of retained earnings need not be computed since the cost of retained earnings is automatically included in the cost of equity share capital.

Therefore,

$$K_r = K_e = D/P + g.$$

Example:

It is given that the cost of equity of a company is 20%, marginal tax rate of the shareholders is 30% and the Broker's Commission is 2% of the investment in share. The company proposes to utilise its retained earnings to the extent of Rs. 6,00,000.

Find out the cost of retained earnings.

Solution:

We know that cost of retained earning

$$K_r = K_e(1-t)(1-f) \qquad \text{Here } K_e = 20\% = 0.20$$

$$or \quad K_r = 0.20(1-0.30)(1-0.02) \qquad t = 30\% = 0.30$$

$$= 0.1372 \; or,\; 13.72\%. \qquad f = 2\% = 0.20.$$

E. Overall or weighted average cost of capital:

A firm may procure long-term funds from various sources like equity share capital, preference share capital, debentures, term loans, retained earnings etc. at different costs depending on the risk perceived by the investors.

When all these costs of different forms of long-term funds are weighted by their relative proportions to get overall cost of capital it is termed as weighted average cost of capital. It is also known as composite cost of capital. While taking financial decisions, the weighted or composite cost of capital is considered.

The weighted average cost of capital is used by an enterprise because of the following reasons:

(i) It is useful in taking capital budgeting/investment decisions.

(ii) It recognises the various sources of finance from which the investment proposal derives its life-blood (i.e., finance).

(iii) It indicates an optimum combination of various sources of finance for the enhancement of the market value of the firm.

(iv) It provides a basis for comparison among projects as a standard or cut-off rate.

I. Computation of weighted average cost of capital:

Computation of weighted average cost of capital is made in the following ways:

(i) The specific cost of each source of funds (i.e., cost of equity, preference shares, debts, retained earnings etc.) is to be calculated.

(ii) Weights (i.e., proportion of each, source of fund in the capital structure) are to be computed and assigned to each type of funds. This implies multiplication of each source of capital by appropriate weights.

Generally, the following weights are assigned:

(a) Book values of various sources of funds

(b) Market values of various sources of capital

(c) Marginal book values of various sources of capital.

Book values of weights are based on the values reflected by the balance sheet of a concern, prepared under historical basis and ignoring price level changes. Most of the financial analysts prefer to use market value as the weights to calculate the weighted average cost of capital as it reflects the current cost of capital.

But the determination of market value involves some difficulties for which the measurement of cost of capital becomes very difficult.

(iii) Add all the weighted component costs to obtain the firm's weighted average cost of capital.

Therefore, weighted average cost of capital (Ko) is to be calculated by using the following formula:

$$K_o = K_1 w_1 + K_2 w_2 + \ldots\ldots\ldots$$

where K_1, K_2 .... are component costs and W_1, W_2 .... are weights.

Example:

Excel Ltd. has assets of Rs. 1,60,000 which have been financed with Rs. 52,000 of debt and Rs. 90,000 of equity and a general reserve of Rs. 18,000. The firm's total profits after interest and taxes for the year ended 31st March 2006 were Rs. 13,500. It pays 8% interest on borrowed funds and is in the 50% tax bracket. It has 900 equity shares of Rs. 100 each selling at a market price of Rs. 120 per share.

What is the weighted average cost of capital?

Solution:

(1) Earnings per share $= \dfrac{\text{Earnings after interest and taxes}}{\text{Number of Equity Shares}} = \dfrac{13,500}{900} = \text{Rs}.15.$

(2) Computation of specific cost of each source:

(i) Cost of Debt $(K_d) = r(1-t) = 8\%(1-0.5) = 4\%$

(ii) Cost of Equity $(K_e) = \dfrac{EPS}{P}. = \dfrac{Rs.15}{Rs.120} = 0.125 \text{ or } = 12.5\%$

(iii) Cost of retained earnings (K_r) is equivalent to cost of equity (K_e) i.e., 12.5%.

Source (1)	Amount (Rs.) (2)	Proportion (3)	After-tax Cost (4)	Weighted Cost (5)=(3)×(4)
Equity share Reserves capital Debt	90,000 18,000 52,000	0.5625 0.1125 0.325	0.125 0.125 0.04	0.070 0.014 0.013
	1,60,000	1.00		0.097

∴ Weighted average cost of capital (K_0)=0.097×100=9.7%

Example:

RIL Ltd. opts for the following capital structure:

$$\begin{array}{ll} \textit{Equity Shares}\,(1,00,000\,\textit{share}) & 50,00,000 \\ 1.5\%\ \textit{Debentures} & 50,00,000 \\ \hline \quad\textit{Total} & 1,00,00,000 \end{array}$$

The company is expected to declare a dividend of Rs. 5 per share. The market price per share is Rs. 50. The dividend is expected to grow at 10%.

Compute weighted average cost of capital of RIL Ltd. assuming 50% tex rate.

Solution:

Computation of specific cost of each source:

(i) Cost of debenture $(K_d) = (I - t) = 15\%(1 - 0.5) = 7.5\%$

(ii) Cost of equity share $(K_e) = \frac{D}{P} + g = \frac{Rs.5}{Rs.50} + 10\% = 20\%$

Statement showing weighted average cost of capital

Source (1)	Amount (Rs.) (2)	Proportion (3)	After-tax Cost (4)	Weighted Cost (5)=(3)×(4)
Equity share capital Debentures	50,00,000 50,00,000	0.50 0.50	0.20 0.075	0.1000 0.75
	10,00,000	1.00		0.1375

You are required to determine the optimum debt-equity mix for the company by calculating composite cost of capital.

Optimal debt-equity mix for the company is at the point where the composite cost of capital is minimum. Hence, the composite cost of capital is minimum (10.75%) at the debt-equity mix of 3: 7 (i.e., 30% debt and 70% equity). Therefore, 30% of debt and 70% equity mix would be an optimal debt-equity mix for the company.

Equivalent Annual Cost

Equivalent annual cost (EAC) is the annual cost of owning and maintaining an asset determined by dividing the net present value of the asset purchase, operations and maintenance cost by the present value of annuity factor. It is a capital budgeting tool used by companies to compare assets with unequal useful lives. The same concept can be applied to analyse projects which have unequal useful lives.

Let's say your company must decide between installing tube-lights or LED lights at its office. A tube light has a useful life of 2 years and an LED lights has useful life of 4 years. 200 tube-lights costs $1,000 and consume electricity of $18,000 per annum. 200 LED lights will cost $3,000 and consume electricity of $12,000 per annum.

Importance

Capital budgeting decisions require distinct methods for determining the costs and potential profitability of new projects. EAC is a method which is most useful for evaluating projects which are assumed to have unequal but repeating life spans. By contrast, when comparing two projects that have equal life spans, or that have unequal life spans but are assumed not to repeat, the best method may be to simply compare the NPVs.

Due to its applicability for projects with life spans that repeat indefinitely, the EAC method is often seen as an indication that the firm itself has a long operating horizon as a going concern, and therefore, is a financially healthy company.

Formula

We just need to find the net present value of both assets. There is no cash inflow here, so it will essentially be negative. Net present value can be calculated by discounting the future cash flows and subtracting the asset cost:

$$NPV = \frac{CF_1}{(1+r)^1} + \frac{CF_2}{(1+r)^2} + \frac{CF_3}{(1+r)^3} + \ldots + \frac{CF_n}{(1+r)^n} - I$$

Now that we have the net present value, we must convert it to annual terms which we can do by treating the net present value obtained as the present value of an ordinary annuity of duration equal to the asset life.

$$NPV = PV\ of\ annuity = EAC \times \frac{1-\left(1+\frac{r}{m}\right)^{-n\times m}}{\frac{r}{m}}$$

Equivalent Annual Cost

$$= \frac{NPV \times \frac{r}{m}}{1 - \left(1 + \frac{r}{m}\right)^{-n \times m}}$$

Where *r* is the annual percentage rate, *n* is the number of years and m is the number of compounding periods per year.

Example

Assuming a discount rate of 10%, find out which type of lights your company must install.

Net present value of the tube-lights is –$26,976:

$$NPV$$
$$= -18,000 \times \frac{1-(1+10\%)^{-2}}{10\%} - \$1,000$$
$$= -\$33,240$$

Net present value of the LED lights is -$33,491:

$$NPV$$
$$= -12,000 \times \frac{1-(1+10\%)^{-4}}{10\%} - \$3,000$$
$$= -\$40,538$$

Now, we need to divide the net present value amount by the present value factor for annuity of 2 years and 4 years respectively at 10% interest rate compounded monthly:

$$EAC\ (tube\,light)$$
$$= \frac{-\$33,240 \times 10\%}{1-(1+10\%)^{-2}}$$
$$= \$19,152$$

$$EAC\ (LED\,light)$$
$$= \frac{-\$40,538 \times 10\%}{1-(1+10\%)^{-4}}$$
$$= \$12,789$$

References

- Capital-budgeting: edupristine.com, Retrieved 12 June 2018
- Payback-method-payback-period-formula: accountingtools.com, Retrieved 29 May 2018
- Types-of-capital-assets, income-tax: taxfinadvisory.com, Retrieved 19 June 2018
- What-is-financial-capital-3305825: thebalance.com, Retrieved 19 March 2018
- The-three-primary-types-of-financial-capital-357332: thebalance.com, Retrieved 10 June 2018
- What-is-working-capital: bajajfinserv.in, Retrieved 10 April 2018
- Capital-expenditure, accounting-dictionary: myaccountingcourse.com, Retrieved 21 May 2018
- How-to-calculate-capital-expenditures: accountingtools.com, Retrieved 11 July 2018

2

Investment: Types and Strategy

Investment is the allotment of money to a particular venture with the expectation of some return in the future. Capital investment may be done through durable goods, real estate, manufacturing processes, product development, etc. All the diverse facts of investment strategy, traditional investments, impact investing, alternative investment and portfolio investment have been carefully analyzed in this chapter.

Investment

An investment is an asset or item acquired with the goal of generating income or appreciation. In an economic sense, an investment is the purchase of goods that are not consumed today but are used in the future to create wealth. In finance, an investment is a monetary asset purchased with the idea that the asset will provide income in the future or will later be sold at a higher price for a profit.

The term "investment" can refer to any mechanism used for generating future income. In the financial sense, this includes the purchase of bonds, stocks or real estate property. Additionally, a constructed building or other facility used to produce goods can be seen as an investment. The production of goods required to produce other goods may also be seen as investing.

Taking an action in the hopes of raising future revenue can also be considered an investment. For example, when choosing to pursue additional education, the goal is often to increase knowledge and improve skills in the hopes of ultimately producing more income.

Investment and Economic Growth

Economic growth can be encouraged through the use of sound investments at the business level. When a company constructs or acquires a new piece of production equipment in order to raise the total output of goods within the facility, the increased production can cause the nation's gross domestic product (GDP) to rise. This allows the economy to grow through increased production based on the previous equipment investment.

Investment Banking

An investment bank provides a variety of services designed to assist an individual or business in increasing associated wealth. This does not include traditional consumer banking. Instead, the institution focuses on investment vehicles such as trading and asset management. Financing options may also be provided for the purpose of assisting with the these services.

Investments and Speculation

Speculation is a separate activity from making an investment. Investing involves the purchase of assets with the intent of holding them for the long term, while speculation involves attempting to capitalize on market inefficiencies for short-term profit. Ownership is generally not a goal of speculators, while investors often look to build the number of assets in their portfolios over time.

Although speculators are often making informed decisions, speculation cannot usually be categorized as traditional investing. Speculation is generally considered higher risk than traditional investing, though this can vary depending on the type of investment involved.

Types of Investment

Different types or kinds of investment are discussed in the following points.

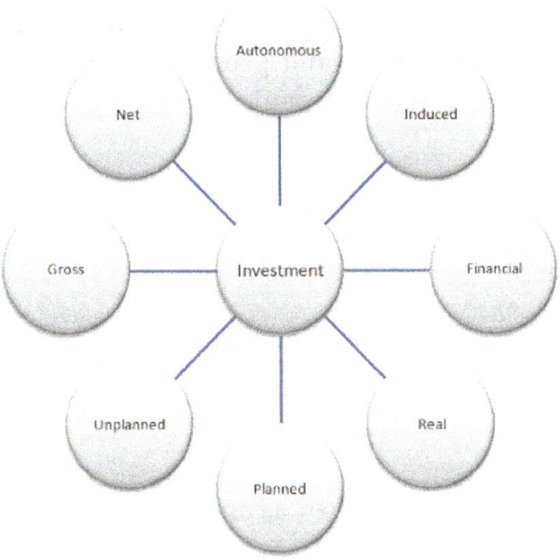

1. Autonomous investment

Investment which does not change with the changes in income level, is called as autonomous or government investment.

Autonomous investment remains constant irrespective of income level. Which means even if the income is low, the autonomous, Investment remains the same. It refers to the investment made on houses, roads, public buildings and other parts of Infrastructure. The Government normally makes such a type of investment.

2. Induced investment

Investment which changes with the changes in the income level, is called as Induced Investment.

Induced investment is positively related to the income level. That is, at high levels of income entrepreneurs are induced to invest more and vice-versa. At a high level of income, Consumption expenditure increases this leads to an increase in investment of capital goods, in order to produce more consumer goods.

3. Financial investment

Investment made in buying financial instruments such as new shares, bonds, securities, etc. is considered as a financial investment.

However, the money used for purchasing existing financial instruments such as old bonds, old shares, etc., cannot be considered as financial investment. It is a mere transfer of a financial asset from one individual to another. In financial investment, money invested for buying of new shares and bonds as well as debentures have a positive impact on employment level, production and economic growth.

4. Real investment

Investment made in new plant and equipment, construction of public utilities like schools, roads and railways, etc., is considered as real Investment.

Real investment in new machine tools, plant and equipments purchased factory buildings, etc. increases employment, production and economic growth of the nation. Thus real investment has a direct impact on employment generation, economic growth, etc.

5. Planned investment

Investment made with a plan in several sectors of the economy with specific objectives is called as planned or intended investment.

Planned Investment can also be called as Intended Investment because an investor while making investment make a concrete plan of his investment.

6. Unplanned investment

Investment done without any planning is called as an Unplanned or Unintended Investment.

In unplanned type of investment, investors make investment randomly without making any concrete plans. Hence it can also be called as Unintended Investment. Under this type of investment, the investor may not consider the specific objectives while making an investment decision.

7. Gross investment

Gross Investment means the total amount of money spent for creation of new capital assets like Plant and Machinery, Factory Building, etc.

It is the total expenditure made on new capital assets in a period.

8. Net investment

Net investment is gross investment less (minus) capital consumption (depreciation) during a period of time, usually a year.

It must be noted that a part of the investment is meant for depreciation of the capital asset or for replacing a worn-out capital asset. Hence it must be deducted to arrive at net investment.

Importance of Investment

In order to build your wealth, you will want to invest your money. Investing allows you to put your money in vehicles that have the potential to earn strong rates of return.

If you don't invest, you are missing out on opportunities to increase your financial worth. Of course, you have the potential to lose your money in investments, but if you invest wisely, the potential to gain money is higher than if you never invest.

Here are the top 10 reasons to invest your money:

1. Grow your money

Investing your money can allow you to grow it. Most investment vehicles, such as stocks, certificates of deposit, or bonds, offer returns on your money over the long term. This return allows your money to build, creating wealth over time.

2. Save for retirement

As you are working, you should be saving money for retirement. Put your retirement savings into a portfolio of investments, such as stocks, bonds, mutual funds, real estate, businesses, or precious metals. Then, at retirement age, you can live off funds earned from these investments.

Based on your personal tolerance of risk, you may want to consider being riskier at a younger age with your investments. Greater risk increases your chances of earning greater wealth. Becoming more conservative with your investments as you grow older can be wise, especially as you near retirement age.

3. Earn higher returns

In order to grow your money, you need to put it in a place where it can earn a high rate of return. The higher the rate of return, the more money you will earn. Investment vehicles tend to offer the opportunity to earn higher rates of return than savings accounts. Therefore, if you want the chance to earn a higher return on your money, you will need to explore investing your money.

4. Reach financial goals

Investing can help you reach big financial goals. If your money is earning a higher rate of return than a savings account, you will be earning more money both over the long term and within a faster period. This return on your investments can be used toward major financial goals, such as buying a home, buying a car, starting your own business, or putting your children through college.

5. Build on pre-tax dollars

Some investment vehicles, like employer-sponsored 401(k)s, allow you to invest your pre-tax dollars. This option allows you to save more money than if you could only invest your post-tax dollars.

6. Qualify for employer-matching programs

Some employers offer to match the money you invest in your 401(k) plan up to a certain amount. Of course, the only way you can qualify and earn these matching funds is if you are actively investing in your 401(k) plan. Thus, many people invest in their 401(k)s to gain the matching employer funds.

7. Start and expand a business

Investing is an important part of business creation and expansion. Many investors like to support entrepreneurs and contribute to the creation of new jobs and new products. They enjoy the process of creating and establishing new businesses and building them into successful entities that can provide them with a strong return on their investment.

8. Support others

Many investors like investing in people, whether they are business owners, artists, or manufacturers. These investors feel good helping others achieve their goals.

9. Reduce taxable income

As an investor, you may be able to reduce your taxable income by investing pre-tax dollars into a retirement fund, like a 401(k). If you generate a loss from an investment, you may be able to apply that loss against any gains from other investments, which lowers the amount of your taxable income.

10. Be part of a new venture

New ventures need the backing of money, and they look to investors for that backing. Some investors may like the excitement of investing in a new, cutting-edge product or service, or being part of something like a business or film that introduces them to a glamorous world.

Disadvantages of Investments

There are also disadvantages of financial investment, such as the following:

1. High Expense Ratios and Sales Charges

If you're not paying attention to mutual fund expense ratios and sales charges; they can get out of hand. Be very careful when investing in funds with expense ratios higher than 1.20%, as they will be considered on the higher cost end. Be wary of 12b-1advertising fees and sales charges in general. There are several good fund companies out there that have no sales charges. Fees reduce overall investment returns.

2. Management Abuses

Churning, turnover and window dressing may happen if your manager is abusing his or her authority. This includes unnecessary trading, excessive replacement and selling the losers prior to quarter-end to fix the books.

3. Tax Inefficiency

Like it or not, investors do not have any choice when it comes to capital gain payouts in mutual funds. Due to the turnover, redemptions, gains and losses in security holdings throughout the year, investors typically receive distributions from the fund that are an uncontrollable tax event.

4. Poor Trade Execution

if you place your mutual fund trade any time before the cut-off time for same-day NAV, you'll get the same closing price NAV is for buy or sell on the mutual fund. For investors searching for faster execution times, maybe because of short investment horizons, day trading, or timing the market, mutual funds provide a weak execution strategy.

5. Volatile Investments

Investment in BSE is subjected to many risks since the market is volatile. The shares of a company fluctuate so many times in just a single day. These price fluctuations are unpredictable most of the times and the investor sometimes have to face severe loss due to such uncertainty.

6. Brokerage Commissions Kill Profit Margin

Every time an investor purchase or sells his shares; he has to pay some amount as a brokerage commission to the broker, which kills the profit margin.

7. Time Consuming

Investment in NSE is not as easy as investing in a lottery as you have to complete many formalities in the process and hence is time consuming.

Cash on Cash Return

Passive investors in crowd funded real estate transactions may not be familiar with some of the various ways that return on investment can be calculated in the real estate world. Here we explore one of the most common measures, the "cash-on-cash" return.

Cash-on-cash (sometimes called the equity dividend rate) is one of the most common return formats used in the real estate industry. It is a ratio (usually converted to a percentage) that is derived by dividing cash flow (before tax) by the amount of equity initially invested.

The cash flow figure equals the net operating income of the property – the gross rental income less the usual operating expenses – minus the debt service on any mortgages to which the property is (or will be) subject. That number is then divided by the equity investment in order to get a measure of the "return on equity," or cash-on-cash return. A simple example might be as follows:

$$\begin{array}{lll} \text{Effective gross income} & \$180{,}000 & \\ \text{Less: operating expenses} & (\$70{,}000) & \\ \quad\text{Net operating income} & \$110{,}000 & \\ \quad\text{Total investment (all-cash)} & \$1{,}000{,}000 & \\ \quad\text{Cash-on-cash return} \quad = & \dfrac{\$110{,}000}{\$1{,}000{,}000} = & 11.0\% \end{array}$$

The cash-on-cash figure doesn't take into account any income tax effects, resale implications (including changes in property value), future cash flows, or reductions in loan principal. It does, however, give a good feel for the immediate and on-going periodic return that a cash flow investor can expect.

The cash-on-cash figure can also show the effects of leverage – using a mortgage loan to finance part of the property's purchase price. Let's assume now that in the above example $800,000 of the total purchase price is financed by a mortgage loan – so that the investor is only paying $200,000 cash for the same property. Although this will result in debt repayment expenses (interest and, oftentimes, principal amortization), the much lesser equity investment required often makes this additional expense worthwhile. Let's look at the same property with leverage in place, assuming an 8% interest-only loan:

$$\begin{array}{llll} \textit{Net operating income} & \$110{,}000 & & \\ \textit{Less: debt service } (8\%) & (\$64{,}000) & & \\ \textit{Net cash flow } \$46{,}000 & & & \\ \text{Cash-on-cash return} = & \dfrac{\$46{,}000}{\$200{,}000} & = & 23.0\% \end{array}$$

Our cash-on-cash return would thus more than double if this mortgage loan were to be used to finance the greater part of the property's purchase price. Loans bring with them risks, of course – any decrease in the property's projected net operating income will be borne entirely by the owner, since the bank must be paid back in any event. Yet this cash-on-cash return analysis shows how leverage can also greatly increase the return on equity, and thus the proportionate cash flow returns to the investor, if the interest rate on the loan offers favorable financial leverage to the person making the equity investment.

There are other measures that may be needed to decide whether an investment should be purchased; investors need to consider income taxes, riskiness, whether more or less money should be borrowed, and possible alternative means of financing. A potential real estate investment requires a sophisticated level of in-depth analysis. The cash-on-cash return measure remains a basic and important yardstick, however, in indicating whether an investment might be a good one.

Investment Function

The investment function is a summary of the variables that influence the levels of aggregate investments. It can be formalized as follows:

$$I = f(r, \Delta Y, q)$$

where r is the real interest rate, Y the GDP and q is Tobin's q. The signs under the variables simply tell us if the variable influences investment in a positive or negative way (for instance, if real interest rates were to rise, investments would correspondingly fall).

The reason for investment being inversely related to the Interest rate is simply because the interest rate is a measure of the opportunity cost of those resources. If the resources instead of financing the investment could be invested in financial assets, there is an opportunity cost of (1+r), where r is the interest rate. This implies higher investment spending with a lower interest rate. When GDP increases, the output and the capacity utilization increases. This results in an increase of capital investment. At last, a higher Tobins q is represented when the market puts a high value of the installed capital and buys stocks in the firm for a higher price. The firm can then raise more resources per share issued and increase their investments.

Investment Fund

An investment fund is a supply of capital belonging to numerous investors used to collectively purchase securities while each investor retains ownership and control of his own shares. An investment fund provides a broader selection of investment opportunities, greater management expertise and lower investment fees than investors might be able to obtain on their own. Types of investment funds include mutual funds, exchange-traded funds, money market funds and hedge funds.

With investment funds, individual investors do not make decisions about how a fund's assets should be invested. They simply choose a fund based on its goals, risk, fees and other factors. A fund manager oversees the fund and decides which securities it should hold, in what quantities and when the securities should be bought and sold. An investment fund can be broad-based, such as an index fund that tracks the S&P 500, or it can be tightly focused, such as an ETF that invests only in small technology stocks.

While investment funds in various forms have been around for many years, the Massachusetts Investors Trust Fund is generally considered the first open-end mutual fund in the industry. The fund, investing in a mix of large-cap stocks, launched in 1924.

Open-end vs. Closed-end

The majority of investment fund assets belong to open-end mutual funds. These funds issue new shares as investors add money to the pool, and retire shares as investors redeem. These funds are typically priced just once at the end of the trading day.

Closed-end funds trade more similarly to stocks than open-end funds. Closed-end funds are managed investment funds that issue a fixed number of shares, and trade on an exchange. While a net asset value (NAV) for the fund is calculated, the fund trades based on investor supply and demand. Therefore, a closed-end fund may trade at a premium or a discount to its NAV.

Emergence of ETFs

Exchange-traded funds (ETFs) emerged as an alternative to mutual funds for traders who wanted more flexibility with their investment funds. Similar to closed-end funds, ETFs trade on exchanges, and are priced and available for trading throughout the business day. Many mutual funds, such as the Vanguard 500 Index Fund, have ETF counterparts. The Vanguard S&P 500 ETF is essentially the same fund, but came be bought and sold intraday. ETFs frequently have the additional advantage of slightly lower expense ratios than their mutual fund equal.

The first ETF, the SPDR S&P 500 ETF, debuted in 1993. ETFs have more than $4.4 trillion in assets under management, as of September 2017.

Hedge Funds

A hedge fund is another type of fund that pairs stocks it wants to short (bet will decrease) with stocks it expects to go up in order to decrease the potential for loss. Hedge funds also tend to invest in riskier assets in addition to stocks, bonds, ETFs, commodities and alternative assets. These include derivatives such as futures and options that may also be purchased with leverage, or borrowed money.

Investment Style

Everyone has an investment style that is as personal to them as a fingerprint. But how do you find out what yours is? The simple answer is to determine what level of risk you are comfortable with in your investments.

For most people, who don't have the time or the inclination to manage and monitor a portfolio of individual shares, investment funds make a lot of sense:

- You spread your risk across maybe 30, 50 or even 100 different individual investments (known as diversification).
- You have a qualified fund manager whose job it is to monitor those investments and make informed decisions on your behalf.
- You can usually get your money into and out of the fund easily.
- You can often invest for as little as £1,000 (£500 for some funds), or a much smaller regular monthly investment of £20 to £50.
- The costs of buying and selling individual investments are spread across a large number of people.

However, you do pay for this convenience and expertise. The fund management company will take a small slice of your money each year (usually around 1 to 1.5 per cent): some to pay the fund manager, some to cover admin costs, and some to pay for all those marketing people. There may be other costs too.

Choosing Investment Fund

Before you choose an investment fund, you need to ask yourself a number of questions:

- Do you need a regular income?
- How soon might you need to access your money? (your *investment horizon*)
- How much risk you are prepared to take, and how much money you can afford to lose? (your *risk appetite* and *risk tolerance*)
- What investments do you have already, if any? (Investment experts recommend that you *diversify your portfolio*)

Once you have answered these questions, you'll know what kind of fund you are looking for – an equity income fund, a bond fund, or a fund that attempts to provide capital growth over a longer period of time but might take more risk with your capital. If you might need your money in one or two years, it might not be appropriate to invest in a fund at all and you could be better off leaving your money in cash, for example in a cash ISA.

Buying an Investment Fund

The cheapest way to buy and hold an investment fund is normally not to go direct to the fund provider, but to an online *fund supermarket*. Fund supermarkets generally allow you to invest in funds with lower charges. The exception is with some investment trusts, which can offer good-value share plans if you go direct.

Investment Style

Everyone has an investment style that is as personal to them as a fingerprint. But how do you find out what yours is? The simple answer is to determine what level of risk you are comfortable with in your investments.

Types of Investment Style

1. Active Investing

Do you have a high tolerance for risk? Are you looking to be an active participant in the market multiple times a day? If so, an active investing style might be right for you. Active investing is generally used by investors who aren't as concerned with the long-term horizon as they are with the present. Active investors select specific stocks and use market timing to try to outperform the market in an effort to seek short-term profits. Active investing requires an investor to be on constant watch over the market and his/her positions in the market.

2. Passive Investing

If you are more risk-averse and don't want to stare at the market screens on your computer all day, a passive investing style may be more up your alley. Passive investors are those who invest their money with a long-term time horizon. Instead of trying to time the market like an active investor, passive investors create portfolios that track a market-weighted index or portfolio. Tracking an index will generally result in reduced risk due to diversification as well as lower transaction costs due to low turnover.

3. Growth

The growth style of investing is one that focuses on stocks of companies whose earnings are growing faster than most other stocks and are expected to continue to grow. These stocks are oftentimes referred to as being overvalued and have a high price to earnings ratio. It is important to note that these stocks generally pay either a low or no dividend.

4. Value

Unlike growth investors who seek out overvalued securities, value investors look for those stocks that are out-of-favour or undervalued. Value investors expect that these securities will rise and seek to buy them before they do.

5. Market Capitalization

Those investors who select stocks based on the size of the company are using a market capitalization investing style. Market capitalization, or market cap, is computed as the number of shares outstanding multiplied by earnings per share. Small cap companies have a market capitalization of $300 million to $2 billion, mid-cap companies have a market capitalization of $2 billion to $10 billion, and large-cap companies have a market capitalization of over $10 billion. Small-cap stocks are generally riskier investments than large cap stocks.

While their returns may be higher, their volatility is also higher. On the other hand, large cap companies are those that have been around a much longer time and tend to be more stable. Many people use large cap stocks in their portfolio because of the dividends and stability.

6. Buy and Hold

A buy and hold investing style falls under the umbrella of passive investing. An investor who is engaged in buy and hold investing rarely trades in their portfolio and is mostly concerned with long-term growth.

7. Indexing

Another popular form of passive investing is indexing. With this style of investing, an investor creates a portfolio that mirrors the companies of a particular stock index. The portfolio generally will perform in-line with the index. This kind of investing is good for people that are more risk-averse because of the diversification of the index. The costs, including transaction costs and taxes, related to managing these kinds of the portfolio are relatively low in large part due to less turnover.

8. Diversification

There are two kinds of risk that every investor must be concerned about: systematic risk and unsystematic risk. Systematic risk is a market risk that cannot be diversified away. But unsystematic risk, or the risk that comes from investing in one particular company or sector, can be diversified away. For example, if you were to invest only in technology companies, you would have a high level of risk due to owning stocks in only one sector. By diversifying your portfolio and adding in or replacing some of the technology companies with consumer goods companies, your risk level would be reduced.

Investment Strategy

Having an investment strategy is like having an instruction booklet guiding you through the investment process. It will help you discard many potential investments that may perform poorly overtime or that are not right for the investment goals you are looking to achieve.

When creating an investment strategy, it is important to quantitatively figure out what you are seeking to accomplish. Stating that you simply want to make money or become wealthy is not helpful. A better objective would be to say "I want to achieve an 8% average annual return on my investment contributions over the next 10 years in order to amass $200,000 that will be used to purchase a cottage home." The more specific the objective, the better. And it doesn't stop there. An investment strategy is useless without a proper understanding of it.

Types of Investment Strategies

There are many different strategies that apply to different investment objectives, the key is pairing the right strategy with the right objective.

5 Types of investment strategies

1. Value investing

An investment strategy made popular by Warren Buffet, the principle behind value investing is simple: buy stocks that are cheaper than they should be. Finding stocks that are under-priced takes a lot of research on the fundamentals of the underlying companies. And once you've found them, it often takes a long time for their price to rise. This buy and hold technique requires a patient investor but should the right call be made, handsome payoffs could be earned. All investors should understand at least the basics of value investing.

2. Income investing

A great way to build wealth over time, income investing involves buying securities that generally pay out returns on a steady schedule. Bonds are the best known type of fixed income security, but the category also includes dividend paying stocks, exchange-traded funds (ETFs), mutual funds, and real estate investment trusts (REITs). Fixed income investments provide a reliable income stream with minimal risk and depending on the risk the investor is looking to take should comprise at least a small portion of every investment strategy.

3. Growth investing

An investment strategy that focuses on capital appreciation. Growth investors look for companies that exhibit signs of above-average growth, through revenues and profits, even if the share price appears expensive in terms of metrics such as price-to-earnings or price-to-book ratios. What Warren Buffet did for value investing, Peter Lynch did for growth investing. A relatively riskier strategy, growth investing involves investing in smaller companies that have high potential for growth, blue chips and emerging markets.

4. Small cap investing

An investment strategy fit for those looking to take on a little more risk in their portfolio. As the name suggests, small cap investing involves purchasing stock of small companies with smaller market capitalization (usually between $300 million and $2 billion). Small Cap stocks are appealing to investors due to their ability to go unnoticed. Large-cap stocks will often have inflated prices since everyone's paying attention to them. Small cap stocks tend to have less attention on them because: a) investors stay away from their riskiness and b) institutional investors (like mutual funds) have restrictions when it comes to investing in small cap companies. Small cap investing should only be used by more experienced stock investors as they are more volatile and therefore difficult to trade.

5. Socially Responsible Investing

A portfolio built of environmentally and socially friendly companies while staying competitive alongside other kinds of securities in a typical market environment. In today's modern world, investors and the general public expect companies to maintain some social conscience, and they're putting their money where their mouth is. SRI is one path to seeking returns that poses a significant collateral benefit for everyone.

Choosing the Right Investing Strategy

Setting up your investment strategy is like buying a new car, before you look at the different models, you need to figure out what style suits you best. And just like cars, there are many styles to choose from when creating an investment strategy. When choosing the right investing strategy, there are questions that need to be answered first. What is your investment horizon? What returns are you seeking to achieve? What amount of risk are you able to tolerant? What are the funds in this investment to be used for? Answering these questions will ultimately also help in building your portfolio.

Determining what will be your breakdown between cash, fixed-income securities and stocks is a good start towards creating your investment strategy. The breakdown of your asset allocation ultimately depends on your risk tolerance. A conservative investor may prefer to hold 80% of his portfolio in fixed-income and 20% in stocks. The reverse would be true for an aggressive investor, while a balanced investor will follow a 50-50 split.

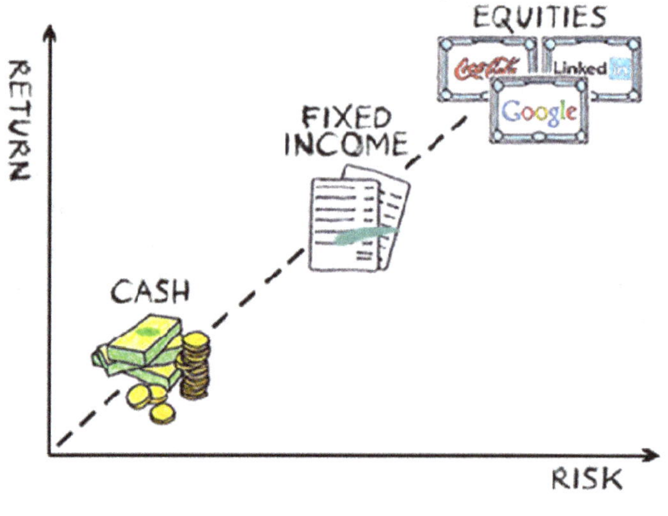

In terms of specific investment strategies within your asset allocation, if you are a high risk investor with a long investment horizon, you may want to include small cap and growth investing in your portfolio. If you have a moderate risk tolerance and shorter investment horizon, you may be more suitable for value and income investing. If you have a low risk tolerance and short investment horizon, you may want to focus solely on income investing. For those looking for companies that aim to do no harm, you can add socially responsible assets to your portfolio with relative ease. It is also important to adapt to the investment strategy you are most comfortable with. Someone with a knack for choosing growth stocks may make that strategy the priority in their portfolio.

Liability-driven Investment

A liability-driven investment, otherwise known as liability-driven investing, is primarily slated toward gaining enough assets to cover all current and future liabilities. This type of investing is common when dealing with defined-benefit pension plans because the liabilities involved quite frequently climb into billions of dollars with the largest of the pension plans.

The liabilities of defined-benefit pension plans, accrued as the direct result of the guaranteed pensions they are designed to provide upon retirement, are perfectly positioned to benefit from liability-driven investments. However, liability investing is a treatment that a variety of clients can use.

Liability-Driven Investment for Individual Clients

For a retiree, using the LDI strategy starts with estimating the amount of income the individual will need for each future year. All potential income, including Social Security benefits, is deducted from the yearly amount that the retiree needs, helping determine the amount of money the retiree will have to withdraw from his or her retirement portfolio to meet the established income needed annually. The yearly withdrawals then become the liabilities that the LDI strategy must focus on. The retiree's portfolio must invest in a manner that provides the individual with the necessary cash flows to meet the yearly withdrawals, accounting for intermittent spending, inflation and other incidental expenses that arise throughout the year.

For example: if an investor needs an additional $10,000 in income beyond what Social Security payments provide, he or she can implement an LDI strategy by purchasing bonds that will provide at least $10,000 in annual interest payments.

Liability-driven Investment for Pension Funds

For a pension fund or pension plan that utilizes the LDI strategy, the focus must be placed on the pension fund's assets. More specifically, the focus should be on the assurances made to pensioners and employees. These assurances become the liabilities the strategy must target. This strategy directly contrasts the investing approach that directs its attention to the asset side of a pension fund's balance sheet.

There is not one agreed upon approach or definition for the specific actions taken in regard to the LDI. Pension fund managers quite often use a variety of approaches under the LDI strategy banner. However, there's a number of key tactics that seem to repeat under this strategy. Hedging is often involved, either in part or in whole, to block or limit the fund's exposure to inflation and interest rates, as these risks often take a bite out of the fund's ability to make good on the promises it has made to members.

In the past, bonds were often used to partially hedge for interest-rate risks, but the LDI strategy tends to focus on using swaps and various other derivatives. Whatever approach is used typically pursues a "glide path" that aims to reduce risks – such as interest rates – over time and achieve returns that either match or exceed the growth of anticipated pension plan liabilities.

Passive Strategy

A passive portfolio strategy focuses on maximizing diversification with little expectational input. A passive portfolio fund essentially mirrors a market index. It is the opposite of an active management portfolio strategy, which aims to beat the market with several investing strategies and trading decisions.

Passive portfolio strategy is also known as 'passive investing', 'passive strategy' and 'index investing'.

It follows the efficient market hypothesis, which states that financial markets are 'informationally efficient'.

What this means is that the strategy assumes that the marketplace provides all information regarding the price paid for securities, and as a result does not try and beat the market by buying 'mispriced' securities.

In passive investment management, no attempt is made to distinguish attractive from unattractive securities, forecast their prices, time markets or market sectors.

Passive managers expect average returns on various asset classes – they invest in broad sectors of the market. Asset class refers to a broad group of securities that act in a similar way in the marketplace, such as stocks, fixed-income securities and cash equivalents.

Advocates of a passive portfolio strategy believe that the best and most risk free strategy is to invest in index funds, which have historically performed better than most actively managed funds. Investors who use this strategy are minimally involved in directing the portfolio.

Active Portfolio Management Strategy

Active portfolio management strategy refers to a portfolio management strategy that involves making precise investments for outperforming an investment benchmark index. The portfolio manager that follows the active management strategy exploits the market inefficiencies by buying undervalued securities or by short selling overvalued securities. Any of these procedures can be used alone or in combination.

Active portfolio managers may create less volatility (or risk) than the benchmark index depending on the targets of the specific hedge fund or mutual fund or investment portfolio. The risk reduction is considered as goal of creating an investment return larger than the benchmark. They use large number of factors and strategies for constructing their portfolio.

Strategies for Constructing the Portfolio

- Quantitative measures like price/earnings ratio (P/E ratios) and PEG ratios
- Sector investments that are expected to deliver long-term macroeconomic trends
- Buying stocks of companies that are disliked temporarily
- Selling at a discount of their intrinsic value

- Merger arbitrage
- Short positions
- Option writing
- Asset allocation

Active Portfolio Management Strategy Performance

The performance of an actively-managed investment portfolio relies on the proficiency of the portfolio manager and research staff. There are many mutual funds that are supposed to be actively managed and they stay invested irrespective of market conditions along with only negligible adjustments in allocation over time. In conditions of prolonged market declines, the managers may use hedging strategies. The performance characteristics are different with two groups of active managers.

Benefits of Active Management

- The active portfolio management strategy allows the portfolio managers to select a variety of investments rather than investing in the market as a whole. There may be different kinds of motivations for the investors to follow active management strategy.
- In order to generate profits, the investors consider that some market segments are less efficient than others.
- Portfolio Manager may manage the volatility or risks of market by investing in less-risky and high-quality companies instead of investing in market as a whole.
- Investors may take additional risk for achieving higher-than-market returns.
- Those investments which are not vastly correlated to the market function as portfolio diversifier and decrease the portfolio volatility as a whole.
- Investors may follow a strategy for avoiding certain industries in comparison to the market as a whole.
- Investors that follow actively-managed fund are more aligned for achieving their specific investment goals.

Drawbacks of Active Management

- There are chances of bad investment choices to be made by fund manager.
- Fund Manager may follow an unsafe theory for the management of the portfolio.
- The costs related to the active management are higher in comparison to passive management in case of lack of frequent trading.
- Fund managers should actively evaluate the fund's prospectus before investing in an actively-managed mutual fund because most of the actively-managed large and mid-cap stock funds fail to beat or outperform their passively managed counterparts.

- Higher transaction costs results due to frequent trading with active fund management strategies that reduces the fund's return.
- The short-term capital gains due to frequent trading have an unfavourable income tax impact.

Growth Investing

Growth investing is a type of investment strategy that concentrates on increasing the value of the financial assets one has, i.e. capital appreciation rather than annual income or dividends.

Growth investing is highly attractive to many investors because buying the right companies early can lead to life-changing returns. However, companies that promise huge upside potential usually trade at lofty valuations. That amps up the risk that they will fail in spectacular fashion if they don't meet expectations.

Principles of Growth Investing

1. A large and expanding market opportunity

The greatest growth stocks move their top line higher at a double-digit rate for decades. That's a nearly impossible feat to pull off unless the company is attacking a massive market opportunity.

A few great recent examples of successful growth companies that are going after large market opportunities include Amazon. com's aim to disrupt the world of retail and Tesla's (NASDAQ: TSLA) foray into the automotive business. Both of these industries literally pull in trillions of dollars in annual worldwide sales. That backdrop provides both companies with a massive runway for future growth.

What's more, Amazon and Tesla have also succeeded in expanding their addressable market opportunity over time. They've each accomplished this by rolling out products or services in new business segments as they've grown. For example, Amazon started out as an online retailer, but it now boasts a thriving web services business. Tesla was initially founded to create automotive products, but the company now sells energy storage systems.

A company's ability to enter adjacent markets is often referred to as "optionality" and is a wonderful trait for growth investors to keep in mind when they considering a potential growth investment.

2. A durable competitive advantage

Warren Buffett is widely believed to be the greatest stock picker of all time, so it makes sense to follow his lead when he speaks about what to look for in great businesses. One of Buffett's investing tenants is to buy businesses with a durable competitive advantage, which he lovingly refers to as a company's "moat." Simply put, this is a company's ability to maintain its competitive advantage over its rivals for a long period, thus keeping its profits protected from the forces of capitalism.

Broadly speaking, there are four main types of competitive advantage:

- Network effect: When a new customer joins a network, it creates additional value for all other members of that network. A classic example is eBay (NASDAQ: EBAY). As more buyers joined eBay's network it created additional demand for goods. Sellers signed on to eBay to meet that growing demand and added even more goods to the network in the process. That attracted even more buyers to the platform. This cycle repeated itself until eBay became a premier destination to buy and sell goods online.

- High switching costs: If it is costly in terms of time or money to switch to a competing product, customers tend to stay loyal even in the face of price increases. A great example of this is in consumer banking. Once a person's paycheck and bills become linked to their checking account, it becomes a large pain for them to consider switching to another bank, even if the interest rate they earn is lower or their fees are higher. This fact keeps many customers loyal to their banks for years.
- Low-cost producer: If a company enjoys a technological, scale, or geographic advantage that allows it to produce a good service for a lower cost than its competition, it can charge a lower price and still earn good returns. Walmart is the classic example of a company that uses its huge buying power and an ultra-efficient supply chain to sell consumers goods at a much lower price than its competition.
- Intangible assets: This is a catch-all category that includes things like patents, branding, trade secrets, and regulatory protection. A great example of this is Tiffany's & Co's use of its strong brand name to convince consumers to pay a huge premium for its jewellery.

The best growth stocks have at least one competitive advantage working for them that will keep their profits protected from market forces.

3. Financial resilience

The economy is inherently unpredictable, so you can bet that sooner or later every company will face hard times. That's why it makes sense to strongly favour growth companies that can fund their future growth needs with internally generated profits instead of being dependent on functional financial markets (or as Warren Buffett likes to say, the "kindness of others.")

That's why I generally steer clear of growth companies that are operating at a loss or rely on a continual stream of acquisitions to grow. Companies that are operating at a loss will constantly need to tap shareholders for fresh capital in order to keep the doors open. That can lead to high levels of dilution which can mute future returns.

Slow or no-growth businesses that rely on acquisitions to post growth are in a similar situation. Buying other companies outright can be expensive and can often require the acquirer to issue new shares or take on debt to fund the deals. This can also lead to high levels of dilution or a severely weakened balance sheet.

These businesses are ultimately dependent on a factor that is outside of their control (functional capital markets or a high stock price) and might see their growth grind to a halt if the economy was to sputter.

For example,

Consider the music-streaming service Pandora Media as a great example. While the company has a great brand name and has grown its revenue quickly for many years, it consistently racks up hundreds of millions of dollars in losses each year. That's forced the company to dilute shareholders with secondary stock offerings and tap the debt markets for fresh capital. The company's financial fragility is a big reason why its stock price has been in free fall for many years.

By contrast, growth companies that are already profitable and sport a clean balance sheet are in far more control of their future. In fact, investors can often benefit when these companies face hard times.

4. Repeat purchase business model

Attracting new customers to a business is difficult and expensive. That's why it is far better for a business to make money by selling products or services to existing customers instead of relying on an endless stream of new customers to drive growth.

For example

Consider the music-streaming service Pandora Media as a great example. While the company has a great brand name and has grown its revenue quickly for many years, it consistently racks up hundreds of millions of dollars in losses each year. That's forced the company to dilute shareholders with secondary stock offerings and tap the debt markets for fresh capital. The company's financial fragility is a big reason why its stock price has been in free fall for many years.

By contrast, growth companies that are already profitable and sport a clean balance sheet are in far more control of their future. In fact, investors can often *benefit* when these companies face hard times.

Repeat Purchase Business Model

Attracting new customers to a business is difficult and expensive. That's why it is far better for a business to make money by selling products or services to *existing* customers instead of relying on an endless stream of new customers to drive growth.

For Example:

This is a big reason why once high-flying growth companies like GoPro and Fitbit ultimately turned into losing investments. These companies each sell electronic products that last for years, which negates the needs for existing customers to make a second purchase. After all, do consumers really need to own multiple sports action cameras or fitness trackers once they already have one?

This simple truth made these companies reliant on pulling in an endless stream of new customers to drive year-over-year growth. While that was possible when these businesses were small, it became an insurmountable challenge once they saturated their initial market niche.

Compare these companies' business model to a wonderful repeat purchase business.

For example

Like Starbucks. Coffee is purchased and consumed daily (and sometimes multiple times each day), so once a consumer warms up to the Starbucks brand, they tend to buy from the company continuously. This fact makes it much easier for Starbucks to post year-over-year growth as it expands its store empire and wins over new consumers.

5. Strong past price appreciation

For investors who grew up with the phrase "buy low, sell high" drilled into their brain (like me), this can be an exceedingly difficult principle to wrap your head around. After all, why would you seek out companies that have already performed well? Isn't it a better strategy to buy companies that are down on their luck and are thus "cheap?".

6. A great corporate culture

All growth businesses will need to bring on an endless stream of talented employees over time to enable them to meet the demands of their customers. However, the competition for top talent has become fierce, so it is critically important for a company to be able to retain its key employees for long periods of time and attract high-caliber new ones. That's why having a great company culture in place is critically important.

So how can investors judge whether or not a business has a thriving culture?

Do employees approve of the CEO? Would they recommend that their friends work there? Do they give the company's culture high marks? These are all questions that can be easily answered with a few minutes of research.

7. Talented leadership with skin in the game

The final thing in a great growth stock is a CEO who is deeply committed to the company's mission and is highly incentivized to make the business a success. Often times these leaders are also the founders or co-founder of the business and remain heavily invested in the company's success. Recent examples of founder-led businesses that went on to drive huge returns for shareholders include Jeff Bezos at Amazon.com, Reed Hastings at Netflix, and Mark Zuckerburg at Facebook.

Quality Investing

Quality investing is an investment strategy based on a set of clearly defined fundamental criteria that seeks to identify companies with outstanding quality characteristics. The quality assessment is made based on soft (e.g. management credibility) and hard criteria (e.g. balance sheet stability). Quality investing supports best overall rather than best-in-class approach.

Identification of Corporate Quality

As a rule, systematic quality investors identify quality stocks using a defined set of criteria that they have generally developed themselves and revise continually. Selection criteria that demonstrably influence and/or explain a company's business success or otherwise can be broken down into five categories:

1. Market positioning: Quality company possesses an economic moat, which distinguishes it from peers and allows to conquer leading market position. The company operates in the industry which offers certain growth potential and has global trends (e.g. ageing population for pharmaceuticals industry) as tailwinds.

2. Business model: According to the BCG matrix, the business model of a quality company is usually classified as star (growing business model, large capex) or cash cow (established business model, ample cash flows, and attractive dividend yield). Having a competitive advantage, quality company offers good product portfolio, well-established value chain and wide geographical span.

3. Corporate governance: Evaluation of corporate management execution is mainly based on soft-criteria assessment. Quality company has professional management, which is limited in headcount (6-8 members in top management) and has a low turnover rate. Its corporate governance structure is transparent, plausible and accordingly organized.

4. Financial strength: Solid balance sheet, high capital and sales profitability, ability to generate ample cash flows are key attributes of quality company. Quality company tends to demonstrate positive financial momentum for several years in a row. Earnings are of high quality, with operating cash flows exceeding net income, inventories and accounts receivables not growing faster than sales etc.

5. Attractive valuation: Valuation ultimately is related to quality, which is similar to investments in real estate. Attractive valuation, which is defined by high discounted cash flow (DCF), low P/E ratio and P/B ratio, becomes an important factor in quality investing process.

According to a number of studies the company can sustain its quality for about 11 months in average, which means that quantitative and qualitative monitoring of the company is done systematically.

Comparison to other Investment Models

Quality investing is an investment style that can be viewed independent of value investing and growth Investing. A quality portfolio may therefore also contain stocks with Growth and Value attributes.

Nowadays, Value Investing is based first and foremost on stock valuation. Certain valuation coefficients, such as the price/earnings and price/book ratios, are key elements here. Value is defined either by valuation level relative to the overall market or to the sector, or as the opposite of Growth. An analysis of the company's fundamentals is therefore secondary. Consequently, a Value investor will buy a company's stock because he believes that it is undervalued and that the company is a good one. A quality investor, meanwhile, will buy a company's stock because it is an excellent company that is also attractively valued.

Modern Growth Investing centers primarily on Growth stocks. The investor's decision rests equally on experts' profit forecasts and the company's earnings per share. Only stocks that are believed to generate high future profits and a strong growth in earnings per share are admitted to a Growth investor's portfolio. The share price at which these anticipated profits are bought, and the fundamental basis for growth, are secondary considerations. Growth investors thus focus on stocks exhibiting strong earnings expansion and high profit expectations, regardless of their valuation. Quality investors, meanwhile, favor stocks whose high earnings growth is rooted in a sound fundamental basis and whose price is justified.

Socially Responsible Investing

Socially responsible investing, or SRI, is the act of choosing your investments on the basis of social good as well as financial gain. Socially responsible investors aim to invest in companies that do business in positive and responsible ways. In general, they look for companies that have a good record on what are known as ESG issues: environment, social justice, and corporate governance.

Although most investors in the U.S. aren't socially responsible investors, their ranks are growing. According to a 2014 report by US SIF, an organization for socially responsible investors, the total amount of money invested in managed funds that use SRI strategies has grown from less than $1 trillion in 1995 to more than $6.5 trillion at the beginning of 2014. That's more than one out of every six dollars under professional management in the country.

The roots of socially responsible investing go back hundreds of years. In the 1700s, members of the Religious Society of Friends – better known as Quakers – refused to take part in the slave trade or to invest in weapons of war. Around 1750, John Wesley, an early leader of the Methodist church, wrote a famous sermon, "The Use of Money," in which he declared that it was a sin to make money at the expense of your own or your neighbour's welfare. He specifically urged his congregants not to be involved in gambling, usury (loaning out money at unreasonably high interest rates), and industries that used toxic chemicals such as arsenic and lead.

For centuries, many socially responsible investors focused on avoiding "sin industries" such as gambling, tobacco, and liquor. However, that began to change in the 1960s, when investors became interested in using their money to promote civil rights, equality for women, and better treatment of workers. SRI achieved one of its most notable successes in the 1980s, when both individual investors and institutions began pulling their money out of South Africa because of its policy of apartheid, or strict separation between races. Their efforts played a major part in bringing an end to apartheid in 1994.

It was also during the 1980s that SRI began to attract more attention from mainstream investors. The oldest investment advisor devoted specifically to SRI, Trillium Asset Management, was founded in 1982. Today, Trillium is just one of many companies that offer socially responsible funds to investors. According to the US SIF report, in 2014, there were 480 registered investment companies in the U.S. that considered ESG factors in choosing their investments.

Types of Socially Responsible Investments

Socially responsible investors have a wide range of investments to choose from. Major types include:

- Mutual Funds and ETFs: There are hundreds of mutual funds on the market that use ESG criteria. On its website, US SIF publishes a list of more than 200 socially responsible mutual funds offered by its member firms, with information about both their financial performance and the criteria they use for choosing their investments. In addition, US SIF's 2010 report on social investing trends identifies 26 exchange-traded funds (ETFs) that use social and environmental screens.

- Alternative Investments: Alternatives to traditional investments, such as hedge funds and property funds, are also getting into the SRI game. According to US SIF, alternative investment funds for SRI are growing at a dramatic rate. In 2012, there were a total of 177 alternative SRI funds in the country managing about $38 billion in assets. By 2014, the number had jumped to 336 funds with $224 billion in assets.
- Community Investments. Socially responsible investors can also lend money directly into community organizations: One way to do this is to put money into community development financial institutions (CDFIs), including banks, credit unions, and loan funds, which provide credit and other financial services in low-income areas. You can find CDFI banks through the website of the National Community Investment Fund (NCIF) and credit unions through the National Federation of Community Development Credit Unions (NFCDCU).
- Microfinance: Another way for investors to invest money where it can do the most good is through microloans, small loans made directly to start up businesses. Kiva and Zidisha are two organizations that offer microloans to entrepreneurs in developing countries, while Kabbage focuses on small businesses in the U.S.

Goals of Socially Responsible Investors

The essence of SRI is choosing investments that are in line with your values. However, those values aren't the same for all investors.

Socially responsible investors choose their investments to promote a variety of different goals, including the following:

- Cleaner Environment: "Green" investors prefer companies that don't pollute the environment. Some refuse to invest in fossil fuels, while others look for companies that minimize the carbon footprint of their products and services.
- Social Justice: Some investors refuse to do business in countries with a record of human rights violations. Others look for companies that provide their workers with fair wages and decent working conditions.
- Promoting Peace: Like the early Quakers, peace investors won't invest in war in any way. They avoid all companies that make weapons or profit from conflict in foreign countries.
- Promoting Health: Many socially responsible investors refuse to invest in companies that sell tobacco or alcohol. Others refuse to invest in products that they think pose a threat to human health, such as genetically modified organisms. Since some of these products can also be seen as threats to the environment, this category overlaps with green investing.
- Promoting Morality: Many socially responsible investors today continue the time-honored practice of avoiding "sin industries." Different investors see this category as including different types of enterprises, such as liquor, gambling, pornography, and contraception.

Although many of these issues are popular with the political left, SRI isn't defined by politics. Both the liberal who refuses to invest in companies that make weapons and the conservative who refuses to invest in hospitals that perform abortions are considered to be socially responsible investors – they just choose their investments based on different standards.

Ways to be a Socially Responsible Investor

To promote their social goals, socially responsible investors rely on four main strategies:

1. Negative Screening: Negative screening means refusing to invest in companies that don't meet your social standards. For instance, many socially responsible mutual funds screen out tobacco companies. An extreme form of negative screening is divestment: pulling all your assets out of specific companies because of how or where they do business. This is the strategy investors used against South African companies in the 1980s.

2. Positive Investing: Although negative screening is the strategy people most often associate with SRI, an equally important tool is positive screening: choosing companies to include in your portfolio specifically because you approve of their behaviour. One example is choosing companies that have signed the CERES principles, a code of environmental conduct for businesses developed in 1989. Positive investing is also known as impact investing, or ESG incorporation.

3. Community Investing: This is a specific subcategory of positive investing that focuses specifically on investing in community-based organizations, especially in low-income areas. Community investment provides loans to people and organizations that would have trouble getting them otherwise. These loans can be used to fund small businesses and provide needed services such as housing and education. Community investment can also focus on making communities more sustainable by financing projects such as green energy and smart growth, a type of urban planning designed to reduce sprawl and protect green space.

4. Shareholder Action: Socially responsible investors don't just use their values to choose companies for their portfolios – they also try to influence the behavior of companies in which they hold stock. One way to do this is by filing shareholder resolutions – proposals for management about how to run the company. One popular example is a resolution requiring the company to disclose all the donations it makes to political campaigns. Under the Securities and Exchange Act of 1934, any investor or group of investors who owns at least 1% of a company's stock (or $2,000 worth) can submit a proposal to be voted on at the next shareholder meeting. Even if a proposal doesn't win a majority vote at the meeting, it can still influence the management's decisions if it attracts a significant amount of support.

Getting Started with SRI

Putting your money into SRI isn't all that different from making any other investment. All you're really doing is adding an extra step to the process: deciding what your social goals are, and then choosing investments to promote those goals. True, this limits your investing options, but that can actually be helpful. With such a huge array of funds out there, it's much easier to choose if you have a way of narrowing down the field first.

Here are some basic steps to follow when making your first socially responsible investment:

1. Choose Your Social Criteria. You can't choose socially responsible investments until you know what social goals you want to promote. Don't worry at this point about what's actually available or how the funds perform. Instead, just think about your values and what you want to achieve with your money. Then, write down a list of criteria that your investments need to meet to put them in line with your conscience.

2. Choose Your Financial Criteria. Next, consider your investment goals – just as you would when making any other investment. Think about what you're investing your money for, when you expect to need it, how much risk you can handle, and how big a return you need to meet your goals. And don't worry that you'll hurt your bottom line any more than in traditional investments by investing in a socially responsible way. Studies by numerous financial and academic institutions – including the Morgan Stanley Institute for Responsible Investing, the Global Impact Investing Network, and TIAA-CREF Asset Management – show that SRI provides returns at least as good as conventional investing.

3. Find Funds that Meet your Needs. Once you've nailed down your social and financial goals, the next step is to find investments that meet them. One good place to look is the US SIF website, which offers handbooks on investing to advance women, fight climate change, and fight corporate money in politics. US SIF also publishes a list of funds that shows how different funds perform and what social screens they apply.

4. Compare and Choose. Look at the investments on your short list and ask yourself which ones do the best job of meeting both your social goals and your financial goals. Of course, depending on what those goals are, you may need to make some trade-offs. For example, one of my aims as an investor is to keep fees as low as possible, but the SRI funds with the lowest overall expenses don't do the best job of meeting my social goals. So try to strike a balance based on what's most important to you.

Moving your money into socially responsible investments is really a win-win. It lets you make the most of your money in two different ways: You can earn good returns, and promote values that are important to you.

The only real downside is that it takes a bit more work to find the right investments to meet two sets of goals – social and financial – instead of just one. But the good news is, that's a job you only have to do once. Once you've made your investment choices, you can just keep putting your money in the same place, secure in the knowledge that it's going toward companies you can approve of.

Goal-based Investing

A goals-based approach to investing is beneficial to investors because it puts them in the driver's seat as they are actively involved in the decision making process. The success of a goals-based strategy is not about outperforming benchmarks or competitors. Success is measured by how well an investor's portfolio is tracking against a stated goal. It's about being more relevant to investors and their needs, not only in terms of product design but in terms of communications and reporting.

By focusing on how an investment is on track to meet investors' needs, it should help investors fight the urge to respond inappropriately and irrationally when markets aren't performing as they might expect.

Applying Goal-based Investing Practically

Don't Fall Short on Savings

The income you earn has to be first allocated to your regular expenses. What is left out of your income is normally your savings. These savings forms the corpus for you to intelligently invest in wealth creating assets. That is where the basic conceptual problem arises. Most of us tend to believe that (Savings = Income - Expenses). This definition will not take you too far. You need to make savings your target. Your actual formula should be (Discretionary spending = Income - necessary expenses – target savings). Here you have to set a target savings out of your total income and look to reduce routine expenses to the bare minimum and look at all your discretionary spending as residual. That is the only way you will have adequate savings to fund your long term goals through intelligent investing.

You Can Achieve More by Saving Less

In economics we call it the power of compounding. The beauty of money is that it compounds because not only your principal but even the income earned by your investment generates income. That is why equity funds are able to give returns in excess of 17-18% annualized over a longer period of time. The earlier you start the better. For example, if you started a mutual fund SIP with a monthly investment of Rs.10,000 for a 20 year period and earned 18 % returns then at the end of 20 years you would have invested Rs.24 lakhs but your portfolio will be worth Rs.2.35 crore. And all this with a monthly outlay of just Rs.10,000! Now if you started 10 years later, you will have only 10 years of investing left with you. In that case, hold your breath, you will have to invest a whopping Rs.70,000 per month to reach the same target. That is why in any savings plan, you can achieve more through your investments if you start off early.

Let your Investment Goals be Driven by Data

The beauty of goal based investing is that your decisions are actually driven by credible data. For example, when expected returns on equity, volatility and inflation are factored in after considering the empirical data for a longer period for a longer period of time, then your assumptions become more fine-tuned and therefore your results become more achievable.

Your Investment Must be Towards a Tangible Outcome

This is one of the most important contributions of goal-based investing. Because you know what your long term goals is you know the monetary implication of that goal. Since you know the monetary outcome of that goal, you know the tangible outcome that you need to work towards.

This enables you to plan your savings, tweak your investments and monitor their performance with that tangible goal in mind. Vague goals really cannot take you too far and therefore your investment will become more haphazard rather than being focused on your goal.

Goals will Automatically Balance the Risk/Return of Equity Portfolio

The big advantage of goal based investing is that it compels you to automatically shift out of high risk situations. Take the example of your equity exposure of 60 % which has gone up to 75 % purely because the markets are up by 70 % in the last 2 years. That creates a big mismatch in your original asset allocation. As a result you will be forced to reduce your equity component accordingly. This instils in you a discipline to automatically take money out of the market when it gets overpriced. Of course, in the process you may miss out on the last ditch bull market but then that is not the essence of goal-based investing anyways.

Avoid the Maturity Mismatch Blunder

Have you even wondered what the maturity mismatch is all about? Let us understand what the Indian investment anomaly is all about. In India long term money belonging to insurance endowments and provident funds and pensions are invested in debt at ridiculously low yields. On the other hand, the short term money is getting invested into equities with disappointing results. A goal-based approach to investing will automatically rectify this maturity mismatch. The funds that you require after a long period will go into equities and the funds that you require sooner will automatically go into debt and similar products. The mismatch is dangerous because it results in higher risk and also in sub-optimal returns.

To cut a long story short, goal based investing has a lot of inherent advantages. It not only forces a sense of discipline into your investing but also ensures that you are working towards a tangible long term goal. That is a good point to start with.

Factor Investing

Factor investing has received considerable attention recently, primarily because factors are the cornerstones of "smart" or "strategic" beta strategies that have become popular among individual and institutional investors. In fact, these strategies had net inflows of nearly $250 billion during the past five years. But investors actually have been employing factor based techniques in some form for decades, seeking the potential enhanced risk-adjusted-return benefits of certain factor exposures.

Key Factors

The following five factors have been identified by academics and widely adopted by investors over the years as key exposures in a portfolio.

1. Size

In pinpointing the first of their two identified factors, Fama and French demonstrated that a return premium exists for investing in smaller-cap stocks. This could be due to their inherently riskier nature: Smaller companies are typically more volatile and have a higher risk of bankruptcy, and investors expect to be compensated for taking on that additional level of risk. As shown in figure empirical evidence demonstrates that over longer periods of time, smallcap stocks outperform large caps.

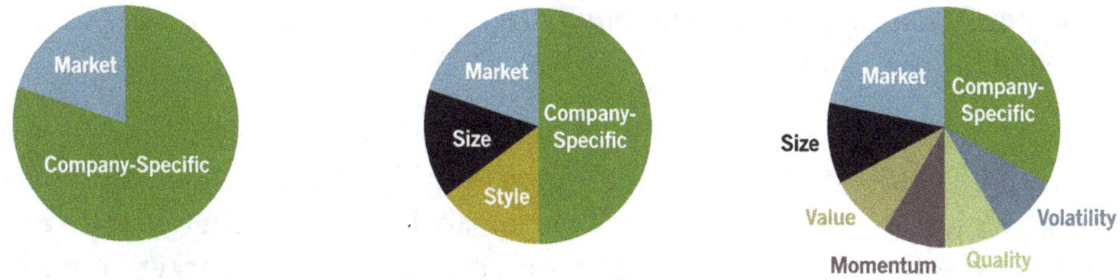

CAPM: Stock returns are driven by exposure to the market factor (beta) and company-specific drivers

Fama and French account for additional factors: size and style

Research proves the case for multiple factors as components of stock returns and risk

Exposure to small-cap stocks can be achieved relatively easily by using standard market capitalizations. For most investors, holding a small-cap fund or ETF, for example, is a straightforward and relatively efficient way to harvest the small-cap premium. However, the inherently riskier nature of investing in smaller companies is important to bear in mind.

2. Value

The second factor introduced in the Fama–French model is value, suggesting that inexpensive stocks should outperform more expensive ones. Research on the field of value investing stretches back many decades. In 1949, Benjamin Graham urged investors to buy stocks at a discount to their intrinsic value. He argued that expensive stocks with lofty expectations leave little room for error, while cheaper stocks that can beat expectations may afford investors more upside.

Small caps have beaten large caps over time, even though this leadership can shift over shorter periods

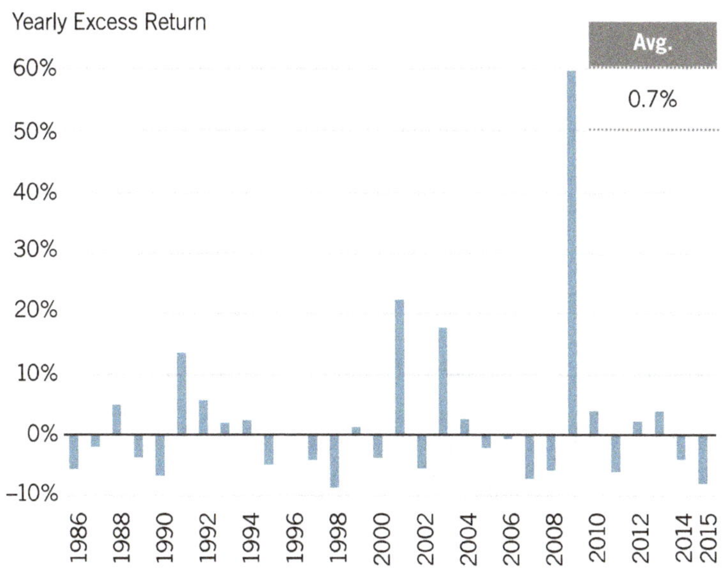

Figure: Small-Cap Excess Returns

Small-cap returns shown are yearly returns of the equal-weighted bottom quintile (by market capitalization) of the Russell 1000 Index. All excess returns are relative to the equal-weighted Russell 1000 Index. All factor portfolios are sector neutral, assume dividend reinvestment, and exclude fees and implementation costs. Avg.: compound average of yearly excess returns. Past performance is no guarantee of future results.

With this in mind, one view is that value investing works because stocks follow earnings over time. Investors tend to be overly optimistic about expensive, high-growth stocks and overly pessimistic about cheap, slower-growth stocks. When cheap stocks report higher-than-expected earnings (even versus low expectations), they can outperform as a result of the market's improved optimism in their earnings potential.

Empirical results also seem to indicate that value investing can generate excess returns over time. Fama and French demonstrated that stocks with high book-to-price ratios outperformed stcks with lower ratios. Many commonly used indexes still place a heavy emphasis on that definition, and exposure to that particular valuation factor is easy to gain with available products. Yet there are many different ways to define value. For example, investors may examine earnings, sales, or cash flows to judge whether a stock appears inexpensive, and performance can vary based on which metric is used. Figure shows the performance differential between two common measures of value: book-to-price ratio and earnings yield (earnings-to-price ratio).

The performance of a value portfolio can vary based on how value is defined

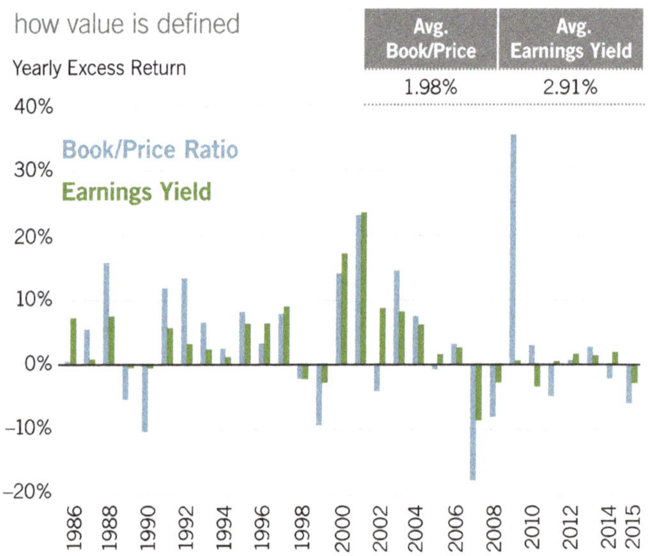

Figure: Excess returns of two value measures

Earnings yield: last 12 months of earnings per share divided by price per share. Book/price ratio: the ratio of a company's reported accumulated profits to its price per share. Returns shown are yearly returns of the equal-weighted top quintile (based on these two value metrics) of the Russell 1000 Index. Past performance is no guarantee of future results.

In fact, a single-factor definition of value may expose investors to greater volatility and larger declines, and a multifactor approach to finding value stocks is typically preferred due to its diversification benefits, which tend to lead to higher returns over time. Figure shows that a stock portfolio created using a composite of high book-to-price ratio and high earnings yield outpaced the broader market by 3.50% on average each year, beating both independent underlying metrics.

3. Momentum

The concept of momentum investing is similar in spirit to what technical analysts have been doing for decades, namely, examining price trends to forecast future returns. Empirical evidence of the momentum anomaly was first published in 1993 by Narasimhan Jegadeesh and Sheridan Titman, and demonstrated that stocks that had outperformed in the medium term would continue to perform well, and vice versa for stocks that had lagged.

Inexpensive stocks have outperformed the broader market over the long term.

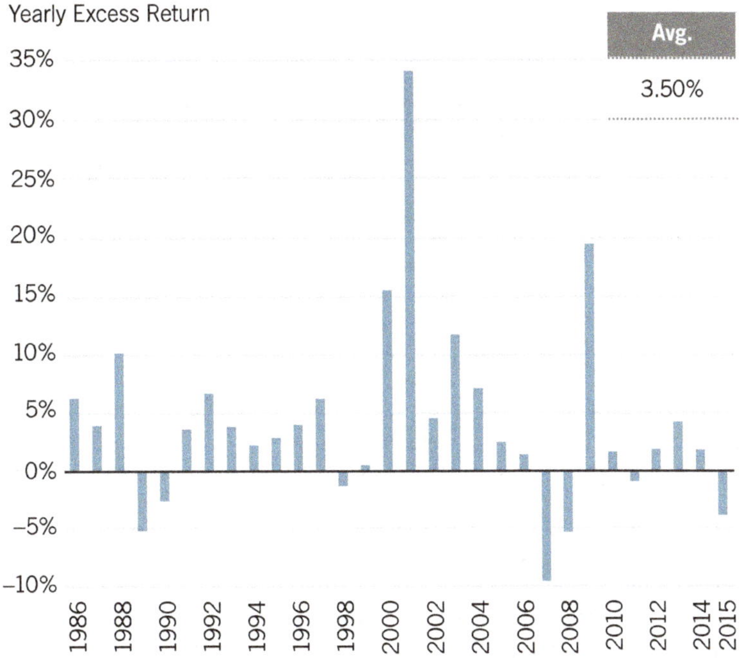

Figure: Excess returns of value stocks

Value composite is a combined average ranking of stocks in the equal weighted top quintile (by book/price ratio) and stocks in the equal-weighted top quintile (by earnings yield) of the Russell 1000 Index. Returns shown are yearly returns of this value composite. Past performance is no guarantee of future results.

Value composite is a combined average ranking of stocks in the equal weighted top quintile (by book/price ratio) and stocks in the equal-weighted top quintile (by earnings yield) of the Russell 1000 Index. Returns shown are yearly returns of this value composite. Past performance is no guarantee of future results.

The explanation for why momentum investing works has been a topic of much debate, but many make a behavioural argument that investors tend to underreact to improving fundamentals or company trends. It's not until a stock is outperforming that it catches investors' attention and they pile onto the trade. This dynamic allows winners to keep winning and momentum investing to work. The cycle tends to continue until there is a catalyst that causes it to stop (e.g., an earnings miss or overvaluation, indicating a negative fundamental change). A common way to measure momentum is to classify stocks by 12-month price returns, which has proven to be an effective strategy for outperforming the broader market over time.

4. Quality

Due to common investor behaviors, momentum investing has led to outperformance over time

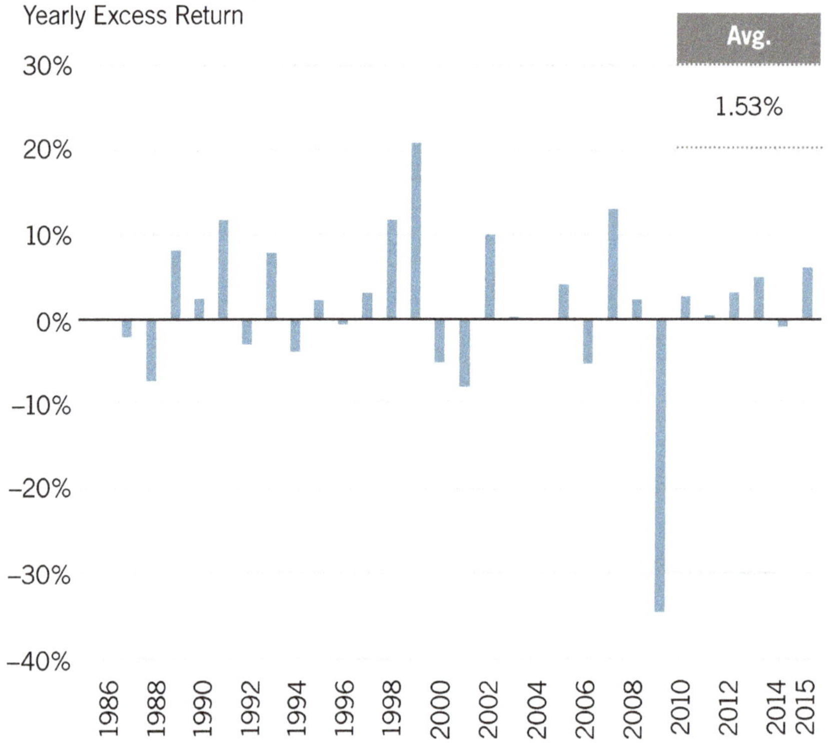

Figure: Excess Returns of Momentum Portfolios

Momentum returns shown are yearly returns of the equal-weighted top quintile (as measured by trailing 12-month returns) of the Russell 1000 Index. Past performance is no guarantee of future results.

Although investors have been seeking out high-quality companies for decades, empirical evidence validating the merits of this approach has only emerged relatively recently. This may be due to the lack of consensus on how best to define "quality." For example, Richard Sloan and Scott Richardson conducted important work suggesting that companies with higher earnings quality or lower accruals (roughly measured as the difference between operating cash flow and net income) have outperformed over time. Many observers agree, however, that higher profitability, more stable income and cash flows, and a lack of excessive leverage are hallmarks of quality companies. For a company to have higher margins and profits than its competitors, it must boast some competitive advantage. Competitive advantages tend to be sticky, and companies that have them are thus able to earn higher profits than their peers over long periods of time. Put simply, companies that generate superior profits, possess strong balance sheets, and demonstrate stable cash flows should be able to provide consistent outperformance over the long term. Even by examining only a single measure of quality—such as return on equity—it is evident that stocks that exhibit strong profitability tend to outpace the market over time (Exhibit).

High-quality stocks with strong profitability tend to exhibit long-term outperformance

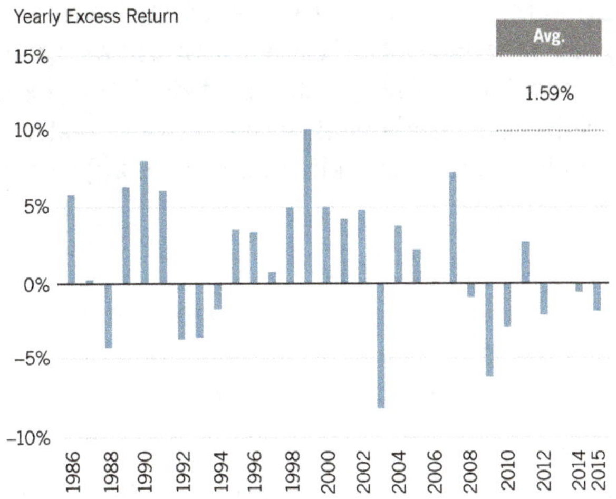

Figure: Excess Returns of Quality Portfolios

Return on equity: a measure of profitability that calculates how many dollars of profit a company generates with each dollar of shareholders' equity. Quality returns shown are yearly returns of the equal-weighted top quintile (as measured by return on equity) of the Russell 1000 Index. Past performance is no guarantee of future results.

5. Low Volatility

As the name suggests, the primary objective of a low-volatility approach is to own stocks that have lower risk or return volatility than the broader market, which has historically resulted in higher risk-adjusted returns. Considerable research has shown that low-volatility portfolios may also outperform the broader market over time. For example, work by Robert Haugen and James Heins stated that stock portfolios with less variance in monthly returns tend to produce higher returns on average than those that are "riskier." Some argue, however, that the relative outperformance of these strategies is actually attributable to the size anomaly or sector biases inherent to this category of stocks, and not to the low-volatility characteristic itself. Generally, robust factors should outperform even when their size and sector biases are controlled.

In addition to reducing risk, a low-volatility portfolio may beat the market over time

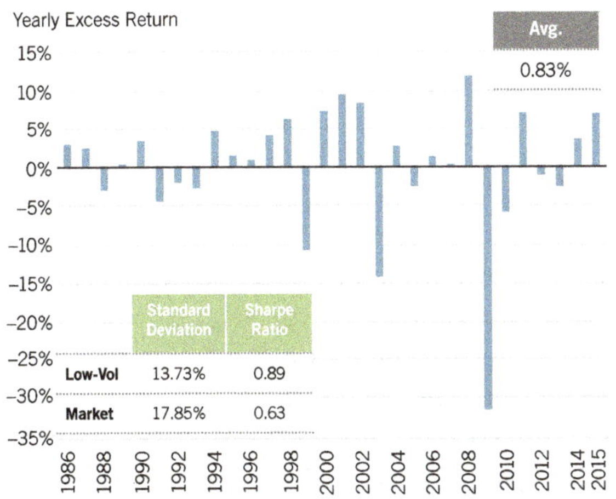

Figure: Excess returns of low-volatility portfolios

Low-volatility returns shown are yearly returns of the equal-weighted bottom quintile (by standard deviation of weekly price returns) of the Russell 1000 Index. Standard deviation: a measure of return dispersion. A portfolio with a lower standard deviation exhibits less return volatility. Sharpe ratio compares portfolio returns above the risk-free rate relative to overall portfolio volatility (a higher Sharpe ratio implies better risk-adjusted returns). Past performance is no guarantee of future results.

Even if the jury is still out on whether low-volatility investing can lead to outperformance on its own, the strategy can still be compelling. By classifying stocks in this way, investors may generate returns similar to the market over time, but with a less bumpy ride. The benefits of a low-volatility approach can also be achieved by investing in stocks with more stable revenues and earnings, which are less susceptible to recessions and other macroeconomic events.

This approach is designed to perform best when volatility is high and markets decline rapidly, because lower-risk stocks tend to hold up better during down markets when investor uncertainty is elevated. Low-volatility portfolios tend to experience smaller drawdowns, and investors can benefit from the compounding of positive excess returns in a down market.

Exhibit shows that stocks exhibiting low price volatility have narrowly outperformed the market over time, with less risk—leading to higher risk-adjusted returns.

Cyclicality of Factor Performance

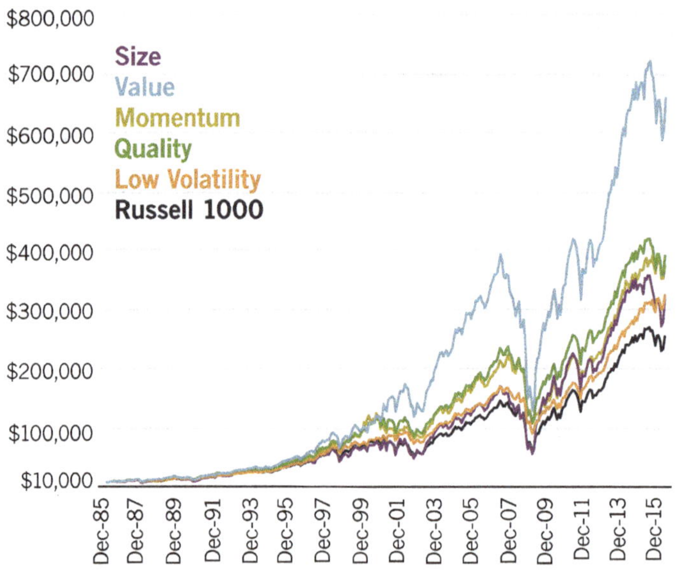

Figure: Growth of $10,000 Investing in Factor Portfolios vs. the Broader Market (1985–2015)

The evidence suggests that these five key factor exposures can be compelling additions to a portfolio. But no single factor works all the time and returns tend to be cyclical. For example, small-caps can underperform large-caps for multiyear periods, as they did during the technology "bubble" in the late 1990s and during the financial crisis in 2007–08. Value stocks also fell out of favour during the high-growth tech bubble but managed to earn back their losses (and then some) in the years that followed. Swift changes in market direction are typically detrimental to momentum strategies—such as in 2000, following the collapse of the tech bubble, and in 2009, following the rapid recovery from the financial crisis. Quality portfolios typically lag during low-quality rallies—when the most beaten-down stocks lead the market in a rebound, as they did in 2003. Finally, low-volatility stocks tend to underperform during market rallies following bear markets—such as in 2009. These performance swings can be unsettling to investors, causing them to sell and miss out on rebounding performance.

These five factors have outperformed over time

Returns are cumulative and assume reinvestment of dividends. Past performance is no guarantee of future results. Factor definitions consistent with those shown in previous exhibits.

The good news is that most factors are not highly correlated with one another—they are driven by different market anomalies and therefore tend to pay off at different times. For example,

Most factors are not highly correlated, so diversifying among them may improve risk-adjusted returns over.

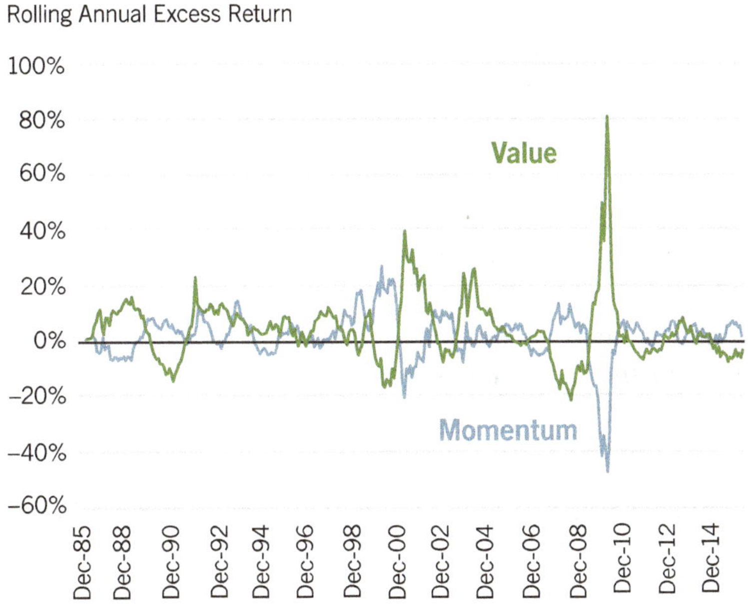

Figure: Value and momentum cyclicality

Value represented by the equal-weighted top quintile (by book-to-price ratio) of the Russell 1000 Index. Momentum represented by the equal-weighted top quintile (by trailing 12-month returns) of the Russell 1000 Index.

by definition, value and momentum strategies are poles apart (Exhibit). Value investors buy stocks that have declined in price and are cheap, while momentum investors buy stocks that have been on the rise and should continue to run.

The distinct cyclicality of factor returns may tempt investors to try and time their exposures. Indeed, factor strategies can provide a useful tool for tactically minded investors to get the right exposure at the right time. But, similar to market timing, effective factor timing can be challenging, and diversifying across multiple factor strategies may be a sound option for long-term investors. For more detail on how to implement factor-based strategies.

Investment Implications

Factor-based investment strategies can be compelling options because they provide investors with targeted and streamlined access to factor exposures. It's important to also note that the factor-investing universe is broad and extends beyond single factor strategies targeting the five key factors. Many factor-based strategies provide exposure to multiple factors within one vehicle and others provide exposure to stock characteristics that address specific investor needs or desired outcomes—such as income—but do not explicitly seek to improve returns or adjust risk in any way.

The factor-investing marketplace has become more crowded, and these strategies can vary significantly in how they are constructed and in how they perform. As a result, it can be a difficult investment landscape to navigate. For example, a naively constructed factor-based strategy may also contain unintended exposures (e.g., a small-cap bias or sector tilts) that could alter the overall exposures of a broader portfolio. Further, some factor definitions and the best metrics t capture these exposures are still up for debate.

Although not all factor-based strategies are created equal and careful evaluation may be required to select among them, academic research and historical performance have proven the case for factors and exposures as potentially compelling components of a broader portfolio.

Traditional Investments

Essentially, this is where you invest your money into assets that are well-known. There are three types of traditional investments cash, stocks and bonds.

Traditional Ways to Invest your Money

If you're a first time investor, you should concentrate your money in traditional asset classes. The classes below should be at the top of your list.

1. Bonds

This is a debt security issued by a company, government, or government agency. They are typically available in denominations of $1,000 and pay interest to the holder on a periodic basis. There are three major categories of bonds:

Municipal bonds are sold by states and local governments, and pay interest that is free from federal income taxes, as well as taxes in the issuing jurisdiction.

Treasury bonds are issued by the United States government and are considered the safest type of bonds since they're backed by the full faith, credit, and taxing power of the federal government.

Corporate bonds are issued by companies and can come with a variety of different features, including convertibility to the company's stock, and early call provisions (the corporation has the ability to pay the bonds early).

2. Mutual Funds and Exchange Traded Funds (ETFs)

These are portfolios of stocks, bonds, and other securities, that are offered for sale to the general public. They typically include money from thousands of investors, and can have anywhere from a few securities to several hundred in the fund.

They are an excellent way to invest in a ready-made portfolio of diversified securities, and are typically less risky than investing in individual stocks. The funds typically pay dividends and capital gains distributions based on the performance of the securities in the portfolio.

3. Certificates of Deposit (CDs)

These are contracts between a bank and a depositor in which the bank borrows money from the depositor at a fixed rate of interest. They typically have minimums of $500 or $1,000, and terms can range anywhere from 90 days to several years.

The principal invested in CDs is completely safe, as are the interest payments, as long as the security is held until maturity. Normally, there are prepayment penalties should you liquidate the CD prior to its maturity date and that will reduce the amount of interest you will receive. CDs are an excellent place to park cash or invest your emergency fund.

4. Money Markets

These are essentially mutual funds comprised entirely of interest-bearing cash type investments, typically US treasury bills. Unlike a CD, interest rates tend to fluctuate based on prevailing rates in the financial markets. Principal invested, while theoretically not guaranteed by the issuer, is nonetheless highly stable.

Money markets can be issued by banks and investment brokers. When provided by investment brokers, they are an outstanding place to park cash in between risk investments, like stocks and bonds.

5. Stocks

Stocks trade in shares since they represent a form of ownership in a business entity. Holding stock in a company not only entitles you to a share of the entity's revenues (paid through dividends), but also the ability to participate in the growth of the stock price if the company is successful. While stocks represent an ownership share in the business, the price is not stable, being completely dependent upon market fluctuations.

Stock held in a strong company can provide steady price appreciation over many years, while stock held in a weak company could drop to nearly zero.

Investment Real Estate

Investment real estate is real estate that generates income or is otherwise intended for investment purposes rather than as a primary residence. It is common for investors to own multiple pieces of real estate, one of which serves as a primary residence while the others are used to generate rental income and profits through price appreciation. The tax implications for investment real estate are often different than those for residential real estate.

Common examples of investment properties are apartment buildings and rental houses in which the owners do not live in the residential units but use them to generate ongoing rental income from tenants. Those who invest in real estate also expect to generate capital gains as property values increase over time.

Ways Investment Real Estate can be Managed

Leveraging investment real estate can follow numerous paths. An investor might join a real estate investment group that pools its funds to acquire properties. The owner or owners of investment property may hire property managers to oversee the day-to-day upkeep and rent collection for a piece of real estate or an entire portfolio.

A real estate investor could also look to serve on the lending or funding side of projects with an expectation of a return on their investment. For example, investors could be the lenders behind hard money loans for real estate. The borrower in such an instance will likely pay higher interest rates to receive the funds and will need to repay the loan in short order. The lender might agree to the loan in the hopes of taking ownership of the property should the borrower default especially if the property has the potential for greater resale value.

Investment real estate can take the form of a piece of property that is in disrepair or otherwise underdeveloped that is built up with the intent to rent the space for a long-term return. The owner of the property might seek financing to cover the cost to improve the real estate and make it more attractive to tenants.

A real estate investor could acquire a property based on an expectation that demand for the space will increase because of external factors. New attractions such as a sports arena or infrastructure development, such as a highway extension, could make neighboring properties highly desirable. For example, a real estate investor might buy a commercial property next door to the site for a new theater that is under construction. The assumption is that there would be increased foot traffic passing by the purchased property, which would make the location a prime choice for retailers. The increased demand could give the owned cause to alleviate rent prices as well.

Impact Investing

Impact investments are investments made into companies, organizations, and funds with the intention to generate social and environmental impact alongside a financial return. Impact investments can be made in both emerging and developed markets, and target a range of returns from below market to market rate, depending on investors' strategic goals.

The growing impact investment market provides capital to address the world's most pressing challenges in sectors such as sustainable agriculture, renewable energy, conservation, microfinance, and affordable and accessible basic services including housing, healthcare, and education.

Core Characteristics of Impact Investing

The practice of impact investing is further defined by the following four core characteristics:

- Intentionality: An investor's intention to have a positive social or environmental impact through investments is essential to impact investing.
- Investment with return expectations: Impact investments are expected to generate a financial return on capital or, at minimum, a return of capital.
- Range of return expectations and asset classes: Impact investments target financial returns that range from below market (sometimes called concessionary) to risk-adjusted market rate, and can be made across asset classes, including but not limited to cash equivalents, fixed income, venture capital, and private equity.

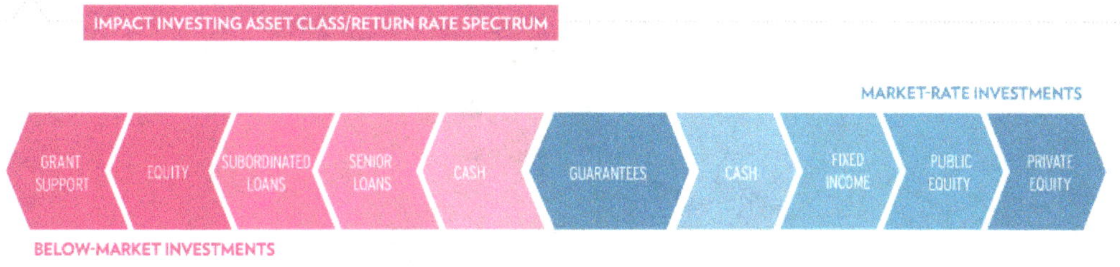

- Impact measurement: A hallmark of impact investing is the commitment of the investor to measure and report the social and environmental performance and progress of underlying investments, ensuring transparency and accountability while informing the practice of impact investing and building the field.

Investors' approaches to impact measurement will vary based on their objectives and capacities, and the choice of what to measure usually reflects investor goals and, consequently, investor intention. In general, components of impact measurement best practices for impact investing include:

- Establishing and stating social and environmental objectives to relevant stakeholders
- Setting performance metrics/targets related to these objectives using standardized metrics wherever possible

- Monitoring and managing the performance of investees against these targets
- Reporting on social and environmental performance to relevant stakeholders

Reasons for Impact Investing

Impact investing challenges the long-held views that social and environmental issues should be addressed only by philanthropic donations, and that market investments should focus exclusively on achieving financial returns.

The impact investing market offers diverse and viable opportunities for investors to advance social and environmental solutions through investments that also produce financial returns.

Many types of investors are entering the growing impact investing market. Here are a few common investor motivations:

- Banks, pension funds, financial advisors, and wealth managers can provide client investment opportunities to both individuals and institutions with an interest in general or specific social and/or environmental causes.
- Institutional and family foundations can leverage significantly greater assets to advance their core social and/or environmental goals, while maintaining or growing their overall endowment.
- Government investors and development finance institutions can provide proof of financial viability for private-sector investors while targeting specific social and environmental goals.

Investors of Impact Investments

Impact investment has attracted a wide variety of investors, both individual and institutional.

- Fund Managers
- Development finance institutions
- Diversified financial institutions/banks
- Private foundations

- Pension funds and insurance companies
- Family Offices
- Individual investors
- NGOs
- Religious institutions

Performance of Impact Investments Financially

Impact investors have diverse financial return expectations. Some intentionally invest for below-market-rate returns, in line with their strategic objectives. Others pursue market-competitive and market-beating returns, sometimes required by fiduciary responsibility.

Figure : Target financial returns principally sought by percentage of respondents

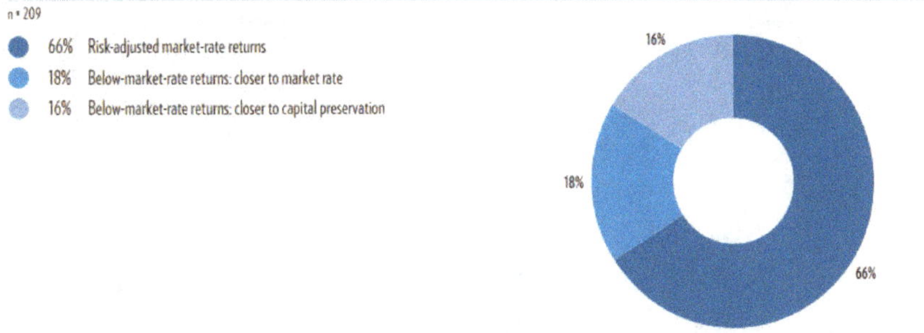

Respondents also report that portfolio performance overwhelmingly meets or exceeds investor expectations for both social and environmental impact and financial return, in investments spanning emerging markets, developed markets, and the market as a whole.

Figure : Performance relative to expectations

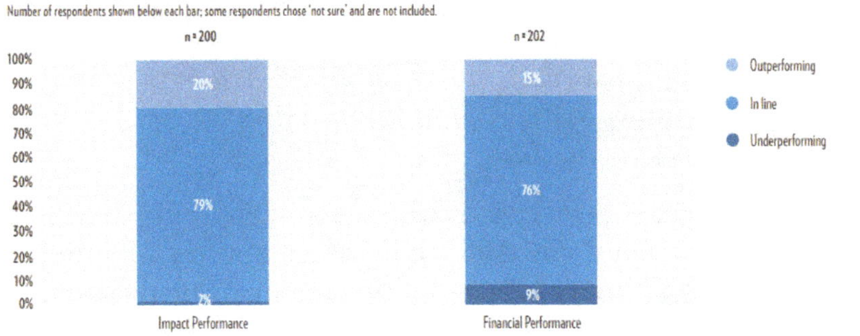

Although very few investors report significant risk events in their impact investing portfolios, business model execution and management is by far the most often cited contributor to risk.

Current State of the Impact Investing Market

While some investors have been making impact investments for decades, recently there has emerged a new collaborative international effort to accelerate the development of a high- functioning market that supports impact investing. While this market is still relatively new, investors are optimistic overall about its development and expect increased scale and efficiency in the future.

Impact investors generally recognize broad progress across key indicators of market growth but also acknowledge that some challenges remain.

Figure : Progress on indicators of market growth

Number of respondents shown above each indicator; some respondents chose 'not sure' and these responses are not included. Ranked by percent selecting 'some progress' or 'significant progress.'

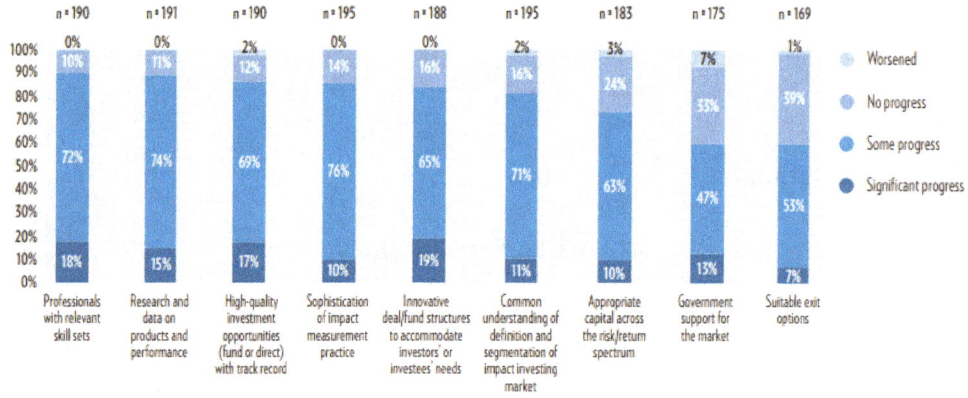

Figure : Challenges to the growth of the impact investing industry

Number responding for each option shown above each column. Some respondents chose 'not sure' and these responses are not included. Ranked by percent selecting 'very significant challenge.'

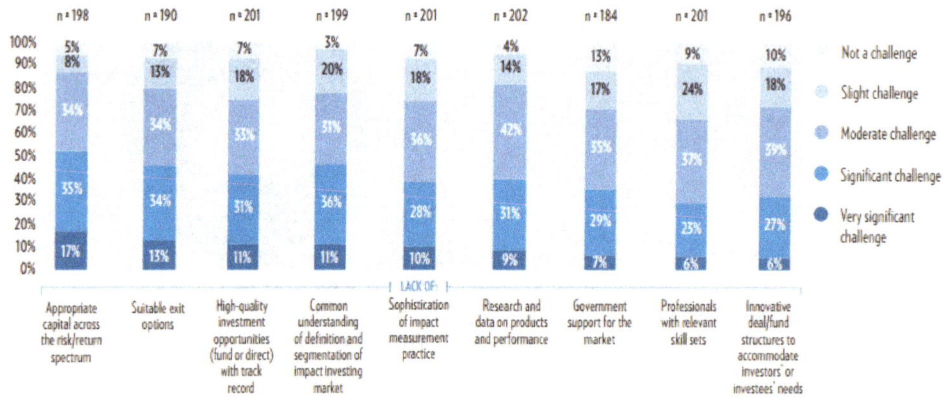

Alternative Investment

Alternative investments represent asset classes of just about anything outside the realm of traditional stocks, bonds and cash equivalents. Many investment options fall into this category including but not limited to, real estate, commodities, hedge funds, private debt and equity.

Alternative investments, or alternatives, have gained favour among financial advisors in recent years. As markets have become more unpredictable, investors have sought assets that are less correlated with the variations experienced with daily market pricing. This has advanced an allocation model with four general investment options:

1. Traded stocks, where a company issues securities representing ownership in a company.
2. Bonds, where a company borrows money for a specific time period at a fixed interest rate.
3. Cash equivalents, such as actual cash or assets that can be quickly converted into cash.
4. Alternative investments, such as real estate, commodities, hedge funds, private debt and equity.

Alternative investments are not as much of a substitute as a complement to portfolio's assets by adding diversification features. Alternative investment options are not suitable for all investors. Government bonds are guaranteed by the full faith and credit of the United States government as to the timely payment of principal and interest, while returns in non-traded REITs, stocks, and real estate are subject to losses and/or gains. Stock reflects traded securities and shares are easily redeemed. However, the markets experience daily price swings, sometimes based upon market sentiment.

Large institutional investors have successfully invested in alternative investments for years and now certain individuals have the opportunity to invest in these assets.

Institutional investors invest with strategies, terms and conditions different from those of individual investors, who have a shorter investment time horizon, lower risk capacity, greater liquidity needs and pay higher fees and expenses for retail offerings.

Types of Alternatives

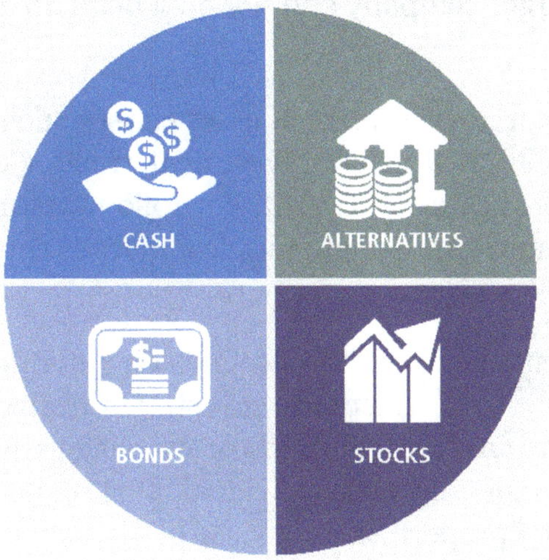

Asset classes can be allocated in varying amounts to help meet an individual's personal investment needs.

Alternative investments can be traded and non-traded. For example, traded real estate investment trusts (REITs) can be bought and sold just like stocks or bonds on public exchanges. The advantage here is that investments in traded alternatives are highly liquid.

Alternately, there is no secondary marketplace for non-traded investments — which are typically only available to qualified investors through their financial advisors — making the investment comparatively illiquid. Non-traded REITs invest in real estate and real estate-related assets, offering a diversification option for the higher risk long-term investment portion of certain qualified investors' portfolios.

Common Alternative Investments

1. Private equity. There are more private companies than public companies, and many of them take

on investor capital. Private equity is a broad term encompassing the entire investment spectrum of the private capital markets, and different private equity firms specialize in multiple investment strategies. Private equity firms typically raise funds and take capital from both non-institutional and institutional investors. The funds will then be used to place investments in promising private companies. The capital is returned to investors upon an exit event such as an IPO or acquisition after the firm takes its management and performance fee. As mentioned, private equity is a general classification that includes the investment in start-ups, venture capital, and financing throughout phases of a company's growth.

Portfolio Investment

A portfolio investment is a hands-off or passive investment of securities in a portfolio, and it is made with the expectation of earning a return. This expected return is directly correlated with the investment's expected risk. Portfolio investment is distinct from direct investment, which involves taking a sizable stake in a target company and possibly being involved with its day-to-day management.

Portfolio investments can span a wide range of asset classes such as stocks, government bonds, corporate bonds, treasury bills, real estate investment trusts (REITs), exchange-traded funds (ETFs), mutual funds and certificates of deposit. Portfolio investments can also include options, derivatives such as warrants and futures, and physical investments such as commodities, real estate, land and timber.

The composition of investments in a portfolio depends on a number of factors. Some of the most important include the investor's risk tolerance, investment horizon and amount invested. For a young investor with limited funds, mutual funds or exchange-traded funds may be appropriate portfolio investments. For a high net worth individual, portfolio investments may include stocks, bonds, commodities and rental properties.

Portfolio investments for the largest institutional investors such as pension funds and sovereign funds include a significant proportion of infrastructure assets like bridges and toll roads. Portfolio investments for institutional investors generally need to have very long lives so that the duration of their assets and liabilities match.

Impact of Risk Tolerance, Age and Time Horizon

The investments that are made in a portfolio are dependent on the investor's individual circumstances. Those with a greater risk tolerance may favour investments in stocks, real estate, international securities and options, while more conservative investors may opt for government bonds and the stocks of large well-known companies.

These risk preferences should also be weighed against the investor's goals and time horizon. A young person saving for retirement may have 30 years or more to save but isn't comfortable with the risks of the stock market. This individual may want to favour a more conservative mix of portfolio investments despite the long time horizon. Conversely, individuals with high risk tolerances may want to avoid large allocations to riskier growth stocks if they are nearing retirement age. A progression to a portfolio of more conservative investments is generally recommended as an investment goal nears.

Portfolio Investments for Retirement

Investors saving for retirement should focus on a diversified mix of low-cost investments for their portfolios. Index funds have become popular in individual retirement accounts (IRAs) and 401(k) accounts, due to their broad exposure to a number of asset classes at a minimum expense level. These types of funds make ideal core holdings in retirement portfolios. Those wishing to take a more hands-on approach may tweak portfolio allocations by adding additional asset classes such as real estate, private equity and individual stocks and bonds to their portfolio mix.

Investment Performance

Choosing investments is just the beginning of our work as an investor. As time goes by, we'll need to monitor the performance of these investments to see how they are working together in our portfolio to help we progress toward our goals. Generally speaking, progress means that our portfolio value is steadily increasing, even though one or more of our investments may have lost value.

If our investments are not showing any gains or our account value is slipping, we'll have to determine why, and decide on our next move. In addition, because investment markets change all the time, we'll want to be alert to opportunities to improve our portfolio's performance, perhaps by diversifying into a different sector of the economy or allocating part of our portfolio to international investments. To free up money to make these new purchases, we may want to sell individual investments that have not performed well, while not abandoning the asset allocation we've selected as appropriate.

Performance of Investments

To assess how well our investments are doing, we'll need to consider several different ways of measuring performance. The measures we choose will depend on the information we're looking for and the types of investments we own. For example, if we have a stock that we hope to sell in the short term at a profit, we may be most interested in whether its market price is going up, has started to slide, or seems to have reached a plateau. On the other hand, if we're a buy-and-hold investor more concerned about the stock's value 15 or 20 years in the future, we're likely to be more interested in whether it has a pattern of earnings growth and seems to be well positioned for future expansion.

In contrast, if we're a conservative investor or we're approaching retirement, we may be primarily interested in the income our investments provide. We may want to examine the interest rate our bonds and certificates of deposit (CDs) are paying in relation to current market rates and evaluate the yield from stock and mutual funds we bought for the income they provide. Of course, if market rates are down, we may be disappointed with our reinvestment opportunities as our existing bonds mature. We might even be tempted to buy investments with a lower rating in expectation of getting a potentially higher return. In this case, we want to use a performance measure that assesses the risk we take to get the results we want.

In measuring investment performance, we want to be sure to avoid comparing apples to oranges. Finding and applying the right evaluation standards for our investments is important. If we don't, we might end up drawing the wrong conclusions. For example, there's little reason to compare yield from a growth mutual fund with yield from a Treasury bond, since they don't fulfil the same role in our portfolio. Instead, we want to measure performance for a growth fund by the standards of other growth investments, such as a growth mutual fund index or an appropriate market index. Here are some concepts to consider when evaluating the performance of our investments including yield, rate of return and capital gains and losses.

Yield

Yield is typically expressed as a percentage. It is a measure of the income an investment pays during a specific period, typically a year, divided by the investment's price. All bonds have yields, as do dividend-paying stocks, most mutual funds, and bank accounts including CDs.

- Yields on Bonds: When we buy a bond at issue, its yield is the same as its interest rate or coupon rate. The rate is figured by dividing the yearly interest payments by the par value, usually $1,000. So if we're collecting $50 in interest on a $1,000 bond, the yield is 5 percent. However, bonds we buy after issue in the secondary market have a yield different from the stated coupon rate because the price we pay is different from the par value. Bond yields go up and down depending on the credit rating of the issuer, the interest rate environment and general market demand for bonds. The yield for a bond based on its price in the secondary market is known as the bond's current yield. For more information on bond yields, see Bond Yield and Return.
- Yields on Stocks: For stocks, yield is calculated by dividing the year's dividend by the stock's market price. We can find that information online, in the financial pages of our newspaper and in our brokerage statement. Of course, if a stock doesn't pay a dividend, it has no yield. But if part of our reason for investing is to achieve a combination of growth and income, we may have deliberately chosen stocks that provided a yield at least as good as the market average. However, if we're buying a stock for its dividend yield, one thing to be aware of is the percentage of earnings that the issuing company is paying to its shareholders. Sometimes stocks with the highest yield have been issued by companies that may be trying to keep up a good face despite financial setbacks. Sooner or later, though, if a company doesn't rebound, it may have to cut the dividend, reducing the yield. The share price may suffer as well. Also remember that dividends paid out by the company are funds that the company is not using to reinvest in its businesses.
- Yields on CDs: If our assets are in conventional CDs, figuring our yield is easy. Our bank or other financial services firm will provide not only the interest rate the CD pays, but its annual percentage yield (APY). In most cases, that rate remains fixed for the CD's term.

Rate of Return

Our investment return is all of the money we make or lose on an investment. To find our total return, generally considered the most accurate measure of return, we add the change in value—up or down—from the time we purchased the investment to all of the income we collected from that investment in interest or dividends. To find percent return, we divide the change in value plus income by the amount we invested.

Here's the formula for that calculation:

(Change in value + Income) ÷ Investment amount = Percent return

For example, suppose we invested $2,000 to buy 100 shares of a stock at $20 a share. While we own it, the price increases to $25 a share and the company pays a total of $120 in dividends. To find our total return, we'd add the $500 increase in value to the $120 in dividends, and to find percent return we divide by $2,000, for a result of 31 percent.

That number by itself doesn't give us the whole picture, though. Since we hold investments for different periods of time, the best way to compare their performance is by looking at their annualized percent return.

For example, we had a $620 total return on a $2,000 investment over three years. So, our total return is 31 percent. our annualized return is 9.42 percent. This is derived by doing the following calculation: $(1+.31)^{(1/3)} - 1 = 9.42$ percent. The standard formula for computing annualized return is $AR=(1+return)^{1/years} - 1$.

If the price of the stock drops during the period we own it, and we have a loss instead of a profit, we do the calculation the same way but our return may be negative if income from the investment hasn't offset the loss in value.

Remember that we don't have to sell the investment to calculate our return. In fact, figuring return may be one of the factors in deciding whether to keep a stock in our portfolio or trade it in for one that seems likely to provide a stronger performance.

In the case of bonds, if we're planning to hold a bond until maturity we can calculate our total return by adding the bond income we'll receive during the term to the principal that will be paid back at maturity. If we sell the bond before maturity, in figuring wer return we'll need to take into account the interest we've been paid plus the amount we receive from the sale of the bond, as well as the price we paid to purchase it.

Helpful Tips

Whatever type of securities we hold, here are some tips to help we evaluate and monitor investment performance:

- Don't forget to factor in transaction fees. To be sure our calculation is accurate, it's important to include the transaction fees wew pay when we buy our investments. If we're calculating return on actual gains or losses after selling the investment, we should also subtract the fees we paid when we sold.
- Review and understand our account statements. In addition to fees, our account statement—specifically the Account Summary section—offers a high-level picture of our account performance from the end point of the previous statement, including the total value of our account.

- Calculate total return. If we reinvest our earnings to buy additional shares, as is often the case with a mutual fund and is always the case with a stock dividend reinvestment plan, calculating total return is more complicated. That's one reason to use the total return figures that mutual fund companies provide for each of their funds over various time periods, even if the calculation is not exactly the same result we'd find if we did the math our self. One reason it might differ is that the fund calculates total return on an annual basis. If we made a major purchase in May, just before a major market decline, or sold just before a market rally, our result for the year might be less than the fund's annual total return.
- Consider the role of taxes on performance. Computing after-tax returns is important. For example, interest income from some federal or municipal bonds may be tax-exempt. In this case, we might earn a lower rate of interest but our return could actually be greater than the return on taxable bonds paying a higher interest rate. It's especially important to figure after-tax returns in taxable accounts. This is often helpful to do with a tax professional. We may find that the gains made in a taxable account are not as robust as we thought, leading we to consider other investments for our taxable accounts (for instance investments that appreciate in value, but don't pay income that can itself be taxed).
- Factor in inflation: With investments we hold for a long time, inflation may play a big role in calculating our return. Inflation means our money loses value over time. It's the reason that a dollar in 1950 could buy a lot more than a dollar in 2015. The calculation of return that takes inflation into account is called real return. We'll also see inflation-adjusted dollars called real dollars. To get real return, we subtract the rate of inflation from our percentage return. In a year in which our investments returned 10 percent but inflation sent prices rising three percent, our real return would be only seven percent.

As we gain experience as an investor, we can learn a lot by comparing our returns over several years to see when different investments had strong returns and when the returns were weaker. Among other things, year-by-year returns can help we see how our various investments behaved in different market environments. This can also be a factor in what we decide to do next.

However, unless we have an extremely short-term investment strategy or one of our investments is extremely time-sensitive, it's generally a good idea to make investment decisions with a view to their long-term impact on our portfolio rather than in response to ups and downs in the markets.

Capital Gains and Losses

Investments are also known as capital assets. If we make money by selling one of our capital assets for a higher price than we paid to buy it, we have a capital gain. In contrast, if we lose money on the sale, we have a capital loss. Capital gains and losses may be a major factor in our portfolio performance, especially if we are an active investor who buys and sells frequently.

In general, capital gains are taxable, unless we sell the assets in a tax-free or tax-deferred account. But the rate at which the tax is calculated depends on how long we hold the asset before selling it.

Profits we make by selling an asset we've held for over a year are considered long-term capital gains and are taxed at a lower rate than our ordinary income. However, short-term gains from selling assets we've held for less than a year don't enjoy this special tax treatment, so they're taxed at the same rate as our ordinary income. That's one reason we may want to postpone taking gains, when possible, until they qualify as long-term gains.

With some investments, such as stocks we own outright, we can determine when to buy and sell. We will owe taxes only on any capital gains we actually realize—meaning we've sold the investment for a profit. And even then we may be able to offset these gains if we sold other investments at a loss. With other investments, capital gains can become more complicated.

Mutual funds, for example, are different from stocks and bonds when it comes to capital gains. As with a stock or a bond, we will have to pay either short- or long-term capital gains taxes if we sell our shares in the fund for a profit. But even if we hold our shares and do not sell, we will also have to pay our share of taxes each year on the fund's overall capital gains. Each time the managers of a mutual fund sell securities within the fund, there's the potential for a taxable capital gain (or loss). If the fund has gains that cannot be offset by losses, then the fund must, by law, distribute those gains to its shareholders.

If a fund has a lot of taxable short-term gains, our return is reduced, which is something to keep in mind in evaluating investment performance. We can look at a mutual fund's turnover ratio, which we can find in a mutual fund's prospectus, to give us an idea of whether the fund might generate a lot of short-term gains. The turnover ratio tells we the percentage of a mutual fund's portfolio that is replaced through sales and purchases during a given time period—usually a year.

Unrealized gains and losses—sometimes called paper gains and losses—are the result of changes in the market price of our investments while we hold them but before we sell them. Suppose, for example, the price of a stock we hold in our portfolio increases. If we don't sell the stock at the new higher price, our profit is unrealized because if the price falls later, the gain is lost. Only when we sell the investment is the gain realized—in other words, it becomes actual profit.

This is not to say that unrealized gains and losses are unimportant. On the contrary, unrealized gains and losses determine the overall value of our portfolio and are a large part of what we assess in measuring performance, along with any income generated by our investments. In fact, many discussions of performance in the financial press, especially regarding stocks, focus entirely on these price changes over time.

References

- What-is-an-investment-fund-2347543: whatinvestment.co.uk, Retrieved 28 June 2018
- Weckherlin, P. / Hepp, M. (2006). Systematische Investments in Corporate Excellence, Verlag Neue Zürcher Zeitung. ISBN 3-03823-278-5
- Different-investing-styles-1289917: thebalance.com, Retrieved 18 May 2018
- Investment-strategies, starter-guides: wallstreetsurvivor.com, Retrieved 28 March 2018
- Passive-portfolio-strategy, financial-glossary: marketbusinessnews.com, Retrieved 15 April 2018
- Active-portfolio-management-strategy: portfoliomanagement.in, Retrieved 25 May 2018
- Socially-responsible-investing: moneycrashers.com, Retrieved 21 April 2018
- Goals-based-investing: ampcapital.com, Retrieved 11 July 2018
- Understanding-how-to-apply-goal-based-investing-practically-1389: motilaloswal.com, Retrieved 21 July 2018

3

Cash Flow Management

Cash flow refers to the virtual or real movement of money. The total cash flow of a company is a combination of the operating cash flow, investment cash flow and financing cash flow. This chapter has been carefully written to provide an easy understanding of the varied facets of cash flow and cash management, such as free cash flow, cash flow statement, valuation using discounted cash flows, burn rate and discounted payback period.

Cash Flow

The amount of cash or cash-equivalent which the company receives or gives out by the way of payment(s) to creditors is known as cash flow. Cash flow analysis is often used to analyse the liquidity position of the company. It gives a snapshot of the amount of cash coming into the business, from where, and amount flowing out.

Cash flows can either be positive or negative. It is calculated by subtracting the cash balance at the beginning of a period which is also known as opening balance, form the cash balance at the end of the period (could be a month, quarter or a year) or the closing balance.

If the difference is positive, it means you have more cash at the end of a given period. If the difference is negative it means that you have less amount of cash at the end of a given period when compared with the opening balance at the starting of a period.

To analyse where the cash is coming from and going out, cash flow statements are prepared. It has three main categories – operating cash flow which includes day-to-day transactions, investing cash flow which includes transactions which are done for expansion purpose, and financing cash flow which include transactions relating to the amount of dividend paid out to stockholders.

However, the level of cash flow is not an ideal metric to analyse a company when making an investment decision. A Company's balance sheet as well as income statements should be studied carefully to come to a conclusion.

Cash level might be increasing for a company because it might have sold some of its assets, but that doesn't mean the liquidity is improving. If the company has sold off some of its assets to pay off debt then this is a negative sign and should be investigated further for more clarification.

If the company is not reinvesting cash then this is also a negative sign because in that case it is not using the opportunity to diversify or build business for expansion.

Types of Cash Flow

There are various types of Cash Flow, so it's important to have a solid understanding of what each of them is. When someone refers to CF, they could mean any of the types listed below, so be sure to clarify which one it is.

Types of cash flow include:

- Cash from operating activities: This is found on the company's statement of cash flows.
- Free cash flow to equity (FCFE): This represents the cash that's available after reinvestment back in the business (capital expenditures).
- Free cash flow to the firm (FCFF): This is a measure that assumes a company has no leverage (debt) and is used in financial modeling and valuation.
- Net change in cash: This is found at the bottom of the cash flow statement.

Uses of Cash Flow

Cash Flow has many uses in both operating a business and performing financial analysis. In fact, it's one of the most important metrics in all of finance and accounting.

The most common uses are:

- Net Present Value: calculating the value of a business by building a DCF Model and calculating the net present value (NPV)
- Internal Rate of Return: determining the IRR an investor achieves for making an investment
- Liquidity: assessing how well a company can meet its short-term financial obligations
- Cash Flow Yield: measuring how much cash a business generates per share relative to its share price, expressed as a percentage
- Cash Flow Per Share (CFPS):cash from operating activities divided by the number of shares outstanding results in CFPS
- P/CF Ratio: the price of a stock divided by the CFPS (see above), sometimes used as an alternative to the Price-Earnings or P/E ratio
- Cash Conversion Ratio: the amount of time between when a business pays for its inventory (cost of goods sold) and receives payment from its customers is the cash conversion ratio
- Funding Gap: a measure of the shortfall a company has to overcome (how much more cash it needs)
- Dividend Payments: CF can be used to fund dividend payments to investors
- Capital Expenditures: CF can be used to fund reinvestment and growth in the business

Cash Flow vs Income

Investors and business operators care deeply about CF because it's the lifeblood of a company. You may be wondering, how is CF different from what's reported on a company's income statement? Income and profit are based on accrual accounting principles, which smooths-out expenditures and matches revenues to the timing of when products/services are delivered. Due to revenue recognition policies and the matching principle, a company's net income or net earning can actually be materially different from its cash flow.

Companies pay close attention to the cash flow and seek to manage it as carefully as possible. Professionals working in the finance, accounting, and financial planning & analysis (FP&A) functions at a company will spend significant time evaluating the flow of funds in the business and identifying potential problems.

Cash Flow Generation Strategies

Since CF matters so much, it's only natural that managers of businesses do everything in their power to increase it. Let's explore how operators of businesses can try to increase the flow of cash in a company. Below is an info graphic that demonstrates how CF can be increased using different strategies.

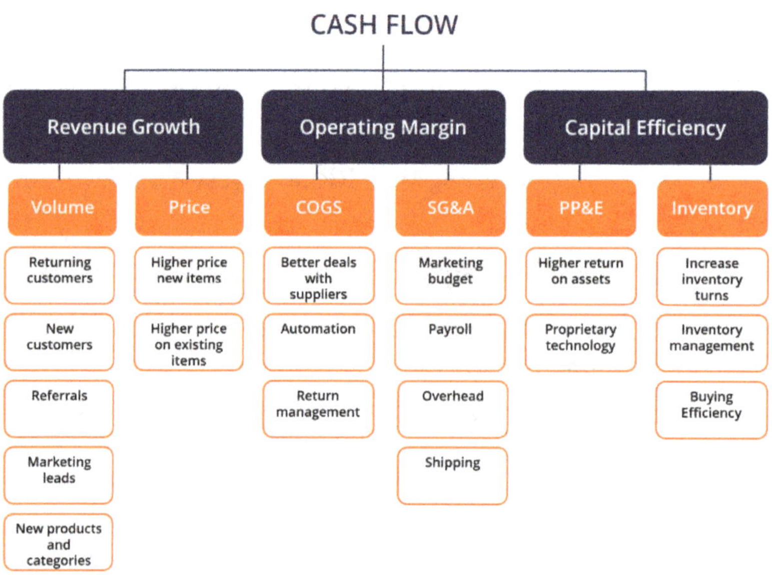

Managers of business can increase CF using any of the levers listed above. The strategies fall into three categories: revenue growth, operating margins, and capital efficiency. Each of those can then be broken down into higher volume, higher prices, lower cost of goods sold, lower SG&A, more efficient property plant & equipment (PP&E), and more efficient inventory management.

Importance of Cash Flow

Lack of cash is one of the biggest reasons small businesses fail. The Small Business Administration says that "inadequate cash reserves" are a top reason start-ups don't succeed. It's called "running out of money," and it will shut you down faster than anything else.

Cash Flow when Starting a Business

Dealing with cash flow issues is most difficult when you are starting a business. You have many expenses and money is going out fast. And you may have no sales or customers who are paying you. You will need some other temporary sources of cash, like through a temporary line of credit, to get you going and on to a positive cash flow situation.

Cash Flow in a Seasonal Business

Cash flow is particularly important for seasonal businesses - those that have a large fluctuation of business at different times of the year, like holiday businesses and summer businesses. Managing cash flow in this type of business is tricky, but it can be done, with diligence.

It's possible for your business to make a profit, but have no cash. How can that happen? The short answer is that profit is an accounting concept, while cash, as noted above, is only the amount in the business checking account. You can have assets, like accounts receivable (money owed to you by customers) but if you can't collect on what's owed, you won't have cash.

Your accounting system may also show a difference between cash and profits. If your business runs on accrual accounting, you recognize income when the invoice is sent, even though the customer hasn't paid. In this case, you might show a profit but not have the cash.

Analysing Cash Flow

The best way to keep track of cash flow in your business is to run a cash flow report.

A cash flow statement looks at the change to cash (in this case, your business checking account), from different business activities and increases or decreases in other accounts on the business balance sheet.

For example:

- What happens to cash if a customer pays a bill?
- What happens to cash if your business purchases supplies?
- What happens to cash if you buy a computer?
- What happens to cash if you pay an employee or independent contractor?

At times, you may need to keep track of cash flow on a weekly, maybe even a daily basis.

Cash Management

The term cash management refers to the management of cash resource in such a way that generally accepted business objectives could be achieved. In this context, the objectives of a firm can be unified as bringing about consistency between maximum possible profitability and liquidity of a firm. Cash management may be defined as the ability of a management in recognizing the problems related with cash which may come across in future course of action, finding appropriate solution to curb such problems if they arise, and finally delegating these solutions to the competent authority for carrying them out. The choice between liquidity and ij profitability creates a state of confusion. It is cash management that can provide solution to this dilemma. Cash management may be regarded as an art that assists in establishing equilibrium between liquidity and profitability to ensure undisturbed functioning of a firm towards attaining its li business objectives.

Cash itself is not capable of generating any sort of income on its own. It rather is the prime requirement of income generating sources and functions. Thus, a firm should go for minimum possible balance of cash, yet maintaining its adequacy for the obvious reason of firm's solvency. Cash management deals with maintaining sufficient quantity of cash in such a way that the quantity denotes the lowest adequate cash figure to meet business obligations. Cash management involves managing cash flows (into and out of the firm), within the firm and the cash balances held by a concern at a point of time. The words, 'managing cash and the cash balances' as specified above does not mean optimization of cash and near cash items but also point towards providing a protective shield to the business obligations. Cash management is concerned with minimizing unproductive cash balances, investing temporarily excess cash advantageously and to make the best possible arrangement for meeting planned and unexpected demands on the firms' cash.

General Principles of Cash Management

These principles reflecting cause and effect relationship having universal applications give a scientific outlook to the subject of cash management. While, the application of these principles in accordance with the changing conditions and business environment requiring high degree of skill and tact which places cash management in the category of art. Thus, we can say that cash management like any other subject of management is both science and art for it has well-established principles capable of being skill fully modified as per the requirements. The principles of management are follows as:

- Determinable variations of cash needs

A reasonable portion of funds, in the form of cash is required to be kept aside to overcome the period anticipated as the period of cash deficit. This period may either be short and temporary or last for a longer duration of time. Normal and regular payment cf cash leads to small reductions in the cash balance at periodic intervals. Making this payment to different employees on different days of a week can equalize these reductions. Another technique for balancing the level of cash is to schedule i cash disbursements to creditors during that period when accounts receivables collected amounts to a large sum but without putting the goodwill at stake.

- Contingency cash requirement

There may arise certain instances, which fall beyond the forecast of the management. These constitute unforeseen calamities, which are too difficult to be provided for in the normal course of the business. Such contingencies always demand for special cash requirements that was not estimated and provided for in the cash budget. Rejections of wholesale product, large amount of bad debts, strikes, lockouts etc. are a few among these contingencies. Only a prior experience and investigation of other similar companies prove helpful as a customary practice. A practical procedure is to protect the business from such calamities like bad-debt losses, fire etc. by way of insurance coverage.

- Availability of external cash

Another factor that is of great importance to the cash management is the availability of funds from outside sources. There resources aid in providing credit facility to the firm, which materialized the firm's objectives of holding minimum cash balance. As such if a firm succeeds in acquiring sufficient funds from external sources like banks or private financers, shareholders, government agencies etc., the need for maintaining cash reserves diminishes.

- Maximizing cash receipts

Every financial manager aims at making the best possible use of cash receipts. Again, cash receipts if tackled prudently results in minimizing cash requirements of a concern. For this purpose, the comparative cost of granting cash discount to customer and the policy of charging interest expense for borrowing must be evaluated on continuous basis to determine the futility of either of the alternative or both of them during that particular period for maximizing cash receipts. Yet, the under mentioned techniques proved helpful in this context:

(A) Concentration Banking: Under this system, a company establishes banking centres for collection of cash in different areas. Thereby, the company instructs its customers of adjoining areas to send their payments to those centres. The collection amount is then deposited with the local bank by these centres as early as possible. Whereby, the collected funds are transferred to the company's central bank accounts operated by the head office.

(B) Local Box System: Under this system, a company rents out the local post offices boxes of different cities and the customers are asked to \ forward their remittances to it. These remittances are picked by the authorized lock bank from these boxes to be transferred to the company's central bank operated by the head office.

(C) Reviewing Credit Procedures: It aids in determining the impact of slow payers and baddebtors on cash. The accounts of slow paying customers should be reviewed to determine the volume of cash tied up. Besides this, evaluation of credit policy must also be conducted for introducing essential amendments. As a matter of fact, too strict a credit policy involves rejections of sales. Thus, curtailing the cash in flow. On the other hand, too lenient, a credit policy would increase the number of slow payments and bad debts again decreasing the cash inflows.

(D) Minimizing Credit Period: Shortening the terms allowed to the customers would definitely accelerate the cash inflow side-by-side revising the discount ofered would prevent the customers from using the credit for financing their own operations profitably.

(E) Others: Introducing various procedures for special handling of large to very large remittances or foreign remittances such as, personal pick up of large sum of cash using airmail, special delivery and simitar techniques to accelerate such collections.

Minimizing Cash Disbursements

The motive of minimizing cash payments is the ultimate benefit derived from maximizing cash receipts. Cash disbursement can be brought under control by preventing fraudulent practices, serving time draft to creditors of large sum, making staggered payments to creditors and for payrolls etc.

Maximizing Cash Utilization

Although a surplus of cash is a luxury, yet money is costly. Moreover, proper and optimum utilization of cash always makes way for achievement of the motive of maximizing cash receipts and minimizing cash payments. At times, a concern finds itself with funds in excess of its requirement, which lay idle without bringing any return to it. At the same time, the concern finds it unwise to dispose it, as the concern shall soon need it. In such conditions, efforts should be made in investing these funds in some interest bearing securities. There are certain basic strategies suggested by Gitman, which prove evidently helpful in managing cash if employed by the cash management. They are:

Pay accounts payables as late as possible without damaging the firm's credit rating, but take advantage of the favourable cash discount, if any.

Turnover, the inventories as quickly as possible, avoiding stock outs that might result in shutting down the productions line or loss of sales.

Collect accounts receivables as early as possible without losing future loss sales because of high-pressure collections techniques. Cash discounts, if they are economically justifiable, may be used to accomplish this objective.

Function of Cash Management

Cash management is concerned with minimizing unproductive cash balances, investing temporarily excess cash advantageously and to make the best possible arrangements for meeting planned and unexpected demands on the firm's cash. Cash Management must aim to reduce the required level of cash but minimize the risk of being unable to discharge claims against the company as they arise. All these aims and motives of cash management largely depend upon the efficient and effective functioning of cash management. Cash management functions can be studied under five heads, namely, cash planning, managing cash flow, controlling cash flow, optimizing the cash level and investing idle cash. All these functions are discussed below in details:

Cash Planning

Good planning is the very foundation of attaining success. For any management decision, planning is the foremost requirement. Planning is basically an intellectual process, a menfal pre-disposition to do things in an orderly way, to think before acting and to act in the light of facts rather than of a guess. Cash planning is a technique, which comprises of planning for and controlling of cash. It is a management process of forecasting the future need of cash, its available resources and various uses for a specified period. Cash planning, thus, deals at length with formulation of necessary cash policies and procedures in order to carry on business continuously and on sound lines. A good cash planning aims at providing cash, not only for regular but also for irregular and abnormal requirements.

Managing Cash Flows

The heading simply suggests an idea of managing properly the flow of cash coming inside the business i.e. cash inflow and cash moving out of the business i.e. cash outflow. These two are said to be properly managed only, if a firm succeeds in accelerating the rate of cash inflow together with minimizing the cash outflow. As observed expediting collections, avoiding unnecessary inventories, improving control over payments etc. contribute to better management of cash. Whereby, a business can conserve cash and thereof would require lesser cash balance for its operations.

Controlling the Cash Flows

As forecasting is not an exact science because it is based on certain assumptions. Therefore, cash planning will inevitably be at variance with the results actually obtained. For this reason, control becomes an unavoidable function of cash management. Moreover, cash controlling becomes essential as it increases the availability of usable cash from within the enterprise. As it is obvious that greater the speed of cash flow cycle, greater would be the number of times a firm can convert its goods and ' services into cash and so lesser will be the cash requirement to finance the desired volume of business during that period. Furthermore, every enterprise is in possession of some hidden cash, which if traced out substantially decreases the cash requirement of the enterprise.

Optimizing the Cash Level

A financial manager should concentrate on maintaining sound liquidity position i.e. cash level. All his efforts relating to planning, managing and controlling cash should be diverted towards maintaining an optimum level of cash. The foremost need of maintaining optimum level of cash is to meet the necessary requirements and to settle the obligations well in time. Optimization of cash level may be related to establishing equilibrium between risk and the related profit expected to be earned by the company.

Investing Idle Cash

Idle cash or surplus cash refers to the excess of cash inflows over cash outflows, which do not have any specific operations or any other purpose to solve currently. Generally, a firm is required to hold cash for meeting working needs facing contingencies and to maintain as well as develop goodwill of bankers.

The problem of investing this excess amount of cash arise simply because it contributes nothing towards profitability of the firm as idle cash precisely earns no returns. Further permanent disposal of such cash is not possible, as the concern may again need this cash after a short while. But, if such cash is deposited with the bank, it definitely would earn a nominal rate of interest paid by the bank. A much better returns than the bank interest can be expected if a company deploys idle cash in marketable securities. There are yet another group of enterprise that neither invest in marketable securities nor willing to get interest instead they prefer to deposit excess cash for improving relations with banks by helping them in meeting bank requirements for compensating balances for services and loans.

Motives of Holding Cash

Every business transaction whether carried on credit or on cash basis ultimately results in either cash inflow or cash outflows. The pivotal point in present day financial management is to maximize cash generation and to minimize cash outflows in relation to the cash inflows. Keynes postulated three motives for holding cash:-

1. Transaction Motive,
2. Precautionary Motive, and
3. Speculative Motive.

To which one more motive for holding cash has been added:

4. Compensation Motive

1. Transaction Motive

It refers to holding of cash for meeting routine cash requirements and financing transactions carried on by the business in the normal course of action. This motive requires cash for payment of various obligations like purchase of raw materials, the payment of usage and salaries, dividend, income tax, various other operating expenses etc. However, there exists regular and counter inflow of cash in the business by way of return on investments, sales etc. However, cash receipts and cash payments do not perfectly synchronies with each other. Therefore, a firm requires an additional cash balance during the periods when payments are in excess of cash receipts. Thus transaction motive stresses on holding cash to meet anticipated obligations that are not counter balanced by cash receipts due to disparity of timings.

2. Precautionary Motive

Under precautionary motive, the need to hold cash arises for meeting any unforeseen, unpredicted contingencies or unexpected disbursements. Such motives provide a cushion to withstand unexpected cash requirements arising spontaneously at short notice due to various causes. In this regard, two factors largely influence the precautionary cash balance, degree of predictability and availability of short-term credit. If a cash management succeeds in estimating the cash requirements adequately, it escapes from maintaining big cash balance for emergency. Likewise, if a management is capable and efficient enough to borrow the required cash from short-term creditors small balance would be held and vise-versa. 'Ready borrowing power is the best antidote to emergency cash drains and facilitates release of available cash resources for remunerative

3. Speculative Motive

The speculative motive finds its origin out of the desire of an enterprise to avail itself the benefits of the opportunities arising at unexpected moments that do not happen to exist in the normal course of business. This motive represents a positive and aggressive approach. Reasonable cash reserve is maintained by concerns for exploiting profitable opportunities like bulk purchase of raw materials at discounted prices, purchasing securities when interest rates are expected to fall, postpone purchase of raw material if decline in prices is anticipated, etc.

4. Compensation Motive

Such motives require holding cash balance in case the concern enters into some loan agreement with the bank. Bank provides a great variety of services to its customers. For some of such services it charges commission or fee. While for other an indirect compensation is demanded by it by asking its customers to keep a minimum bank balance sufficient to earn a return equal to cost of services provided by it. Such balances are termed as compensating balances.

Financing of Cash Shortage and Cost of Running out of Cash

A situation arises, when the cash outflows of a firm exceeds its inflows during a certain period. Such situation creates cash shortage in a firm. Shortage of cash is highly undesirable in all sort of business holding for the reason of dreadful consequences that it bears. A management is deemed to be over-cautious and highly careful while dealing with the problem of cash shortage even if cash inflows are anticipated in the near future; else a concern may even reach the stage of final liquidation. Cash flow statement should be prepared to acknowledge the repercussions of transactions involving the movement of cash. As cash flow statement is made to show the impact of various transactions on the cash position of a firm, it takes into consideration only such transactions that have relationship with cash.

In case of temporary shortage of cash, a concern is required to procure essential cash immediately for the anticipated short duration, so as the curb it at the very stage instead of sustaining the long-term implication later on. 'The immediate source to fall back upon remains the bank credit.|| In fact, bank credit is a means to meet cash shortages as well as source of financing the current assets. The various methods from which a [firm can procure funds during the period when its outflows exceed the inflows are stated below -(i) Using bank credit line, (ii) Raising loans from institutions and creditors other than banks. (iii) Liquidity marketable securities, (IV) Resorting to bills discounting schemes, (v) Disposing off surplus fixed assets, (vi) Sheding the quantity of raw materials, (vii) Unloading finished goods even at loss, (viii) By delaying payments.

As a piece of advice, it is recommended by the financial experts that a cash management should not start searching for external finance at the very instance when the cash shortage is anticipated. At the initial stage, a management should take appropriate steps to avoid or minimize the undesirable situation of emerging cash shortage by exercising effective! Control over internal resources. In this respect, the matters of special consideration that can be gainfully employed by the concern for overpowering the situation of cash shortage are -(i) Increasing efforts to speedup collection, (ii) Reduction in purchase of inventories, (ii) Increasing cash sales, (iv) Selling-off redundant assets, (v) Selling short-term investments. (vi) Deferment of capital expenditure, (vii) Postponing and delaying payments.

These considerations are nothing but mere use of tact and skill to overcome a shortage of cash. They are much economical than any other resources (internal or external) for they cost neither interest nor any expenses. "Even if an external resources has to be found, this might be seen as a bridging operation pending the ability to bring on stream an alternative internal source".

No sooner than a firm becomes aware of approaching shortage of cash than it should concentrate its efforts towards the eradication of such situation. The sooner the shortage is provided for, the better it is. Every Concern escapes itself form lending into such a situation as it makes way for numerous costs because of running out cash. A firm bears not only the burden of unnecessary costs but is subjected to various types of pressures pertaining to its dealings. All these factors adversely affect the morale of management, causes damages to the hard-earned reputation and financial credit-worthiness etc. A firm is forced to borrow funds at high rates of interest has to accept higher price demand of suppliers, loses cash discount on payments, enter into further negotiations with banks and other financial institutions on account of slow payment.

Financing Current Assets

Current assets of enterprises may be financed either by short-term sources or long term sources or by combination of both. The main sources constituting long-term financing are shares, debentures, and debts form banks and financial institutions. The long term source of finance provides support for a small part of current assets requirements which is called the working capital margin' Working capital margin is used here to express the difference between current assets and current liabilities. Short-term financing of current assets includes sources of short-term credit, which a firm is mostly required to arrange in advance. Short term bank loans, commercial papers etc. are a few of its components. Current liabilities like accruals and provisions, trade credit, short-term bank finance, short-term deposits and the like warranting the current assets are also referred to a short-term term sources of finance. Spontaneous financing can also finance current assets, which includes creditors, bills payable, and outstanding receipts. A product firm would always opt for utilizing spontaneous sources fully since it is free of cost. Every concerns that can no more be financed by spontaneous sources of financing has to decide between short-term and long-term source of finance along with relevant proportion of the two. There are three approaches of financing current assets that are popularly used.

Matching Approach

As the name itself suggests, a financing instrument would offset the current asset under consideration, bearing financing instrument bearing approximately same maturity. In simple words, under this approach a match is established between the expected lives of current asset to be financed with the source of fund raised to finance the current assets. For this, reason a firm would select long-term financing to finance or permanent current assets to finance temporary or variable current assets. Thus, a ten-year loan may be raised for financing machinery bearing expected life of ten years. Similarly, one-month stock can be financed by means of one-month bank loan. This is also termed as hedging approach.

Conservative Approach

Conservative approach takes an edge over and above matching approach, as it is practically not possible to plan an exact match in all cases. A firm is said to be following conservative approach when it depends more on long-term financial sources for meeting its financial needs. Under this financing policy, the fixed assets, permanent current assets and even a part of temporary current assets is provided with long-term sources of finance and this make it less risky nature. Another advantage of following this approach is that in the absence of temporary current assets, a firm can invest surplus funds into marketable securities and store liquidity.

Aggressive Approach

As against conservative approach, a firm is said to be following aggressive financing policy when depends relatively more on short-term sources than warranted by the matching plan. Under this approach the firm finance not only its temporary current assets but also a part of permanent current assets with short-term sources of finance. In nutshell, it may be concluded that for financing of current assets, a firm should decide upon two important constraints; firstly, the type of financing policy to be selected (whether short-term or long term and secondly, the relative proportion of modes of financing. This decision is totally based on trade-off between risk and return. As short-term financing is less costly but risky, long-term financing is less risky but costly.

Operating Cash Flow

Operating cash flow (OCF), often called cash flow from operations, is an efficiency calculation that measures the cash that a business produces from its principal operations and business activities by subtracting operating expenses from total revenues. Basically, it shows how much cash flow is generated from the business operations without regard to secondary sources of revenue like interest or investments.

For example, a company that manufactures widgets must make more money selling them than it cost to produce them. In other words, cash inflows must always be greater than cash outflows in order for the business to be profitable and able to successfully pay its bills.

This is an important measurement because it allows investors and creditors to see how successful a company's operations are and if the company is making enough money from its primary activities to maintain and grow the company. This concept is particularly important for financial forecasting because it can help show the health of a company. Take Circuit City for example. For the last few years of their operations, they were losing money on all of their retail activities, but they were making money on maintenance contracts and customer financing. What does that tell us about the core business? It's unhealthy and can survive very long.

This is why all public companies must report this number in their quarterly financial reports and annual cash flow statement. GAAP also requires companies to use the indirect method to compute this figure.

Formula

The operating cash flow formula can be calculated two different ways. The first way, or the direct method, simply subtracts operating expenses from total revenues.

Operating Cash Flow		
Operating Cash Flow	=	Total Revenue - Operating Expenses

This calculation is simple and accurate, but does not give investors much information about the company, its operations, or the sources of cash. That's why GAAP requires companies to use the indirect method of calculating the cash flows from operations. This method is exactly what it sounds like. It's an indirect, round about way to calculate it.

The operating cash flow equation for the indirect method adjusts net income for changes in all non-cash accounts on the balance sheet. Depreciation and amortization is added back to net income while it is adjusted for changes in accounts receivable and inventory.

Operating Cash Flow		
Operating Cash Flow	=	Net Income +/- Changes in Assets & Liabilities + Non Cash Expenses

This OCF formula much more complicated, but it gives much more information about the company's operations. It's essentially converting the operating section of the accrual income statement to a cash basis statement.

Now that we know how to calculate operating cash flows, let's look at an example.

Example:

Bill's Guitar Shop is a music retail store that specializes in guitars and other instruments. Bill's main competition is Guitar Center and he wants to analyze ways he can improve his business. Bill's year-end financial statements show the following numbers.

- Net income: $100,000
- Depreciation: $10,000
- Change in accounts receivable: +$50,000
- Change in inventory: -$20,000
- Change in accounts payable: -$25,000

Using the indirect method can be confusing because you are converting the accrual net income to a cash basis net income. Thus, any increase in assets must be subtracted out, while a decrease in assets must be added back in. The opposite is true for liabilities. Increases are added back while decreases are subtracted out. I know this sounds confusing, but you have to think about it in terms of cash. If inventory went down during the year, it means that inventory was sold and cash was received. Therefore, a decrease in inventory must be added back to net income.

Here how to calculate OCF for Bill's store using the indirect method:

Operating Cash Flow		
$55,000	=	$100,000 - $50,000 + $20,000 - $25,000 +$10,000

Bill was able to generate $55,000 of cash flows from his operations. This means that Bill's operations generated enough money to pay its bills and have $55,000 left over at the end of the year. This money could be reinvested back into the business by purchasing more inventory, a bigger storefront, or Bill could pay himself a dividend for a successful year. Either way, it shows that the retail operations are successful enough to pay the associated expenses and fund some level of expansion and company growth.

Analysis

Many investors prefer analysing cash flow number compared with other ratios because they are largely immune from management altering them. For instance, many performance ratios can easily be manipulated by management's choice of accounting principle or practice. Cash flows aren't so easily manipulated. The company earns cash and spends cash. Investors also like analysing cash flows because it presents a stripped down version of the company where it's much easier to see problem areas in the operations.

For instance, a company may have high net income, but low OCF. Why is this? Maybe it's because they are having a difficult time collecting receivables from customers. Conversely, a company might have a low net profit and a high cash flow from operations. This might happen because the company is generating huge revenues but reducing them with accelerated depreciation on the income statement. Since the depreciation is added back into net income in the operating cash flow calculator, the accelerated depreciation doesn't affect OCF.

Operating Cash Flow vs Net Income

Net income and earnings per share (EPS) are two of the most frequently referenced financial metrics, so how are they different than operating cash flow? The main difference comes down to accounting rules such as the matching principle and accrual principle when preparing financial statements.

Net income includes all sorts of expenses that may have have been paid for and may have just been created by accountants (such as depreciation).

In addition, a company's revenue recognition principle and matching of expenses to the timing of revenues can result in a material difference between OCF and net income.

Unfortunately, it is not possible to simply say that one number is always higher or lower than the other. Sometimes OCF is higher than net income (as with Amazon) and sometimes it's the opposite.

AMAZON.COM, INC.

CONSOLIDATED STATEMENTS OF CASH FLOWS
(in millions)

	Year Ended December 31,		
	2015	2016	2017
CASH AND CASH EQUIVALENTS, BEGINNING OF PERIOD	$ 14,557	$ 15,890	$ 19,334
OPERATING ACTIVITIES:			
Net income	596	2,371	3,033
Adjustments to reconcile net income to net cash from operating activities:			
Depreciation of property and equipment, including internal-use software and website development, and other amortization, including capitalized content costs	6,281	8,116	11,478
Stock-based compensation	2,119	2,975	4,215
Other operating expense, net	155	160	202
Other expense (income), net	250	(20)	(292)
Deferred income taxes	81	(246)	(29)
Changes in operating assets and liabilities:			
Inventories	(2,187)	(1,426)	(3,583)
Accounts receivable, net and other	(1,755)	(3,367)	(4,786)
Accounts payable	4,294	5,030	7,175
Accrued expenses and other	913	1,724	283
Unearned revenue	1,292	1,955	738
Net cash provided by (used in) operating activities	12,039	17,272	18,434

As you can see in the image above, there is a major difference between the two metrics, and Amazon has constantly generated more OCF than net income. To be fair though, what OCF doesn't take into account is capital expenditures (Capex) or purchases of PP&E. By deducting Capex from OCF you arrive at free cash flow, which is a more comparable figure.

Operating Cash Flow in Financial Modeling

Calculating the cash flow from operations can be one of the most challenging parts of financial modeling in Excel. Below is an example of what this activity looks like in a spread sheet.

Net earnings are adjusted for depreciation and amortization, as well as the net increase in working capital. In a financial model, there be separate sections for the depreciation schedule and working capital schedule, which then feed into the cash flow statement section of the model.

LBO Model for Retail Co. Live Case -> Base Case | Sponsor IRR -> 26.6% | Error Checks -> OK

Cash Flow Statement

Row		2014A	2015A	2016A	2017A	2018F	2019F	2020F	2021F	2022F	2023F	2024F
159	**Operating Cash Flow**											
160	Net Earnings	1,121	5,466	10,071	13,161	12,124	13,256	14,362	15,667	17,727	19,362	21,299
161	Plus: Depreciation & Amortization	10,921	10,165	9,635	9,265	6,400	6,516	6,650	6,714	6,807	6,924	6,967
162	Less: Increase in Working Capital	5,042	953	434	506	1,172	196	142	144	147	215	221
163	**Cash from Operations**	**6,999**	**14,677**	**19,272**	**21,921**	**17,351**	**19,576**	**20,870**	**22,237**	**24,387**	**26,071**	**28,045**
164												
165	**Investing Cash Flow**											
166	Investments in Property & Equipment	(8,401)	(8,401)	(8,401)	(8,401)	(6,979)	(7,189)	(6,969)	(7,178)	(7,393)	(7,139)	(7,353)
167	Investments in Businesses											
168	**Cash from Investing**	**(8,401)**	**(8,401)**	**(8,401)**	**(8,401)**	**(6,979)**	**(7,189)**	**(6,969)**	**(7,178)**	**(7,393)**	**(7,139)**	**(7,353)**
169												
170	**Financing Cash Flow**											
171	Issuance of Debt (line of credit)	-	-	-	-	-	-	-	-	15,271	3,333	-
172	Repayment of Debt	-	-	(11,201)	-	(10,372)	(12,387)	(13,902)	(15,059)	(32,265)	(22,265)	(20,692)
173	Issuance of equity	39,203	-	-	-							
174	Repurchase of equity											
175	Payment of Dividends	-	-	-	-							
176	**Cash from Financing**	**39,203**	**-**	**(11,201)**	**-**	**(10,372)**	**(12,387)**	**(13,902)**	**(15,059)**	**(16,994)**	**(18,932)**	**(20,692)**
177												
178	Net Increase (decrease) in Cash	37,801	6,277	(329)	13,520	-	-	-	-	-	-	-
179	Opening Cash Balance	-	37,801	44,078	43,749	10,000	10,000	10,000	10,000	10,000	10,000	10,000
180	**Closing Cash Balance**	**37,801**	**44,078**	**43,749**	**57,269**	**10,000**	**10,000**	**10,000**	**10,000**	**10,000**	**10,000**	**10,000**

Cash Flow Forecasting

Cash flow forecasting is the process of obtaining an estimate or forecast of a companys future financial position and is a core planning component of financial management within a company. It might sound obvious but the main output or deliverable of a cash flow forecasting process is a cash flow forecast. A cash flow forecast is a projection of an organisations future financial position based on anticipated payments and receivables. The process of deriving a cash flow forecast is called cash flow forecasting.

Goals of Cash Flow Forecasting

The main goal of a cash flow forecasting is to assist with managing liquidity within an organisation and ensuring that the business has the necessary cash to meet its obligations and avoid funding issues, essentially better management of working capital. Underneath the high level goal of liquidity management, there are often a number of reasons why companies set up a cash flow forecasting process, these include:

- Covenant forecasting and half/ full year reporting visibility.

- Interest and debt reduction.
- Short term liquidity planning.
- Long Term Planning/ Budgeting Purposes (e.g. 3 year plan)

Methods of Cash Flow Forecasting

There are essentially two main types of cash forecasting methods – direct or indirect. Direct cash forecasting is a method of forecasting cash flows and balances for short term liquidity management purposes, typically less than 90 days in duration. Direct cash forecasts often but not always include system based cash flows so as to make the cash forecast as close to real time as possible.

Indirect cash forecasting is often longer term in nature and it relies on various indirect methods of building up a cash forecast such as using projected balance sheets and income statements.

The table below outlines the main differences between direct and indirect cash flow forecasting:

	Direct Forecasting	Indirect Forecasting
Time Horizon	Short term	Longer term
What Should it Show	Cash required to fund working capital	Cash required to fund longer term growth strategies and capital projects
How is it Constructed	Analysis of upcoming receipts/ debtors and payments/ creditors	Various income statement/ balance derivations (adjusted net income, pro-forma balance sheet etc.)

Management of a Cash Flow Forecasting Process

In larger companies, the management of a cash forecasting process is controlled by the head office treasury or finance team. The work to be done in terms of assembling a forecast position generally involves sourcing data from both systems and people. The more complex an organisation, the more systems will contribute to the process, therefore it is critical to have the sources of cashflow data mapped and clearly defined.

Although systems are important, it will be the buy-in and engagement of people that will determine how successful a cash forecasting process will be. Involving the people who will be accountable and ensuring their buy-in is a key factor for success particularly for direct cash flow forecasting.

Cash Flow Loan

A cash-flow loan is a way for a small or mid-sized company to use their expected future revenue and past cash-flow as a way to get a business loan. A cash flow lender will examine a company's bank statements and/or credit card processing transactions for the total cash-flow coming into the company. If a company has decent cash flow (but maybe not profitability) a lender may lend up to 200% of the company's total deposits into their bank accounts and credit card processing statements. Since the cash flow lender is mostly focused on total cash flow, they are less concerned about credit of the business and business owner, and may not care about collateral at all. In fact, almost all cash-flow loans are unsecured (in the sense they don't require commercial real estate or other specific types of collateral) but there are hybrid lenders that can offer cash-flow loans that are enhanced with the use of commercial and personal property.

Working of Cash Flow Loan

Cash-flow loans work differently depending upon the type of cash flow lender you apply with. All lenders will begin by requiring a credit application so they can run credit. As mentioned earlier, having good credit isn't a requirement for most cash flow lenders, as they focus more on revenue that credit history. If the business shows sufficient credit and doesn't have any disqualifying incidents (defaults, current bankruptcy, etc.) the lender will then move on to examining the company's cash flow. By looking at a company's main operating bank account statements and/or the company's credit card processing statements, the lender will get an idea as to how well the company is cash-flowing each month. The lender will analyse the company's cash flow by looking at total deposit amount, number of deposits into the bank account, daily average balance, minimum monthly balance, number of bounced checks and insufficient funds, number credit card processing transactions, total credit card deposits, etc. After analysing the data over past 3-6 months, the lender will then calculate how much they feel the small business will be able to payback comfortably on a daily basis. From there, the lender will then multiply that amount by a term ranging from 3 months up to 60 months, and supply that amount to the merchant or business in the form of a loan or advance. Repayment for a cash flow loan is made either on a daily, weekly or monthly basis in forms including regular monthly payments, or by daily or weekly remittance via bank account ACH or through remitting a percentage of each day's credit card transactions until the loan is fully-repaid.

Types of Cash Flow Loans

Types	Rates	Terms	Funding
Line of Credit	5-15%	1 – 3 years	7-30 days
Alternative	6-25%	1-5 years	5-7 days
Cash Advance	1.16-1.55	3-24 months	1-3 days

Alternative Cash Flow Loans

Alternative cash flow financing is a type of loan offered by non-bank lenders where they focus on the company's cash-flow when deciding upon funding. Most of these lenders provide online approvals that take just minutes, and then decide on pricing and term after analysing the company's bank statements and Profit & Loss statement over past two years. Debt service coverage ratio needed for this type of financing is usually 1.0, meaning the company must show it has the ability to pay off the loan through net profits over past year. Alternative lending is much faster to fund that traditional financing, with funding happening within a week or so of the initial application. Unlike cash advances, these are true loans with a real APR — even if the rate isn't as low as one would see with traditional financing.

- Rates: 9-25%
- Terms: 1-5 years

Cash Flow ACH Cash Advance

There are a number of reasons why a company wouldn't qualify for bank-rate or alternative financing, including bad credit, lack of profitability, short time in business, etc.. If you can't qaulify for other forms of financing, another form of cash-flow financing worth considering is selling future revenues to your company's bank account for immediate funding. ACH loans are the sale of a small business's bank deposit revenue at a discount. Virtually any company can qualify for an advance, but the risk is priced into the funding — meaning the more risk the lender takes, the more expensive the rate will be for the borrower. To qualify a company only needs to supply a credit application and six months bank statements. Approvals take about an hour, and funding can take place quickly — even the same day. After the company is funded, the business cash advance ender will then take a set amount from the company's bank statement on each business day (or sometimes on a weekly basis) until the loan is fully-repaid.

- Factor Rates: 1.16-1.50%
- Terms: 4 months – 2 years

Cash Flow Merchant Cash Advance

A merchant cash advance is similar to an ACH loan in the sense that its also the sale of future revenue at a discount to the lender. The main difference is how the loan is repaid; a merchant cash advance is repaid by the lender collecting a percentage of each day's credit card sales, as opposed to a set amount deducted from their bank accounts.

- Factor Rates: 1.16-1.45%
- Terms: 4 – 21 months

Uses of Cash Flow Loan

- Working capital: Having capital to handle day-to-day operations is essential for all businesses. Having access to fast working capital may be the difference between taking advantage of business opportunities, and missing payments to vendors, suppliers, etc.
- Expansion: Sometimes a business sees an opportunity to move into a new space, or expand the space they have, but don't have the immediate cash to take advantage of the opportunity. In those instances using their expected future revenue to obtain financing may be an option worth pursuing.
- Advertising: having a great product or service does you no good if customers are unaware of what your business has to offer. Dedicating some money toward advertising and marketing may go a long way toward increasing revenue and profits.
- Payroll: a requirement that simply can't be overlooked for many companies. Missing payroll is simply not an option, and a cash flow loan may help ensure all employees are paid on time.
- Tax obligations: While no one enjoys paying taxes, when the IRS demands payment, your business needs to comply. Having a cash-flow funding facility may help keep the government from shutting down your operations.

- Emergency expenses: regardless of how detailed your business plan is, there will always be surprises and occurrences during the business cycle that requires emergency and immediate financing.

Pros of Cash Flow Loan

There are a number of advantages of cash flow loans, especially for companies that may lack profitability or have credit that won't allow them to get approved at a bank. For companies locked-out of traditional financing, a cash-flow loan offers fast financing (1-5 days depending on type) as opposed to months with conventional lenders. A company only needs to show minimal documentation for a cash flow loan (often only application and bank statements) as opposed to traditional financing which requires extensive documentation. While a lien will be placed on the business when financing occurs, no specific collateral is needed to get approved for funding. A company only needs to be in business for 6 months to get approved for some cash flow financing types, where a bank would require a company be in business for at least 2 years.

Cons of Cash Flow Loan

A general downside of most cash-flow loans are the rates and terms offered. As compared to conventional bank loans, a cash flow financing can be expensive – sometimes extremely expensive. Since these lenders are focusing on past bank account cash flow, there is a risk that future performance may not live up to the past. Therefore the lenders are taking increased risk – and such risk will be priced into the loan or advance in the form of higher interest rates, higher fees, and shorter terms than conventional lending.

Cash Sweep

A cash sweep is the use of excess cash flows to maximize interest earnings or to pay off outstanding debts, instead of distributing it to shareholders. Firms use borrowed money for expansion or to finance cash shortages, in which case new liabilities arise. Some debts are healthy (growth) while others could sink the business into a deeper financial crisis. Therefore, clearance of debts is paramount for any borrower, to ensure the steady and stable health of their business. Cash sweeps aid in accelerating the payoff of outstanding debts. Depending on the lender's terms and covenants, debt sweeps may be compulsory.

A cash sweep is an ideal cash management tool to help large firms with accounts that involve great variability in receiving of funds. The cash management arrangement can also work in reverse. That is, if the funds in the sweep account fall beyond a certain point, a drawdown in the credit account is conducted to attain the target balance. Cash sweeps can also refer to investments, where an account can automatically transfer money into the current highest interest-earning options at the end of each day. This ensures that the sweep account earns the optimum amount of money possible.

The easiest way to understand a cash sweep and sweep accounts is to think of a cash sweep as any deliberately chosen and automated transfer ("sweeping") of a portion of a company's cash flow to be used for a specific purpose – such as paying off debt or making an investment. The company makes arrangements with its bank to regularly (usually at the end of each business day) and automatically transfer excess cash flow funds from whatever account(s) they may be in to the sweep account. Then money is again automatically transferred from the sweep account to whatever project it is designated for. For example, if the company wants to do cash sweeps to pay off a loan from the bank, then the money transferred (swept) into the sweep account will automatically be used to make a loan payment of the amount equal to the total amount of money that has been transferred into the sweep account.

The amount of cash available for a cash sweep is calculated as follows:

Cash Sweep = Total Cash at Hand – Minimum Cash Balance for Operations + Debt Service Cash Flow

This can be furthered explained in this sample balance sheet from Company ABC:

	In Thousands
Beginning cash balance (Total cash at hand)	$326.8
(-) Minimum cash balance for operations	$103.2
Excess cash	$223.6
(+) Cash flow available for debt service	$68.2
Cash available for sweep	$291.8

Therefore,

Cash Sweep = $326,800,000 - $103,200,000 + $68,200,000 = $291,800,000

Cash Sweeps for Individuals

Cash sweeps for individuals suit investors who like to automate their investments. A cash sweep account is typically used in brokerages for parking funds ready to be reinvested. Such funds include dividends, cash deposits, etc. Many individuals leave this money untouched in accounts awaiting appropriate long-term investment opportunities. In the meantime, the money can accumulate interest in these cash sweep accounts.

Cash Sweeps for Businesses

Cash sweeps are ideal for businesses because of their automated nature that helps businesses avoid having to make continual decisions and manual money transfers. They are business tools that assist small and medium-sized firms in maximizing revenue earned on idle money reserves in accounts. They diversify the sources of income that would otherwise be underutilized. The business simply sets up a minimum balance for their primary checking account. Any amount over that minimum is automatically swept into high interest earning accounts – or in the case of debt sweeps, automatically dedicated to loan repayment.

Businesses also use cash sweeps to manage their spending. In case the funds in their primary checking account fall below the minimum amount, the funds are swept back from the investment account to ensure that they have adequate operating capital. Some banking institutions encourage sweeping by offering attractive interest rates on sweep accounts.

A Cash Sweep in Financial Modeling

A financial analyst will often build a cash sweep in financial modeling. For example, when building an LBO model it may be necessary for the analyst to use Excel functions and formulas that automatically take all available cash and use it to repay debt.

Advantages of a Cash Sweep

The use of a cash sweep eliminates the aspect of personal intervention. It saves the account owner the time and trouble of having to make separate decisions every day about where to direct the company's cash flow. It also helps them stay on track toward achieving their designated financial goals since the process is automated and ongoing.

In the case of a cash sweep for optimizing investments, it ensures that the account owner earns the optimum amount of interest by making sure that cash is always in the account earning the highest interest rate. Cash sweeps were originally used to get around government regulations prohibiting commercial checking accounts from earning interest. In order to earn interest on their excess cash, companies set up cash sweeps to move excess cash from their commercial checking account that could not pay interest into another account – such as a money market market account – where the money could earn interest.

2016 saw the emergence of brokerage accounts with similar features that allow accounts to earn interest on money lying unused in the account.

Free Cash Flow

Free cash flow, (FCF) is an efficiency and liquidity ratio that calculates the how much more cash a company generates than it uses to run and expand the business by subtracting the capital expenditures from the operating cash flow. In other words, this is the excess money a business produces after it pays all of its operating expenses and CAPEX. This is an important concept because it shows how efficient the business is at generating cash and if it can pay its investors a return after it funds its operations and expansions.

Investors and creditors use this ratio to analyse a business in a number of different ways. Investors like this measurement because it tells the truth about how a business is actually doing. Other financial ratios can be adjusted or changed by management's treatment of accounting principles. That's not really possible with this calculation. It's difficult to fake the cash flow coming in and leaving a company. Thus, investors look at this ratio to gauge how well the business is doing and more importantly will it be able to provide a return on their investment.

Creditors, on the other hand, also use this measurement to analyse the cash flows of the company and evaluate its ability to meet its debt obligations.

Three Ways to Calculate Free Cash Flow

These three ways to calculate free cash flow, also sometimes known as free cash flow to term, are among the easiest to use.

Free cash flow = Sales revenues - Operating costs and taxes - Required investments in operating capital

In this equation, sales revenues are taken from the business's income statement, as are operating costs and taxes. Investments in new operating capital show up as increases in fixed assets on the business's balance sheet.

If Joe's Business has sales revenues of $500,000, this figure might be reduced to $200,000 by $300,000 in operating costs and taxes due. If the business's required investments were $150,000, Joe would have free cash flow of $50,000.

Free cash flow = Net operating profit after taxes (NOPAT) - Net investment in operating capital

Here, NOPAT is the same figure used in the first equation: sales revenue - operating costs and taxes. Net investment in operating capital is the same figure as the third term in the first calculation. You can also use the increase in fixed assets on the balance sheet.

Joe's NOPAT remains at $300,000. We're simply exchanging his required investments in operating capital for his net investment in operating capital. Assuming they're the same, his free cash flow would remain much the same.

Free cash flow = Net cash flow from operations - Capital expenditures

Net cash flow from operations comes from the first section of the statement of cash flows in this equation, while capital expenditures comes from the increase in fixed assets off the balance sheet. If Joe's net cash flow from operations is $200,000, this figure would be reduced by his capital expenditures.

When you examine these equations and work with them for a while, you'll realize that all three methods of calculating free cash flow should yield pretty much the same answer. They just approach the same information from different angles.

Effect of Free Cash Flow

Positive free cash flow is indicative of overall business health. Companies that have a healthy free cash flow have enough funds on hand to meet their bills every month plus some left over. The excess might be distributed among shareholders as dividends or it might be used to seize upon opportunities to generate more income through acquisitions or developing innovative products.

A company with rising or high free cash flow is generally doing well and might want to consider expanding, whereas a company with falling or low free cash flow might need to restructure because there's no money remaining after covering the bills.

Low free cash flow is not always indicative of a failing business, however. It can be expected at times when even a healthy company is actively pursuing growth. Acquisitions and new product development temporarily subtract from the bottom line.

That said, it's not unusual for investors to look for companies with rapidly rising free cash flow because such companies tend to have excellent future prospects. If investors find a company with rising cash flow and an undervalued share price, it can be an even better investment bet.

Analysis

Since the free cash flow equation is both an efficiency and liquidity ratio, it gives investors a great deal of information about the company. Obviously, in most cases a larger FCF is always better than a lesser number because it indicates that the company is doing well and its operations are able to fund all of its activities while throwing off excess cash for its investors.

Going back to our example, Tim's business generated $45,000 in excess of what it needed to run the operations and fund the new capital investments. This $45,000 could be put back into the business to purchase more inventory, or it could be used to issue Tim and his new investors a dividend at the end of the year. This is exactly what Tim's new investors want to see. They want to see that the business operations are healthy and efficient enough to generate excess funds.

It's important to note that excess cash does not always mean the company is doing well or what it should be doing to grow in the future. For example, a company might have positive FCF because it's not spending any money on new equipment. Eventually, the equipment will break down and the business might have to cease operations until the equipment is replaced. For instance, Tim's delivery truck might need to be replaced. If the truck is inoperable, he might lose orders.

Conversely, negative free cash flow might simply mean that the business is investing heavily in new equipment and other capital assets causing the excess cash to disappear. Like with all financial ratios, FCF is a peak into how a company is operated and the strategies that management is taking. You have to measure and analyse the numbers to understand why the ratios are the way they are and whether or not a business is healthy.

Cash Flow Statement

A cash flow statement is a financial statement that provides aggregate data regarding all cash inflows a company receives from its ongoing operations and external investment sources, as well as all cash outflows that pay for business activities and investments during a given period.

The cash flow statement is focused on cash accounting, whereas there are two forms of accounting, accrual and cash. Most public companies use accrual accounting, which means the income statement is not the same as the company's cash position.

For example, a company may sell product and extend its customers credit. It still recognizes that sale as revenue, but the company may not receive cash until a later date. The company is earning a profit on the income statement and will pay income taxes on it, but the business may bring in more or less cash than the sales or income figures. Even profitable companies can fail to adequately manage cash flow, which is why the cash flow statement is a critical tool for companies, analysts and investors.

The cash flow statement is broken down into three different business activities: operations, investing and financing then a final summary section.

Preparing Cash Flow Statement

There are two methods which can be used to prepare cash flow statements:

A. Indirect method

B. Direct method

Whichever method be used, the end result under all three activities i.e. operating, investing and financing will be the same.

1. Preparation under indirect method

I. Operating activities

The cash flow from operating activities are derived under two stages;

A. Calculating the operating profit before changes in working capital

B. The effect of changes in working capital

Stage 1: Operating profit before changes in working capital can be calculated as follows:

Net profit before Tax and extra ordinary Items	**xxx**	
Add: Non-cash and non-operating Items which have already been debited to profit and Loss Account like;		
Depreciation	xxx	
Amortisation of intangible assets	xxx	
Loss on the sale of Fixed assets	xxx	
Loss on the sale of Long-term Investments	xxx	
Provision for tax	xxx	
Dividend paid	xxx	xxx
Less: Non-cash and Non-operating Items which have already been credited to Profit and Loss Account like		
Profit on sale of fixed assets	xxx	
Profit on sale of Long term investment	xxx	xxx
Operating profit before working Capital changes		xxx

Stage 2: Effect of changes in working capital is to be taken into as follows:

a. Current Assets

i. An increase in an item of current assets causes a decrease in cash inflow because cash is blocked in current assets.

ii. A decrease in an item of current assets causes an increase in cash inflow because cash is released from the sale of current assets.

b. Current liabilities

i. An increase in an item of current liability causes a decrease in cash outflow because cash is saved.

ii. A decrease in an item of current liability causes an increase in cash outflow because of payment of the liability.

Thus, in a nutshell

Cash from operating activities = Operating profit before working capital changes + Net decrease in current assets + Net Increase in current liabilities – Net increase in current assets – Net decrease in current liabilities

II. Investing activities

The cash flow from investing activities is derived by adding all the cash inflows from the sale or maturity of assets and subtracting all the cash outflows from the purchase or payment for new fixed assets or investments.

Cash flow arising from investing activities typically are:

i. Cash payments to acquire Fixed Asset

ii. Cash receipts from disposal of fixed asset

iii. Cash payments to acquire shares or debenture investment

iv. Cash receipts from the repayment of advances and loans made to third parties

Furthermore,

Examples of Cash inflow from investing activities are:

i. Cash sale of plant and machinery, land and Building, furniture, goodwill etc

ii. Cash sale of investments made in the shares and debentures of other companies

iii. Cash receipts from collecting the Principal amount of loans made to third parties

Examples of Cash outflow from investing activities are:

i. Purchase of fixed assets i.e. land, Building, furniture, machinery etc.

ii. Purchase of Intangible assets i.e. goodwill, trademark etc.

iii. Purchase of shares and debentures

iv. Purchase of Government Bonds

v. Loan made to third parties

III. Financing activities

Cash flows from financing activities are the cash paid and received from activities with non-current or long-term liabilities and shareholder's capital.

Cash flow arising from financing activities typically are:

1. Cash proceeds from the issue of shares or other similar instruments
2. Cash proceeds from the issue of debentures, loans, notes, bonds, and other short-term borrowings
3. Cash repayment of the amount borrowed

Examples of cash inflow from financing activities are:

i. The issue of equity and preference share capital for cash only

ii. The issue of debentures, bonds and long-term note for cash only

Examples of cash outflow from financing activities are:

i. Payment of dividends to shareholders

ii. Redemption or repayment of loans i.e. debentures and bonds

iii. Redemption of preference share capital

iv. Buyback of equity shares

Illustration of Indirect method:		
Net profit before Tax and extra ordinary Items	xxx	
Cash flow from Operating activities		
Add: Non-cash and non-operating Items which have already been debited to profit and Loss Account like;		
Depreciation	xxx	
Amortisation of intangible assets	xxx	
Loss on the sale of Fixed assets	xxx	
Loss on the sale of Long-term Investments	xxx	
Provision for tax	xxx	
Dividend paid	xxx	xxx
Less: Non-cash and Non-operating Items which have already been credited to Profit and Loss Account like		
Profit on sale of fixed assets	(xxx)	
Profit on sale of Long term investment	(xxx)	(xxx)
Operating profit before working Capital changes (A)		xxx
Changes in working capital:		
Add: Increase in current liabilities	xxx	
Decrease in current assets	xxx	xxx
Less: Increase in current assets	(xxx)	
Decrease in current liabilities	(xxx)	(xxx)
Net increase / decrease in working capital (B)		xxx

Illustration of Indirect method:		
Cash generated from operations (C) = (A+B)		xxx
Less: Income tax paid (Net tax refund received) (D)		(xxx)
Cash flow from before extraordinary items (C-D) = (E)		xxx
Adjusted extraordinary items (+/–) (F)		xxx
Net cash flow from operating activities (E+F) = (G)		xxx
Cash flow from Investing activities		
Proceeds from sale of fixed assets	xxx	
Proceeds from sale of investments	xxx	
Purchase of shares/debentures/fixed assets	(xxx)	
Net cash from investing activities (H)		xxx
Cash flow from Financing activities		
Proceeds from issue of shares	xxx	
Proceeds from issue of debentures	xxx	
Payment of dividend	(xxx)	
Net cash flow from financing activities (I)		xxx
Net increase in cash and cash equivalents (G+H+I) = (J)		xxx
Cash and cash equivalents and the beginning of the period (K)		xxx
Cash and cash equivalents and the end of the period (J+K)		xxx

2. Preparation under the direct method

The fundamentals of preparation of cash flow statement under Direct method is more or less same as in Indirect method with only a few exceptions in terms of its presentation.

The Cash flow statement under direct method is prepared as follows:

Cash flow from Operating activities		
Add: Operating cash receipts: (A)		
Cash sales	xxx	
Cash received from customers	xxx	
Trading commission received	xxx	
Royalties received	xxx	xxx
Less: Operating cash payments: (B)		
Cash purchase	(xxx)	
Cash paid to suppliers	(xxx)	
Cash paid for business expenses	(xxx)	(xxx)
Cash generated from operations (A-B) = (C)		xxx
Less: Income tax paid (Net of tax refund received) (D)		(xxx)
Cash flow before extraordinary items (C-D) = (E)		xxx
Adjusted extraordinary items (+/–) (F)		xxx
Net cash flow from operating activities (E-F) = (G)		xxx
Cash flow from investing activities (calculation same as under indirect method) (H)		xxx

Cash flow from Operating activities		
Cash flow from financing activities (calculation same as under indirect method) (I)		xxx
Net increase in cash and cash equivalents (G+H+I) = (J)		xxx
Cash and cash equivalents and the beginning of the period (K)		xxx
Cash and cash equivalents and the end of the period (J+K)		xxx

Valuation using Discounted Cash Flows

Discounted cash flow (DCF) valuation is one of the fundamental models in value investing. The model is used to calculate the present value of a firm by discounting the expected returns to their present value by using the weighted average cost of capital (WACC).

Performing a DCF Valuation

There are certain steps in performing a DCF valuation. These are:

1. Calculate the WACC

The weighted average cost of capital is fundamental to the capital asset pricing model (CAPM). The WACC is calculated as the weighted average of a firm's cost of debt and cost of equity.

Assuming that you have invested in Novartis (NYSE: NVS), the steps for the calculation of WACC are the following:

Novartis AG				**Input**	**Calculation**		
KEY DRIVERS			**2016**	**2017**	**2018**	**2019**	**2020**
Growth rate			8.00%	8.00%	8.00%	8.00%	8.00%
Growth beyond forecast period		6.00%					
Tax Rate		30.0%					
Cost of Debt (Rd)		**2.81%**					
Total Debt	16,327.0						
Interest expenses	655.0						
Income taxes	196.5						
Cost of equity Rs = RRF + (RPM * b)		**8.83%**					
RRF	5.00%						
RPM	5.10%						
b	0.75						
MVA							
Price per share	75.21						
Number of shares	2,370						
Market Value	**178,248**						
BVPS	31.57						
Book Value	**74,821**						
MVA = Market Value - Book Value	**103,427**						
Total Debt + MVA	**119,754**						
Wd		13.63%					
We		86.37%					
WACC		**8.00%**					
WC/Sales		**6.61%**					

a) The first step is to find the cost of debt and the cost of equity.

The cost of debt is derived as follows:

The company's total debt is $16.33 billion and the interest expenses are $655.0 million. The interest expenses will save Novartis $655 x 30% (tax rate) = $196.50 million. So, the after-tax cost of debt Rd = ($655.0 – $196.5) / $16.33 = 2.81%

The cost of equity is calculated using the formula Rs = RRF + (RPM * b), where,

- RRF: the risk-free rate
- RPM: the return that the market expects
- B: the stock's beta (systemic risk)

Therefore, for a risk-free rate of 5.00%, an expected market return of 5.10% and a b=0.75, the cost of equity is:

Rs = RRF + (RPM * b) = 5.00% + (5.10% x 0.75) = 8.83%

b) The second step is to calculate the weights of debt and equity

First, you need to find the Market value added (MVA) of the company, which represents the difference between the current market value of a firm and its book value. Novartis is currently trading at $75.21 and the number of shares outstanding is 2.37 billion. Therefore, the company's market value is $75.21 x 2.37 = $178.25 billion. Given the company's book value per share (BVPS) of $31.57, its book value is $31.57 x 2.37 = $74.82 billion. Therefore, the market value added is market value – book value = $178.25 – $74.82 = $103.43 billion.

Now that you know the MVA and the total debt, you added them to derive the weights of debt and equity. Therefore:

The book value of debt + MVA of equity = $16.33 + $103.43 = $119.76. Therefore, the weight of debt Wd = $16.33 / $119.76 = 13.63% and the weight of equity We = $103.43 / $119.76 = 86.37%.

c) The final step is to calculate the WACC

The formula for WACC is (Rd*Wd) + (Rs*We). Therefore:

WACC = (2.81% x 13.63%) + (8.83% x 86.37%) = 0.38% + 7.62% = 8.00%.

2. Discounting by the WACC

The goal of a DCF valuation is to derive the fair value of the stock and determine whether it trades above this value (overvalued) or below this valued (undervalued). Remember that value investing is set out to find undervalued stocks, i.e. stocks that trade below their fair value and, therefore, they have a room for growth.

a) Once you know the WACC you can create a spread sheet for the calculation of the free cash flow to the firm (FCFF) by using the sales and EBITDA of the current year, and assuming a sales growth of 8% and a tax rate of 30% for the next 5 years. Then, you discount the FCFF to its present value, using the WACC. The changes in working capital are discounted using the WC/Sales ratio (working capital over sales), which in this case is $3,331 / $50,359 = 6.61%.

FCFF Calculation	YEAR	1	2	3	4	5
Sales	50,359	54,388	58,739	63,438	68,513	73,994
EBITDA	8,845	9,553	10,317	11,142	12,034	12,996
Less: Depreciation	0.0	0	0	0	0	0
EBIT	8,845	9,553	10,317	11,142	12,034	12,996
Less: Taxes on EBIT	(2,654)	(2,866)	(3,095)	(3,343)	(3,610)	(3,899)
EBIT*(1-t)	6,192	6,687	7,222	7,800	8,423	9,097
Plus: Depreciation	0	0	0	0	0	0
Less: Capital Expenditures	(3,331)	(3,597)	(3,885)	(4,196)	(4,532)	(4,894)
Less: Change in Working Capital	0	(266)	(288)	(311)	(336)	(363)
Free Cash Flow to the Firm	2,861	2,823	3,049	3,293	3,556	3,840
Present Value of FCF		2,614	2,614	2,613	2,613	2,613

Here is an example of the calculations:

Sales: 50,359 x (1+8%) = $54,388 x (1+8%) = $58,739 x (1+8%) = $63,438 x (1+8%) =$68,513 x (1+8%) = $73,994

EBITDA: $8,845 x (1+8%) = $9,553 x (1+8%) = $10,317 x (1+8%) = $11,142 x (1+8%) = $12,034 x (1+8%) = $12,996

Since there are depreciation expenses, EBITDA is equal to EBIT.

Taxes on EBIT: $8,845 x 30% and so on up to year 5.

Capex: 3,331 x (1+8%) = $3,597 x (1+8%) = $3,885 x (1+8%) = $4,196 x (1+8%) = $4,532 x (1+8%) = $4,894.

Changes in WC: 6.61%* ($54,388-$50,359) = 266 and so on up to year 5.

FCFF: EBIT (1-t) – Capex – Changes in WC.

PV of FCFF: FCFF / $(1+WACC)^1$ for year 1, ^², for year 2 and so on up to year 5.

b) Then, you need to calculate the terminal value, assuming a growth of 6% beyond the forecast period. Therefore, the FCFF in the year 5 with a growth of 6% = $3,840 x (1+6%) = $4,070.90, and the terminal value is $4,070.90 / (WACC – growth) = $4,070.90 / (8% – 6%) = $4,070.90 / 2% = $203,544.90. Then, you discount the terminal value to its present value, using the WACC. So, the Present value of terminal value is $203,544.90 / (1+8%)5 = $138,175.48.

Terminal Value Calculation	
Growth beyond forecast period	6.00%
FCFF (n+1)	$4,070.90
Terminal value	$203,069.16
Present Value of Terminal Value	$138,175.48

Calculating the total PV of the FCF = $13,067.1c) Then, you need to calculate the equity value of the firm by:

Present Value of FCF	2,614	2,614	2,613	2,613	2,613

3. Add the PV of the terminal value to find the total equity value. So, $13,067.1 + 138,175.48 = $151,242.6

4. Deduct the debt of last year (in this case of 31/12/2015) to find the net asset value. So, $151,242.6 – $21,901 = $129,341.6.

Equity Value	
PV of FCF	$13,067.10
PV of Terminal Value	$138,175.48
Total Entity Value	**$151,242.58**
Less Debt 31/12/2015	$21,901.00
Net Asset (Equity) Value	**$129,341.58**

d) Finally, you need to adjust the net asset value for the present day, as follows:

Adjustment for Present Day	
Today	18-Feb-17
End of last financial year	31-Dec-15
Days since end of year	415
Adjusted Net Asset Value	**$141,176.34**
Number of Shares	2,370,000
Value per share	**$59.57**

So, according to the DCF valuation, Novartis is overvalued, as it trades at $75.21 and the DCF shows that the value per share should be $59.49 based on the company's FCFF.

Some Limitations of the DCF valuation

DCF Valuation is an extremely useful tool, provided that the growth rate assumed for the series of period is justifiable by the firm's operating performance. Although the growth rate cannot be accurately estimated, a firm that is expanding and seek to enter into new markets is more likely to sustain an average growth of 10% for the next five years than a company that is contracting or losing market share. Also, the WACC calculation may not really apply to the real world.

Another area that requires attention is the capex projections. In the above example, we assumed Novartis' capex is growing at 8% annually over the next five years. In the real world, this may not be so true. If, for example, a company is expanding in year 3, its capex will be higher in year 3 and lower in years 1,2,4 and 5. So, before using a constant growth for Capex, you need to dig into the company' balance sheet to investigate the trend of capex throughout the investigation period.

Burn Rate

Burn rate measures how quickly your cash holdings are decreasing. Gross burn rate is the total amount of cash you've spent each month. Net burn rate is the difference between cash out and cash in. Profitable companies have a negative net burn rate because they are bringing in more than they are spending.

Measuring Burn Rate allows you to forecast when you'll run out of money (if you're burning more than you're making) or when you'll be able to expand.

Calculating Burn Rate

To find the burn rate, select the period you want to measure. Find the difference between the starting and ending account balances for the period. Then, divide the difference by the number of months in the period. The result is the cash burn rate.

To find the burn rate:

1. Starting Balance – Ending Balance = Balance Difference
2. Balance Difference / Number of Months in the Period = Burn Rate

For example, let's look at a five-month period. At the beginning of the period, my account balance was $40,000. At the end of the period, a balance of $30,000 was present.

Step 1: Find the difference between the starting and ending balances.

$40,000 – $30,000 = $10,000

Step 2: Divide the balance difference by the number of months in the period.

$10,000 / 5 months = $2,000

The burn rate is $2,000 per month.

Cash Runway

The cash runway is the amount of time you have until you run out of capital.

To find the cash runway, divide the money left in your account at the end of the period by the burn rate.

Using the previous example, the balance at the end of the period is $30,000. The burn rate is $2,000.

$30,000 / $2,000 = 15 months

The cash runway is 15 months. It will take 15 months for you to run out of capital.

Gross Burn Rate vs. Net Burn Rate

Burn rate can be separated into two different categories: gross burn rate and net burn rate.

Gross burn rate is the total capital you spend monthly. Gross burn rate includes all your outgoing money.

Net burn rate is the total amount of capital you lose each month.

Gross and net burn rates sound similar. But, there is a big difference between the amount you spend and the amount you lose. Let's look at an example:

Your business spends $6,000 each month. You make $4,000 in sales each month. Remember, your gross burn rate is the amount you spend. Your gross burn rate is $6,000 per month. No matter what you earn, you still spend $6,000.

But, your net burn rate is the amount you lose. Because you earn $4,000 per month, you only lose $2,000 ($6,000 – $4,000). The net burn rate shows that you have a negative cash flow, since you are earning less than you are spending.

As a small business owner, it's important to know the difference between the gross and net burn rates. The gross burn rate only shows how much you spend each month. But, the net burn rate shows the big picture of how much money you actually lose each month.

Managing your Burn Rate

Knowing your burn rate helps you understand your runway, or the amount of time before you go broke if you continue on the same trend. Your runway is the money you've got in the bank, divided by your monthly net burn rate. This gives you the number of months until Zero Cash Day (aka Doomsday).

It might seem like net burn rate is more important because most companies are happy if they have lots of runway and are growing. But keeping gross burn rate low makes your company more sustainable long term.

Say your net burn rate is reasonable because you've had a couple good months of sales, so you increase your expenses (and therefore your gross burn rate) expecting to grow. If all of a sudden your sales decrease, you won't have a built in cushion anymore – and your runway will shrink quickly.

Balancing the desire to grow with building a sustainable business is tough. As soon as you have that VC money in the bank, the desire to spend it and operate on a high burn rate is ignited.

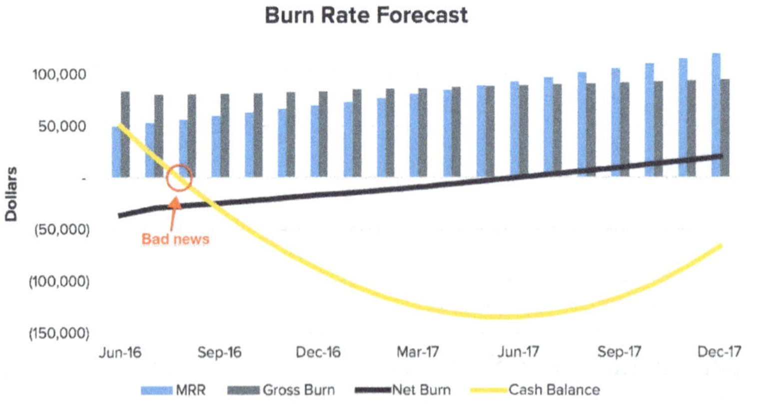

Over the last year we've gone from weeks of runway to being profitable by keeping our gross burn rate low, and turning around our net burn rate.

Discounted Payback Period

The discounted payback period is a capital budgeting procedure used to determine the profitability of a project. A discounted payback period gives the number of years it takes to break even from undertaking the initial expenditure, by discounting future cash flows and recognizing the time value of money. The net present value (NPV) aspect of the discounted payback period does not exist in a payback period in which the gross inflows of future cash flows are not discounted.

The general rule for the calculation of the discounted payback period is to accept projects that result in a payback period that is less than the targeted period. A company is able to compare its required break-even date to when the project will break even in terms of discounted cash flows, to approve or reject the project.

Formulas and Calculation Procedure

In discounted payback period we have to calculate the present value of each cash inflow taking the start of the first period as zero point. For this purpose the management has to set a suitable discount rate. The discounted cash inflow for each period is to be calculated using the formula:

$$\text{Discounted Cash Inflow} = \frac{\text{Actual Cash Inflow}}{(1+i)^n}$$

Where,

i is the discount rate;

n is the period to which the cash inflow relates.

Usually the above formula is split into two components which are actual cash inflow and present value factor (i.e. 1 / (1 + i)^n). Thus discounted cash flow is the product of actual cash flow and present value factor.

The rest of the procedure is similar to the calculation of simple payback period except that we have to use the discounted cash flows as calculated above instead of actual cash flows. The cumulative cash flow will be replaced by cumulative discounted cash flow.

$$\text{Discounted Payback Period} = A + \frac{B}{C}$$

Where,

A = Last period with a negative discounted cumulative cash flow;

B = Absolute value of discounted cumulative cash flow at the end of the period A;

C = Discounted cash flow during the period after A.

In the calculation of simple payback period, we could use an alternative formula for situations where all the cash inflows were even. That formula won't be applicable here since it is extremely unlikely that discounted cash inflows will be even.

The calculation method is illustrated in the example below.

Decision Rule

If the discounted payback period is less that the target period, accept the project. Otherwise reject.

Example:

An initial investment of $2,324,000 is expected to generate $600,000 per year for 6 years. Calculate the discounted payback period of the investment if the discount rate is 11%.

Solution:

Step 1: Prepare a table to calculate discounted cash flow of each period by multiplying the actual cash flows by present value factor. Create a cumulative discounted cash flow column.

Year n	Cash Flow CF	Present Value Factor PV$1=1/(1+i)^n	Discounted Cash Flow CF×PV$1	Cumulative Discounted Cash Flow
0	$ −2,324,000	1.0000	$ −2,324,000	$ −2,324,000
1	600,000	0.9009	540,541	– 1,783,459
2	600,000	0.8116	486,973	– 1,296,486
3	600,000	0.7312	438,715	– 857,771
4	600,000	0.6587	395,239	– 462,533
5	600,000	0.5935	356,071	– 106,462
6	600,000	0.5346	320,785	214,323

Step 2: Discounted Payback Period = 5 + |-106,462| / 320,785 ≈ 5.32 years

Advantages

Discounted payback period incorporates the principle of time value of money into the payback period calculation which provides a more relevant measure of the risk of non-recoverability of investments.

Limitations

Discounted payback period suffers most of the drawbacks of simple payback period summarized below:

- Does not take into account the post-payback period cash flows of investments.
- Its calculation can be problematic where multiple negative cash flows are incurred during the investment period. This problem can be solved however by applying the modified payback period approach.
- Involves the use of judgment in its interpretation as it does not present a definitive decision rule unlike other investment appraisal methods such as NPV (e.g. all positive NPV investment should be accepted).

References

- Cash-flow-how-it-works-to-keep-your-business-afloat-398180: thebalancesmb.com, Retrieved 22 June 2018
- Operating-cash-flow, financial-ratios: myaccountingcourse.com, Retrieved 14 March 2018
- What-is-cash-flow-forecasting: cashanalytics.com, Retrieved 16 May 2018
- What-is-free-cash-flow-and-how-can-you-calculate-it-393111: thebalancesmb.com, Retrieved 26 June 2018
- Free-cash-flow, financial-ratios: myaccountingcourse.com, Retrieved 19 June 2018
- Discounted-payback-period, capital-budgeting, managerial: accountingexplained.com, Retrieved 10 June 2018

4

Real Options Valuation

Real options valuation is the application of the techniques of option valuation to capital budgeting decisions. This chapter discusses in detail the central aspects of real options valuation, such as option, expiration, exercise, valuation of options and real options valuation for a better understanding of the subject.

Option Finance

An option is a financial contract that gives an investor the right, but not the obligation, to either buy or sell an asset at a pre-determined price (known as the strike price) by a specified date (known as the expiration date).

Working of Option

Options are derivative instruments, meaning that their prices are derived from the price of their underlying security, which could be almost anything: stocks, bonds, currencies, indexes, commodities, etc. Many options are created in a standardized form and traded on an options exchange like the Chicago Board Options Exchange (CBOE), although it is possible for the two parties to an options contract to agree to create options with completely customized terms.

There are two types of options: call options and put options. A buyer of a call option has the right to buy the underlying asset for a certain price. The buyer of a put option has the right to sell the underlying asset for a certain price.

Here's a brief look at a few of the most common types of options:

Option Type	Description
Call	Gives the options buyer the right, but not the obligation, to purchase the underlying asset at a pre-determined price, by a specified date.
Put	Gives the options buyer the right, but not the obligation, to sell the underlying asset at a pre-determined price, by a specified date.
Over-the-Counter	Individually tailored options traded between two private parties (generally an investor and an investment bank).They are not listed on an exchange.
Vanilla	A normal option with no special features, terms or conditions -- just the right to buy/ sell a security during a certain time at a set strike price. European and American style options, which make up the majority of options traded, are considered to be "plain" vanilla options.
European	A "plain" vanilla option that can be exercised *only* on the expiration date.

American	A "plain" vanilla option that can be exercised at any time before the expiration date.
Exotic	Any style of option that includes complex structures, terms or conditions, or has a complicated formula to calculate the payoff. It is the opposite of a "plain" vanilla option.

Every option represents a contract between the options writer and the options buyer.

The options writer is the party that "writes," or creates, the options contract, and then sells it. If the investor who buys the contract chooses to exercise the option, the writer is obligated to fulfill the transaction by buying or selling the underlying asset, depending on the type of option he wrote. If the buyer chooses to not exercise the option, the writer does nothing and gets to keep the premium (the price the option was originally sold for).

The options buyer has a lot of power in this relationship. He chooses whether or not they will complete the transaction. When the option expires, if the buyer doesn't want to exercise the option, he doesn't have to. The buyer has purchased the option to carry out a certain transaction in the future - hence the name.

Every option represents a contract between the options writer and the options buyer.

Importance

Investors use options for two primary reasons: to speculate and to hedge risk. Rational investors realize there is no "sure thing," as every investment incurs at least some risk. This risk is what the investor is compensated for when he or she purchases an asset.

Hedging is like buying insurance. It is protection against unforeseen events, but you hope you never have to use it. Should a stock take an unforeseen turn, holding an option opposite of your position will help to limit your losses.

Valuation

Options valuation is a topic of ongoing research in academic and practical finance. In basic terms, the value of an option is commonly decomposed into two parts:

- The first part is the intrinsic value, which is defined as the difference between the market value of the underlying, and the strike price of the given, option
- The second part is the time value, which depends on a set of other factors which, through a multi-variable, non-linear interrelationship, reflect the discounted expected value of that difference at expiration.

Although options valuation has been studied at least since the nineteenth century, the contemporary approach is based on the Black–Scholes model which was first published in 1973.

Valuation Models

The value of an option can be estimated using a variety of quantitative techniques based on the concept of risk neutral pricing and using stochastic calculus. The most basic model is the

Black–Scholes model. More sophisticated models are used to model the volatility smile. These models are implemented using a variety of numerical techniques. In general, standard option valuation models depend on the following factors:

- The current market price of the underlying security,
- The strike price of the option, particularly in relation to the current market price of the underlying (in the money vs. out of the money),
- The cost of holding a position in the underlying security, including interest and dividends,
- The time to expiration together with any restrictions on when exercise may occur, and
- An estimate of the future volatility of the underlying security's price over the life of the option.

More advanced models can require additional factors, such as an estimate of how volatility changes over time and for various underlying price levels, or the dynamics of stochastic interest rates.

The following are some of the principal valuation techniques used in practice to evaluate option contracts.

Black–Scholes

Following early work by Louis Bachelier and later work by Robert C. Merton, Fischer Black and Myron Scholes made a major breakthrough by deriving a differential equation that must be satisfied by the price of any derivative dependent on a non-dividend-paying stock. By employing the technique of constructing a risk neutral portfolio that replicates the returns of holding an option, Black and Scholes produced a closed-form solution for a European option's theoretical price. At the same time, the model generates hedge parameters necessary for effective risk management of option holdings. While the ideas behind the Black–Scholes model were ground-breaking and eventually led to Scholes and Merton receiving the Swedish Central Bank's associated Prize for Achievement in Economics (a.k.a., the Nobel Prize in Economics), the application of the model in actual options trading is clumsy because of the assumptions of continuous trading, constant volatility, and a constant interest rate. Nevertheless, the Black–Scholes model is still one of the most important methods and foundations for the existing financial market in which the result is within the reasonable range.

Stochastic Volatility Models

Since the market crash of 1987, it has been observed that market implied volatility for options of lower strike prices are typically higher than for higher strike prices, suggesting that volatility is stochastic, varying both for time and for the price level of the underlying security. Stochastic volatility models have been developed including one developed by S.L. Heston. One principal advantage of the Heston model is that it can be solved in closed-form, while other stochastic volatility models require complex numerical methods.

Model Implementation

Once a valuation model has been chosen, there are a number of different techniques used to take the mathematical models to implement the models.

Analytic Techniques

In some cases, one can take the mathematical model and using analytical methods develop closed form solutions such as Black–Scholes and the Black model. The resulting solutions are readily computable, as are their "Greeks". Although the Roll-Geske-Whaley model applies to an American call with one dividend, for other cases of American options, closed form solutions are not available; approximations here include Barone-Adesi and Whaley, Bjerksund and Stensland and others.

Binomial Tree Pricing Model

Closely following the derivation of Black and Scholes, John Cox, Stephen Ross and Mark Rubinstein developed the original version of the binomial options pricing model. It models the dynamics of the option's theoretical value for discrete time intervals over the option's life. The model starts with a binomial tree of discrete future possible underlying stock prices. By constructing a riskless portfolio of an option and stock (as in the Black–Scholes model) a simple formula can be used to find the option price at each node in the tree. This value can approximate the theoretical value produced by Black Scholes, to the desired degree of precision. However, the binomial model is considered more accurate than Black–Scholes because it is more flexible; e.g., discrete future dividend payments can be modeled correctly at the proper forward time steps, and American options can be modeled as well as European ones. Binomial models are widely used by professional option traders. The Trinomial tree is a similar model, allowing for an up, down or stable path; although considered more accurate, particularly when fewer time-steps are modelled, it is less commonly used as its implementation is more complex.

Monte Carlo Models

For many classes of options, traditional valuation techniques are intractable because of the complexity of the instrument. In these cases, a Monte Carlo approach may often be useful. Rather than attempt to solve the differential equations of motion that describe the option's value in relation to the underlying security's price, a Monte Carlo model uses simulation to generate random price paths of the underlying asset, each of which results in a payoff for the option. The average of these payoffs can be discounted to yield an expectation value for the option. Note though, that despite its flexibility, using simulation for American styled options is somewhat more complex than for lattice based models.

Finite Difference Models

The equations used to model the option are often expressed as partial differential equations (Black–Scholes equation). Once expressed in this form, a finite difference model can be derived, and the valuation obtained. A number of implementations of finite difference methods exist for option valuation, including: explicit finite difference, implicit finite difference and the Crank-Nicolson method. A trinomial tree option pricing model can be shown to be a simplified application of the explicit finite difference method. Although the finite difference approach is mathematically sophisticated, it is particularly useful where changes are assumed over time in model inputs – for example dividend yield, risk free rate, or volatility, or some combination of these – that are not tractable in closed form.

Other Models

Other numerical implementations which have been used to value options include finite element methods. Additionally, various short rate models have been developed for the valuation of interest rate derivatives, bond options and swaptions. These, similarly, allow for closed-form, lattice-based, and simulation-based modelling, with corresponding advantages and considerations.

Risks

As with all securities, trading options entails the risk of the option's value changing over time. However, unlike traditional securities, the return from holding an option varies non-linearly with the value of the underlying and other factors. Therefore, the risks associated with holding options are more complicated to understand and predict.

In general, the change in the value of an option can be derived from Itō's lemma as:

$$dC = \Delta dS + \Gamma \frac{dS^2}{2} + \kappa d\sigma + \theta dt$$

where the Greeks Δ, Ã, κ and θ are the standard hedge parameters calculated from an option valuation model, such as Black–Scholes, and $dS, d\sigma$ and dt are unit changes in the underlying's price, the underlying's volatility and time, respectively.

Thus, at any point in time, one can estimate the risk inherent in holding an option by calculating its hedge parameters and then estimating the expected change in the model inputs, $dS, d\sigma$ and dt , provided the changes in these values are small. This technique can be used effectively to understand and manage the risks associated with standard options. For instance, by offsetting a holding in an option with the quantity $-\Delta$ of shares in the underlying, a trader can form a delta neutral portfolio that is hedged from loss for small changes in the underlying's price. The corresponding price sensitivity formula for this portfolio Π is:

$$d\Pi = \Delta dS + \Gamma \frac{dS^2}{2} + \kappa d\sigma + \theta dt = \Gamma \frac{dS^2}{2} + \kappa d\sigma + \theta dt$$

Example

A call option expiring in 99 days on 100 shares of XYZ stock is struck at $50, with XYZ currently trading at $48. With future realized volatility over the life of the option estimated at 25%, the theoretical value of the option is $1.89. The hedge parameters Ä, Γ, κ, θ are (0.439, 0.0631, 9.6, and −0.022), respectively. Assume that on the following day, XYZ stock rises to $48.5 and volatility falls to 23.5%. We can calculate the estimated value of the call option by applying the hedge parameters to the new model inputs as:

$$dC = (0.439 \cdot 0.5) + \left(0.0631 \cdot \frac{0.5^2}{2}\right) + (9.6 \cdot -0.015) + (-0.022 \cdot 1) = 0.0614$$

Under this scenario, the value of the option increases by $0.0614 to $1.9514, realizing a profit of

$6.14. Note that for a delta neutral portfolio, whereby the trader had also sold 44 shares of XYZ stock as a hedge, the net loss under the same scenario would be ($15.86).

Pin Risk

A special situation called pin risk can arise when the underlying closes at or very close to the option's strike value on the last day the option is traded prior to expiration. The option writer (seller) may not know with certainty whether or not the option will actually be exercised or be allowed to expire. Therefore, the option writer may end up with a large, unwanted residual position in the underlying when the markets open on the next trading day after expiration, regardless of his or her best efforts to avoid such a residual.

Counterparty Risk

A further, often ignored, risk in derivatives such as options is counterparty risk. In an option contract this risk is that the seller won't sell or buy the underlying asset as agreed. The risk can be minimized by using a financially strong intermediary able to make good on the trade, but in a major panic or crash the number of defaults can overwhelm even the strongest intermediaries.

Common Types of Option

Call Option

A call option is called a "call" because the owner has the right to "call the stock away" from the seller. It is also called an "option" because the owner has the "right", but not the "obligation", to buy the stock at the strike price. In other words, the owner of the option (also known as "long a call") does not have to exercise the option and buy the stock--if buying the stock at the strike price is unprofitable, the owner of the call can just let the option expire worthless.

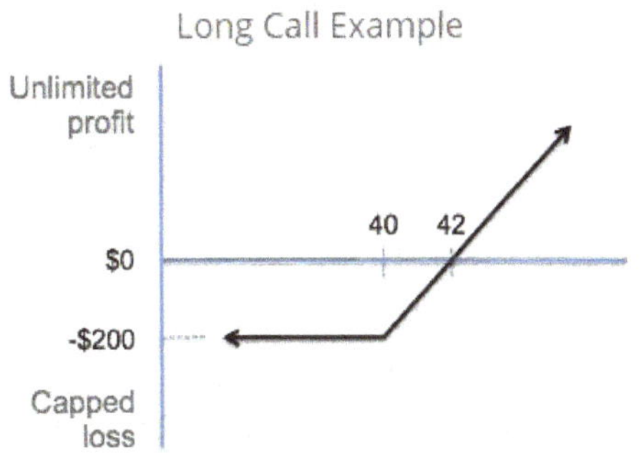

The most attractive characteristic of owning call options is that your profit is technically unlimited. And your loss is limited to the amount that you paid for the option. This diagram shows the payoff for owning call options with a strike price of $40 and a cost of $2. You will notice that if the stock price closes at or below $40, you lose the $200 ($2 price times 100 shares) cost of buying the option (note the horizontal line intersecting the y-axis at -$200). You will also notice that as the stock price increases above $40 the line slopes up indicating your profit. Finally, notice that the up sloping line become profitable at $42, which is the strike price of $40 plus the $2 cost of buying the option. Theoretically the stock price can go to infinity so that is why they say the earnings from owning a call option are unlimited.

Since owning options is always cheaper than owning the stock itself, when you know a stock price is about to move up it is always more profitable to own calls on the stock than it is to own the stock itself.

Best Time to Buy Call Options

If you think a stock price is going to go up, then there are 3 trades that you can make to profit from a rising stock price:

1. You can buy the stock
2. You can buy call options on the stock, or
3. You can write put options on the stock

Calls and puts trading Tip: Before we get too far along in talking about call options and trading call options, you need to understand that a stock price can move in three directions, not just two:

- A stock price can go up
- A stock price can go down, and
- It can stay the same.

Keep these 3 directions in mind as you read on.

Call Options Example:

Suppose YHOO is at $40 and you think YHOO's stock price is going to go up to $50 in the next few weeks. One way to profit from this expectation is to buy 100 shares of YHOO today at $40 and sell it in a few weeks when it goes to $50. This would cost $4,000 today and when you sold the 100 shares of YHOO stock in a few weeks you would receive $5,000 for a $1,000 profit and a 25% return.

That sounds great, but watch how buying a call option on YHOO would have given you a 400% return (instead of the 25% return from buying the stock.

Put Option

Put option is a derivative contract between two parties. The buyer of the put option earns a right (it is not an obligation) to exercise his option to sell a particular asset to the put option seller for a stipulated period of time.

Once the buyer of put exercises his option (before the expiration date), the seller of put has no other choice than to purchase the asset at the strike price at which it was originally agreed. The buyer of put expects the value of asset to decrease so that he can purchase more quantity at lower price.

Time to Buy a Put Option

There is a major difference between a call and a put option – when you buy the two options. The simple rule to maximize profits is that you buy at lows and sell at highs. A put option helps you fix the selling price. This indicates you are expecting a possible decline in the price of the underlying assets. So, you would rather protect yourself by paying a small premium than make losses.

This is exactly the opposite for call options – which are bought in anticipation of a rise in stock markets. Thus, put options are used when market conditions are bearish. They thus protect you against the decline of the price of a stock below a specified price.

WHEN TO BUY PUT OPTIONS

Kinds of Put Options

There are two kinds of put options – American and European – on the basis of when an option can be exercised. American options are more flexible; they allow you to settle the trade before the expiry date of the contract. European options can only be exercised on the day of the expiry. Thus, index options are European options, while stock options are a kind of American options.

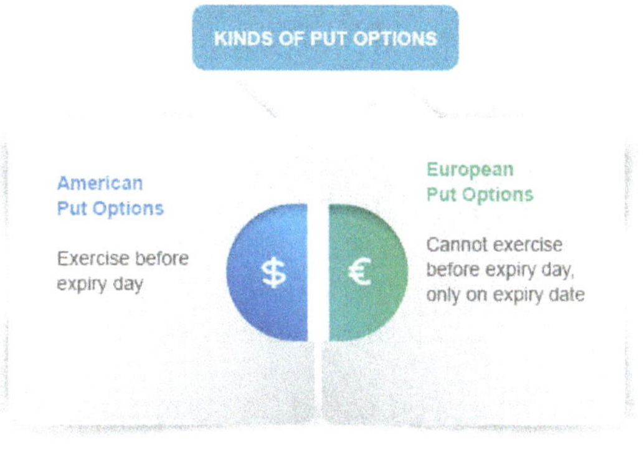

Illustration of a Put Index Option

Suppose the Nifty is currently trading at 6,000 levels. You feel bearish about the market and expect the Nifty to fall to around 5,900 levels within a month. To make the most of your view of the market, you could purchase a 1-month put option with a strike price of 5900. If the premium for this contract is Rs 10 per unit, you will have to pay up Rs 1,000 for the Nifty put option (100 units x Rs 10 per unit).

So, if the index remains above your strike price of 5,900, you would not really benefit from selling at a lower level. For this reason, you would chose to not exercise your option. You just lose your premium of Rs 1,000.

However, if the index falls below 5,900 levels as expected to say 5,850 levels, you are in a position to make profits from your options contract. You will thus choose to exercise your option and sell the index. That said, remember to take into consideration your premium costs. You will need to recover that cost too. For this reason, you will start making profits only once the index level falls below 5,890 levels.

ILLUSTRATION OF PUT INDEX OPTION

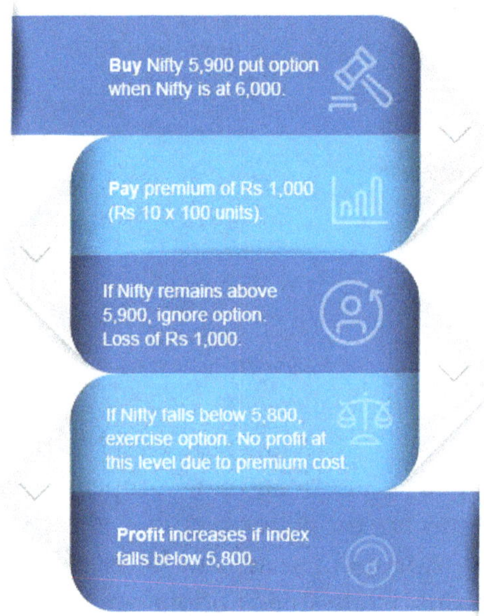

Illustration of a Put Stock Option

Put options on stocks also work the same way as call options on stocks. However, in this case, the option buyer is bearish about the price of a stock and hopes to profit from a fall in its price.

Suppose you hold ABC shares, and you expect that its quarterly results are likely to underperform analyst forecasts. This could lead to a fall in the share prices from the current Rs 950 per share.

To make the most of a fall in the price, you could buy a put option on ABC at the strike price of Rs 930 at a market-determined premium of say Rs 10 per share. Suppose the contract lot is 600 shares. This means, you have to pay a premium of Rs 6,000 (600 shares x Rs 10 per share) to purchase one put option on ABC.

Remember, stock options can be exercised before the expiry date. So you need to monitor the stock movement carefully. It could happen that the stock does fall, but gains back right before expiry. This would mean you lost the opportunity to make profits.

Suppose the stock falls to Rs 930, you could think of exercising the put option. However, this does not cover your premium of Rs 10/share. For this reason, you could wait until the share price falls to at least Rs 920. If there is an indication that the share could fall further to Rs 910 or 900 levels, wait until it does so. If not, jump at the opportunity and exercise the option right away. You would thus earn a profit of Rs 10 per share once you have deducted the premium costs.

However, if the stock price actually rises and not falls as you had expected, you can ignore the option. You loss would be limited to Rs 10 per share or Rs 6,000.

Illustration of Put Stock Option

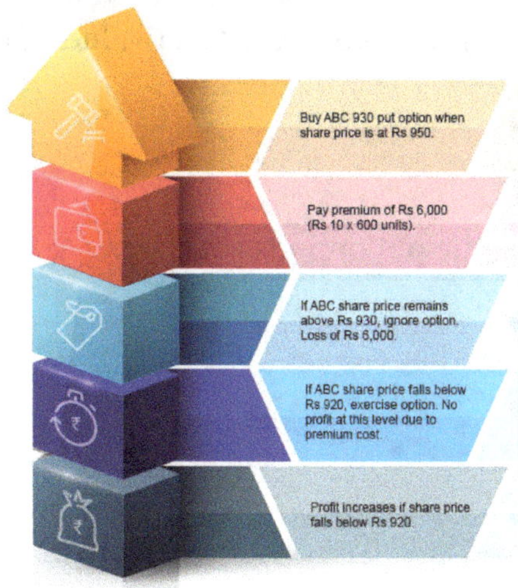

Thus, the maximum loss an investor faces is the premium amount. The maximum profit is the share price minus the premium. This is because, shares, like indexes, cannot have negative values. They can be value at 0 at worst.

What are the payments and margins involved in buying and selling Put Options

Whether you are a buyer or a seller, you have to pay an initial margin as well as an exposure margin. In addition to these two, additional margins are collected. These differ for buyers and sellers, who are at the opposite ends of the spectrum.

Here's a look:

- Buying put options:

  Whether you are a buyer or a seller, you have to pay an initial margin as well as an exposure margin. In addition to these two, additional margins are collected. These differ for buyers and sellers, who are at the opposite ends of the spectrum.

- Selling put options:

  As a seller or writer of a put option, your potential loss is unlimited.This is because prices can rise to any heights theoretically, and as a put option writer, you have to buy at whatever price has been specified.

  For this reason, the buyer of a put option has limited liability – the premium amount, while the seller has a limited gain. Therefore, the seller of a put option has to deposit a higher margin with the exchange as security in case of an adverse movement in the price of the options sold. This is called assignment margin.

  Just like the call option, the margins are levied on the put contract value in percentage terms. This amount the seller has to deposit is dictated by the exchange. Margin requirements typically rise during period of higher volatility.

So, the seller of a put option of ABC at a strike price of 970 with margin requirement of 20%, who receives a premium of Rs 10 per share, would have to deposit a margin of Rs 1,16,400 (20% of 970 x 600) as against the total value of his outstanding position of Rs 5,82,000.

Ways to Settle a Put Option

There are three common ways to settle put options contracts.

Types of Margin Payments

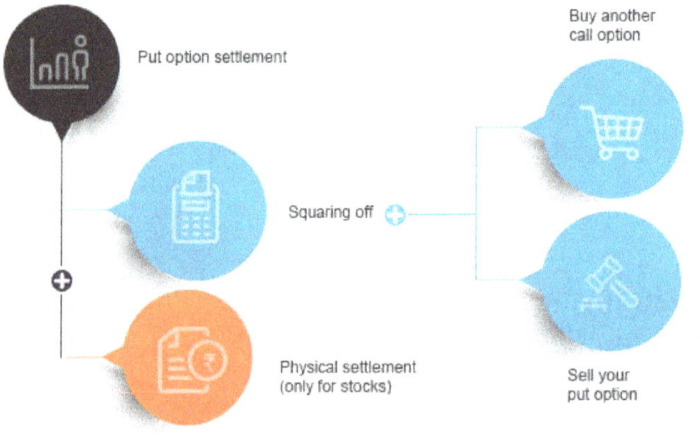

- Squaring off:

  In the case of Stock options, you can buy an opposing contract. This means, if you hold a contract to sell stocks, you purchase a contract to buy the very same stocks. This is called squaring off. You make a profit from the difference in prices and premiums.

- Selling:

  If none of the above options seem profitable, you can simply sell the 'put' option you hold. This is also a kind of squaring off method.

- Physical settlement:

  You can also exercise your option anytime on or before the expiry date of the contract. This means, you will actually sell the underlying stocks as specified in the options contract agreement.

For put index options, you cannot physically settle, as the index is not tangible. So, to settle index options, you can either exit your position through an offsetting trade in the market. You can also hold your position open until the option expires. Subsequently, the clearing house settles the trade.

Now Let's see how this Differs if you are a Buyer or Writer Put Options

For a buyer of a Put Option:

If you decide to square off your position before the expiry of the contract, you will have to buy the same number of call options of the same underlying stock and maturity date. If you have purchased two XYZ put options with a lot size 500, a strike price of Rs 100, and expiry month of August, you will have to buy two XYZ call options contracts with an expiry month of August. Thus, these two cancel each other. Whatever is the difference in strike prices could be your profit or loss.

You can also settle by selling the two put options contracts you hold in order to square off your position. This way, you will earn a premium on the contracts as the seller. The difference between the premium at which you bought the put option and the premium at which you sold them will be your profit or loss.

Or, you can exercise your options on or before the expiration date. The stock exchange will calculate the profit/loss on your positions by measuring the difference between the closing market price of the share or index and the strike price. Your account will be then credited or debited for the amount. However, your maximum loss will be restricted to the premium paid.

- For the seller of a Put Option:

  If you have sold put options and want to square off your position, you will have to buy back the same number of put options that you have written. These must be identical in terms of the underlying asset (stock or index) and maturity date to the ones that you have sold.

  In case the options contract gets exercised on or before the expiration date, the stock exchange will calculate the profit/loss on your position. This will be based on the difference between the strike price and the closing market price of the stock or index on thc day of exercise.

  You losses will be adjusted against the margin that you have provided to the exchange and the balance margin will be credited to your account with the broker.

Strike Price

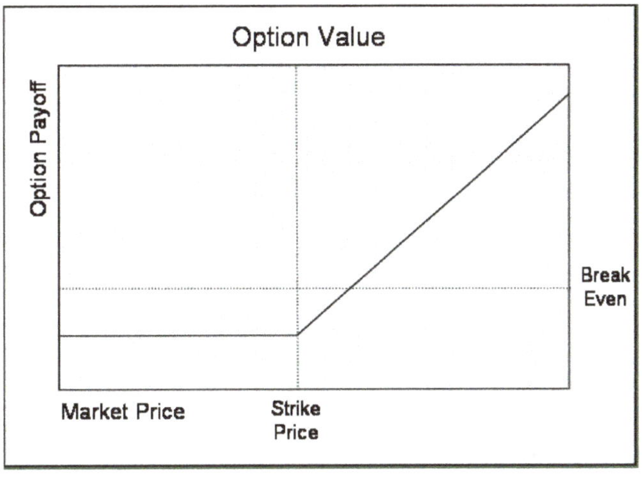

The strike price is the price at which the holder of the option can exercise the option to buy or sell an underlying security, depending on whether they hold a call option or put option. An option is a contract where the option buyer purchases the right to exercise the contract at a specific price, which is known as the strike price.

Buying or selling options is a popular trading strategy. Option trading is not complex, but as with any other investment, having good information is important. In the image below, we can see the strike price for a call option, which confers the right to buy at the strike price, and the break-even point where the option seller starts losing money.

Call Options – Strike Price

The buyer and the seller of a call option enter into an agreement, according to which the buyer gets the right to buy a specified number of shares of stock at a specified price and the seller receives the purchase price for the option in return for agreeing to sell the shares to the option holder at the strike price if the option holder elects to exercise their option. Options are only good for a set period of time, after which the option expires.

The buyer of the option can exercise the option at any time before the specified expiration date. If the call option expires "out of the money", that is with the underlying stock price still below the option strike price, then the option seller will profit by the amount of money received for the sale of the option.

If the option is "in the money" prior to expiration – meaning the underlying stock price has risen to a point above the strike price of the option – then the buyer will profit by the difference between the option strike price and the actual stock price, multiplied by the number of shares in the option. (Stock options are commonly for a lot of 100 shares.)

Put Options – Strike Price

Here, the buyer and the seller of an option also enter into an agreement, according to which the option buyer can exercise the right to sell short shares of the stock at the option strike price. Again, the option seller receives the purchase price of the option, known as the "premium".

The buyer of a put option possesses the right, but not an obligation, to exercise the option and sell short the specified number of shares of stock to the option seller any time before the option expiry, at the predetermined exercise price. In this trade, the buyer of the option will profit if the stock price falls below the option strike price prior to expiration.

The seller will profit from selling the option if the option expires out of the money, which in the case of a put option means the stock price remains higher than the strike price up to the date of the option's expiration.

Example

Maria buys a call option on the shares of company Z at a exercise price of $6. This means that Maria has the right to exercise her option and buy 100 shares of company Z at maturity for $600.

If the stock price increases to $12 before maturity, Maria exercises her option in the money as the exercise price of $6 is lower than the $12 market price. So, Maria can buy 100 shares of company Z for $6 per share and sell them for $12 per share in the open market, thus realizing a profit of ($12 x 100) – ($6 x 100) = $1200 – $600 = $600. At maturity, the difference between the market price and the exercise price is the profit earned by exercising the option.

If the market price falls to $4 at maturity, Maria loses her $600 that she initially paid to buy the shares at the strike price of $6. The seller maintains the shares. This is why the exercise price is one of the most important elements in prices index options, call options, and put options.

Expiration Options

Unlike stocks, options have an expiration date. The option expiration date is the option expires. If the option is out of the money at the expiration date then it just expires worthless and you lose the amount of money you paid for the option. If the option is in the money at the expiration date then you would either sell it or exercise your option.

For example, in the U.S. options technically expire on the third (3rd) Friday of each month. This means that you must either sell or exercise your option by that date. In the U.S., for equity and most index options you can also exercise your option prior to that date. In Europe, you can usually only exercise your options on the expiration date.

However, the option exchanges have begun issuing call and put options that have a weekly expiration. When you buy an option, you need to be 100% clear that you know when it expires. If your option is in the money, you must either sell your option or exercise it by the expiration date. If you have a call option, you would buy the stock at the strike price. If you have a put option, you would sell the stock at the strike price. If the option is "out of the money" then the option just expires worthless and will be removed from your account.

Most brokerages also allow you to setup up your account to receive automated phone, email or text messages to remind you that you have options expiring. These are typically received the Monday of expiration week.

Example of Expiration Date

Look at the first part of the option chain for April call options on AAPL. The first call option in the left column has an expiration date of Apr 10 (since it's not the 3rd Friday of the month, this must be a weekly option). The second series expires on Apr 17 (which is the regular monthly option for April since the 17th is the 3rd Friday).

Stock Symbol: AAPL   Show: Few More Most

APPLE

Last	Change	Bid	Ask	Volume	P/E	Market Ca
127.10	+0.54 (0.43%)	127.07	127.10	40.0M	17	737B

Expiration ▲	Call Strike	Ex-Div & Earnings	Call Bid	Call Ask	Buy Stock Sell Call	Time Premium	Downside Protection
Apr 10	125	-	2.05	2.13	125.05	-0.05	1.6%
Apr 10	126	-	1.05	1.14	126.05	-0.05	0.8%
Apr 10	127	-	0.08	0.11	127.02	-0.02	0.1%
Apr 10	128	-	0.00	0.01	127.10	0.00	0.0%
Apr 10	129	-	0.00	0.01	127.10	0.00	0.0%

Apr 17	125.71	-	2.24	2.28	124.86	0.85	1.8%
Apr 17	126	-	2.05	2.07	125.05	0.95	1.6%
Apr 17	127	-	1.46	1.48	125.64	1.36	1.1%
Apr 17	127.14	-	1.39	1.41	125.71	1.39	1.1%
Apr 17	128	-	0.99	1.00	126.11	0.99	0.8%

Regular Monthly Expiration

All underlyings have standard monthly expirations. Generally, this is the third Friday of each month. Most underlings have a P.M. settlement, which means that you can trade that expiration up until the closing bell on Friday. Most traders use these standard monthly expirations, so they are generally the most liquid.

Some underlyings have irregular monthly expirations. For example, VIX expires on Wednesday, and it is A.M. settled. This means that the last day to trade VIX expiration is Tuesday. Regular SPX monthly expirations are on Friday, but they are A.M. settled. Therefore, the last day to trade a regular SPX monthly expiration is Thursday. It's important to do a little research on your underlying, to ensure you know when the expiration really is.

Weekly Expiration

A lot of the more liquid underlyings have weekly expirations that expire every Friday and are P.M. settled. This includes SPX, which makes that underlying more tricky to keep track of expiration and when the last day to trade it really is. Weekly expirations are usually less liquid than monthly expirations, but they can still be heavily traded. SPY is a great example of this. Weekly expirations that encompass earnings announcements are usually the most liquid.

Impacts of Expiration

At expiration, one of two things happens depending on whether your option is in the money (ITM) or out of the money (OTM).

If an option is ITM, it will be converted to long or short shares of stock. Long calls and short puts will convert to long shares of stock. Long puts and short calls will convert to short shares of stock. Vertical spreads that are completely ITM will offset and result in either max profit or max loss depending on whether the spread is a long or short spread.

If an option is OTM, it will disappear from the account. Calls that are above the stock price & puts that are below the stock price at expiration are OTM, and will expire worthless and disappear. This results in no position and no commission fees for closing the position!

Exercise Options

The basic premise of options are that they are financial contracts that give the holder the right, but not the obligation, to buy or sell an underlying security at a fixed price. Should the holder choose to enforce their right under the terms of the contract, they are said to be exercising their option.

Working of Exercising

If you do have options contracts that you wish to exercise then the process is actually relatively simple; all you have to do is instruct your broker to exercise them for you. If you are using an online broker, then it's usually a simple process of clicking a button in the trading platform. Your broker will then take the necessary steps to exercise.

If you are exercising a call option, then you will purchase the relevant amount of the related underlying security. You can then choose to either sell that underlying security or hold on to it. If you are exercising a put option, then you will sell the relevant amount of the related underlying security, assuming you own it. If you don't own any of the underlying security, then you may have to buy it before exercising.

You should be aware that only American style contracts can be exercised prior to the expiration date. If you own European style contracts, then you cannot exercise them until the expiration date, at which point they will usually be automatically exercised if they are in profit.

Although the process for you to exercise is as simple as described above, there's actually a series of events that take place behind the scenes.

First, your broker would send an exercise notice to the relevant clearing house, depending on what options are being exercised and where. An options clearing house has the responsibility for ensuring that all contracts are settled according to the relevant. The largest clearing organization is the OCC – Options Clearing Corporation.

Once the clearing organization receives the exercise notice, they then select a member firm that is short on the contract being exercised i.e., a firm that has previously written these contracts. The selection process is usually random; any firm that's short on the relevant contracts can be chosen.

The firm that is selected is then responsible for fulfilling the terms of the contract; delivering the underlying security if it's a call option being exercised or paying for the underlying security if it's a put option. In turn, the firm will then selects one of its account holders which is short on the relevant contract and issues them with what is known as an assignment – meaning that they have to fulfil the terms of the contracts that they had previously written.

It should be noted that there is no direct relationship between the holder of options and the writer of them; basically anyone that has written specific contracts can receive the assignment when those specific contracts are exercised. The whole process sounds somewhat complicated, but it actually all happens very quickly and the net result is then reflected in your own trading account.

Advantages of Exercising

When you first start out trading options you should be aware of one very important fact; it isn't necessary to exercise in order to make a profit. A lot of beginner traders look to make profit by exercising options when there's a return to be made, but this isn't the only way to make money and it's rarely the right thing to do. Statistics have shown that traders tend to make their returns through closing positions by buying or selling options rather than exercising them. This is basically because it's usually more profitable to do so.

However, there are some reasons why exercising is the right thing to do, so there may be occasions when you do want to. The most common reason for exercising is when you own call options based on an underlying security and you decide you actually want to own that underlying security.

For example, you may have bought options on a particular stock, expecting that stock to go up in value. If the stock does indeed go up in value, you may decide that the stock represents a solid long term investment and you feel you would like to take a long term position. You could exercise your option, buy the stock at the favorable price, and then hold on to it.

You may also want to exercise a call option if it was based on underlying stock that was due to pay a dividend. You could exercise, buy the stock, receive your dividend, and then either sell the stock or keep hold of it. Another reason for exercising could be if you had specifically bought put options to protect yourself against a fall in price of stocks that you already owned. You could exercise to dispose of your stocks at a favorable price.

A number of possible reasons for exercising depend on what sort of strategies you are using. There isn't necessarily a right or wrong decision when it comes to exercising; it ultimately comes down to what's right for you at any given time and it can also depend on a number of factors. You should always try and determine what course of action gives you the best result, and be aware of the potential disadvantages of exercising.

Disadvantages of Exercising

There are two main disadvantages of exercising, and it's basically these reasons that lead most options traders to sell profitable contracts rather than exercise them. The first disadvantage is a simple one, and that is the cost involved.

The commissions that you incur through exercising call options and then selling the underlying security, or buying the underlying security and then exercising put options, are likely to be noticeably higher than the costs of simply selling the contracts for a profit.

You may also need to have a significant amount of cash on hand to facilitate such transactions, whereas you don't need any additional funds to sell options that you own.

The second disadvantage relates to the extrinsic value of options contracts. The price of an option is made up of two distinct components: intrinsic value and extrinsic value. Intrinsic value is the tangible part of the price and is basically the built in profit option. For example, if you have call options on stock that's trading higher than the strike price of them, then the intrinsic value is the difference between the current trading price of the stock and the strike price. This is the profit you could theoretically make by exercising.

The second part of the price is extrinsic value, and that relates to factors other than the price of the underlying asset. It basically represents the potential for an options contract to deliver profit, and serves to compensate the writer of those contracts for the risk they are taking. At the point of exercising a contract, the contract effectively ceases to exist and so all extrinsic value is therefore lost.

If you own options contracts that are in the money (meaning there is profit to be made through exercising), then the price of those options contact will be made up of both intrinsic value and extrinsic value. If you sell them on the exchanges you would therefore benefit from both the intrinsic value and the extrinsic value, whereas if you exercised them you would only benefit from the intrinsic value.

Although it's not always entirely that straightforward, the basic principle suggests that there's usually more money to be made from selling than there would be from exercising.

Styles

The option style, as specified in the contract, determines when, how, and under what circumstances, the option holder may exercise it. It is at the discretion of the owner whether (and in some circumstances when) to exercise it.

- European - European-style option contracts may only be exercised at the option's expiration date. Thus they can never be worth more than an American-style option with the same underlying strike price and expiration date.
- American - American-style option contracts can be exercised at any time up to the option's expiration. Under certain circumstances early exercise may be advantageous to the option holder.
- Bermudan - Bermudan-style options contracts may only be exercised on specified dates. Bermudan-style options are common in the interest rate options and swaps markets.

Settlement

The option contract specifies the manner in which the contract is to be settled.

- Physical settlement - Physically settled options require the actual delivery of the underlying security. An example of a physically settled contract is U.S.-listed exchange-traded equity options. Delivery settles in two business days. It is the most common form of settlement. Physically settled options are mostly American style.
- Cash settlement - Cash-settled options do not require the actual delivery of the underlier. Instead, the market value, at the exercise date, of the underlier is compared to the strike price, and the difference (if in a favourable direction) is paid by the option seller to the owner of the option. An example of a cash-settled contract is most U.S.-listed exchange-traded index options. This settlement occurs the next business day following the trade.

Considerations

The following guidelines determine whether and when to exercise an option:

1. An option should only be exercised if it is in the money by at least as much as the fees associated with the underlying transaction (e.g. the fee for subsequently selling an underlying which has been physically delivered). The exercise usually costs money as well.
2. In most cases, options should not be exercised before expiration because doing so gives away inherent value. Selling them would almost invariably yield more.

3. For an American-style call option, early exercise is a possibility whenever the benefits of being long the underlier outweigh the cost of surrendering the option early. For instance, on the day before an ex-dividend date, it may make sense to exercise an equity call option early in order to collect the dividend. In general, equity call options should only be exercised early on the day before an ex-dividend date, and then only for deep in-the-money options.

4. For an American-style put option, early exercise is a possibility for deep in-the-money options. In this case, it may make sense to exercise the option early in order to obtain the intrinsic value (K-S) earlier so that it can start to earn interest immediately. This is somewhat more likely to be worthwhile if there is no ex-dividend date (which would probably cause the price of the underlying to fall further) between now and the expiry date.

Early Exercise Strategy

A common strategy among professional option traders is to sell large quantities of in-the-money calls just prior to an ex-dividend date. Quite often, non-professional option traders may not understand the benefit of exercising a call option early, and therefore may unintentionally forgo the value of the dividend. The professional trader may only be 'assigned' on a portion of the calls, and therefore profits by receiving a dividend on the stock used to hedge the calls that are not exercised.

Assignment and Clearing

Assignment occurs when an option holder exercises his option by notifying his broker, who then notifies the Options Clearing Corporation (OCC). The OCC fulfills the contract, then selects, randomly, a member firm who was short the same option contract. The OCC then notifies the firm. The firm then carries out its obligation, and then selects a customer, either randomly, first-in, first-out, or some other equitable method who was short the option, for assignment. That customer is assigned the exercise requiring him to fulfill the obligation that he agreed to when he wrote the option.

Example of Exercising Your Options: If you bought a 100 shares of Apple Computer (AAPL) at $335 and you are afraid the price might drop below $300, you can buy an AAPL Put Option with a strike price of $300. That way if the price drops to $275 you will be able to exercise your option and sell your stock for $300. Please note that you don't "HAVE TO" sell your AAPL shares at $300. If the price in the market is $350 then of course you can sell your shares in the market at $350. That is why it is called an option-it is an option and not an obligation.

Valuation of Options

The option's value is called its premium. This is the current value of each option contract. It is expressed as a single numeral with two decimal places. For example, an option might be priced currently at 2.40. This means it is worth $240.

Value contains three distinct and separate parts, making valuation of options more complex than that of stock. With stock, the current market value is widely understood as the price per share.

With options, the premium is broken out into components based on the proximity between strike and current value of the underlying stock, time to expiration, and volatility of the underlying stock.

The first value is called intrinsic value. This is the value equal to the number of points that the stock is above a call's strike or below a put's strike. For example, a 35 call has intrinsic value of three points ($300) when the stock is worth $38 per share; and a 45 put has intrinsic value of two points ($200) when the stock is worth $43.

Intrinsic value can only exist when the current value of stock is greater than the call's strike or less than the put's strike. In this condition, the option is described as in the money.

In comparison, no intrinsic value exists when the current value of stock is at or below the call's strike, or when the stock's value is at or above the put's strike. When the value and strike are equal, the option is at the money and when the value is lower than the call's strike or higher than the put's strike, the option is out of the money.

The second of three components making up the option's overall premium value is called time value. This is the value assigned solely to the amount of time remaining until expiration. The longer the time remaining in the life of an option, the higher the time value will be. The rate of decline is very slow when options have a long time remaining; as expiration approaches, the time decay of the option accelerates. The rate of decline is faster, so the total history of time value looks much like a 30-year amortization chart; the principal balance falls gradually and then picks up speed in the final years. For options, the same path is seen in the decline of time value.

The third and final type of option premium is the volatility value, usually described as implied volatility of the option. This is also called extrinsic value. Whereas both intrinsic and time value are entirely predictable, extrinsic value is where all of the unknown changes take place, based on volatility of the underlying stock and proximity between current value and strike of the option. Extrinsic value often offsets changes in intrinsic value, resulting in less price reaction to movement in the underlying stock. For example, when in the money an option moves only two points while the stock's price moves three points. The one-point difference reflects a change in extrinsic value.

The option premium is complex when you realize that it contains three distinct parts. However, both intrinsic value and time value are easily understood and completely predictable. So all variables in option valuation are involved with extrinsic value. The factors affecting implied volatility found in extrinsic value include:

- Time to expiration, with a tendency for extrinsic value to offset changes in intrinsic value to a greater degree when more time is involved.
- Proximity between current value of stock and strike of the option, so that when option strikes are deep in the money (more than five points), value is less likely to move point for point with changes in the stock because extrinsic value is more likely to offset intrinsic value.
- Time and proximity in conjunction; as expiration nears and as the current value moves closer to a strike, extrinsic value is likely to become less influential on price movement.

- Changes in volatility of the underlying stock, so that if the stock's breadth of trading expands or if a price breakout occurs and a strong uptrend or downtrend follows, the greater stock volatility causes greater option volatility, as extrinsic value has strong influence on overall option premium.

The premium is complex and changes are likely to be subtle, even when price movement (notably in the money) is obvious. Valuation of options combines known values (intrinsic and time value) with the great unknown influences on the stock's price.

To better understand how extrinsic value works, imagine this situation: A call's strike is 7 points above current value of the stock, meaning it is deep out of the money. The option expires in nine months. The combination of the extended life and the proximity make this a very cheap option. However, within the next month, the stock rises by nine points, so the option is two points in the money. The overall value of the option in terms of intrinsic and extrinsic value increases; intrinsic value moves from zero to two points, but the overall value of the option has risen by five points.

This is a puzzling situation until the relationship between pricing and volatility is understood. In this case, time value has declined slightly because expiration is one month closer. Intrinsic value is equal to the points in the money. However, the difference between 7 points out and 2 points in is significant. It is not only the 9-point change that matters, but the change in status. Now the option is in the money but still has eight months until expiration. Its extrinsic value is much greater now because the opportunities for further intrinsic changes have increased greatly due to the movement in the underlying stock.

Properties of Option Values

1. The minimum value of an option is zero.

This is because an option is only a choice, not an obligation. The value of an option cannot be negative, because you do not have to do anything to get rid of it. The option will always have a zero, or a positive value.

2. The maximum value of a call option is equal to the value of the underlying asset.

This makes a lot of economic sense. An option allows you to buy a given asset at a certain exercise price. The most valuable option will be the one that allows you to acquire the asset at no cost, and the value of this option will be equal to the value of the underlying asset.

3. The total value of an option is the sum of its intrinsic value and its time premium.

Total value of an option	=	Intrinsic value of the option	+	Time premium of the option

The intrinsic value of an option is the value, or benefit, obtained by the holder by exercising the option immediately. The time premium of the option is its value, or benefit, of being able to wait and see. At expiration, the ability to wait is not there and so the time value of the option becomes zero.

For example, when a stock is selling for $60 a share, its call option with exercise price $55 is selling for $8. Then the intrinsic value of the call is $5 and the time value $3. For another option priced at \$3 with stock price \$79 and exercise price \$80, the intrinsic value is zero, and hence the time premium is \$3.

The intrinsic value of a call option equals the difference between the stock price and the exercise price, if the stock price is higher; or the intrinsic value is zero if the stock price is less than the exercise price. We may express it as

Intrinsic value of a call option = S – X, if S > X

= 0, if S ≤ X

These two equations as a single equation,

Intrinsic value of a call = max [S – X, 0]

The value of a put option increases as the stock price drops. This enables us to write,

Intrinsic value of a put = max [X – S, 0]

An option has time value only before its expiration. You lose the time value of an option when you exercise it before its expiration. Therefore, generally, it is not desirable to exercise an option before maturity. There is an important exception to this rule when we are evaluating the call options on dividend-paying stocks. When a stock pays cash dividends its price drops on the ex-dividend date, and the value of the call drops proportionately. If the time value of the option is less than the present value of the dividends paid during the life of the option, then it is better to forgo the time value of the option and capture the present value of the dividends.

4. At expiration, the value of a call option is

$$\begin{aligned} C_T &= 0, \qquad if\ S_T \le X \\ &= S_T - X,\ if\ S_T > X \end{aligned}$$

where S_T is the stock price at time T when the option matures, and X is the exercise price. Another way of expressing this is

$$C_T = \max\left[0, S_T - X\right]$$

The value of an option is zero if one cannot derive any economic benefit out of it. This is the case when the final stock price is less than the exercise price. One could buy the stock directly at a cheaper price and not use the call option. If we are not going to use an option, its value is zero. On the other hand, if the stock price is greater than the exercise price, then it is desirable to use the option and get the stock at a lower price, equal to the exercise price. The net advantage of using the option is just the difference between the final stock price and the exercise price.

For a put option, $C_T = \max\left[0, S_T - X\right]$ becomes

$$P_T = \max\left[0, X - S_T\right]$$

5. In general, the value of an American option is higher than that of a European option.

One may exercise an American option at any time before expiration, but one can exercise a European option at its expiration only. This means that an American option offers greater flexibility to the option holder. A European is more restrictive, because you can utilize it only at its expiration. Thus, an American option is more desirable.

6. The maximum value of an American put is equal to its exercise price X.

We may exercise an American put at any time before expiration, allowing us to sell the stock at the exercise price. Therefore, the maximum amount that a put can realize is the exercise price.

7. The maximum value of a European put equals Xe^{-rT}

An investor can exercise a European option only at expiration. Then it can fetch at the most X. The present value of that X is $X(1 + r)^{-T}$, where r is the interest rate and T is the time to expiration. If we think of time to be a continuous variable, and r to be the continuously compounded rate of interest, then we may write the above expression as,

$$\lim_{n \to \infty} X\left(1+r/n\right)^{-nT} = Xe^{-rT}$$

If the time to maturity of a European put is infinity, then the present value of X is zero. Therefore, the value of a European put with a very long time to maturity is close to zero.

8. A call with a higher exercise price has lower value compared to a similar call with lower exercise price.

$$C(S,X_2,T) \le C(S,X_1,T), \textit{for } X_2 > X_1$$

At expiration, the calls are in the money, if the stock price is higher than the exercise price. They are out of the money when the stock price ends up being less than the exercise price. For the call option to be of any value, the stock price must cross over the exercise price hurdle. Before maturity, the higher the exercise price, the lesser is the probability of jumping over it. Thus, the higher exercise price option is less valuable.

9. For European calls C_E, with different exercise prices, X_2 and X_1, the relationship between call prices is,

$$\left(X_2 - X_1\right)e^{-rT} \ge C_E\left(S,X_1,T\right) - C_E\left(S,X_2,T\right)$$

At expiration, the difference in the value of the options can be zero if they are both out of money and at most $(X_2 - X_1)$ if they are both in the money. Thus at expiration, $(X_2 - X_1)$ is always greater than or equal to the difference in the values of the options. The present value of this quantity, $(X_2 - X_1)\, e^{-rT}$ is always greater than the difference between the present values of the two options. This proves the result.

For American options C_A, the following relationship holds

$$\left(X_2 - X_1\right) \ge C_A\left(S,X_1,T\right) - C_A\left(S,X_2,T\right)$$

This is because we may exercise the American options at any time before maturity and realize their present value immediately.

Examples:

1. Show that before maturity, the value of a call option is

$$C \geq max\left[0, S - X e^{-rT}\right]$$

To prove this proposition, let us make a portfolio by buying a call at C, selling a share of stock at S, and also buying a bond whose face amount is X. The bond will mature after time T, at the same time when the option matures. We buy the bond at a discount, and so its present value is X(1 + r) −T. For continuous time, the present value is X e^{-rT}. The initial investment in the portfolio is

$$V_0 = C - S + X e^{-rT}$$

At expiration, the value of the bond is its face amount, X. In addition, at expiration, if the option is in money, then the final value of the portfolio is,

$$V_T = S_T - X - S_T + X = 0$$

If the final stock price is less than or equal to the exercise price, the option is out of money, and its value is zero. The total value of the portfolio is then,

$$V_T = 0 - S_T + X \geq 0$$

Since the final value of the portfolio is greater than or equal to zero, its initial value is also greater than or equal to zero. This means,

$$C - S + X e^{-rT} \geq 0$$

Or, $$C \geq S - X e^{-rT}$$

2. Show that an American call with a longer time to maturity is more valuable than an otherwise similar call with shorter maturity. That is,

$$C_2(T_2) \geq C_1(T_1), \; where \; T_2 \geq T_1$$

To prove this proposition, let us consider its converse. Suppose the longer-term call is cheaper than the shorter-term call. Then we make a portfolio by buying the cheaper call (with longer time) and selling the more expensive one. We may write the initial value of the portfolio as,

$$V_0 = C_2(T_2) - C_1(T_1) \leq 0$$

Since the initial value is zero or less, setting up this portfolio will actually make money for us. We liquidate the portfolio when the first option matures after time T1. If the shorter-term option is out of money, we simply sell the longer-term option and make some more money. The net value of the portfolio at expiration is positive. If the first option is in the money, and the buyer exercises it, then we deliver the stock by exercising the other option. This will not cost us anything, and the final value of the portfolio is zero. Now, it is impossible for a portfolio with negative initial value to have zero or positive final value. The converse being impossible proves the proposition.

3. Consider the following options on Google, trading on May 23, 2008. The options were to expire on June 21, 2008. The time to maturity is thus 29 days. The closing stock price for the day was 544.62, with a change −4.84. The risk-free rate was 1.85%.

Exercise price	Calls	Intrinsic value	Time value	Puts	Intrinsic value	Time value
510.0	41.30	34.62	6.68	5.27	0	5.27
520.0	34.20	24.62	9.58	8.30	0	8.30
530.0	27.10	14.62	12.48	11.50	0	11.50
540.0	21.20	4.62	16.58	15.50	0	15.50
550.0	16.30	0	16.30	20.60	5.38	15.22
560.0	12.50	0	12.50	26.80	15.38	11.42
570.0	9.00	0	9.00	33.30	25.38	7.92

The intrinsic and time value of the options have been calculated and added to the table. Now we make the following observations

1. The intrinsic value of an option can be positive, or zero.
2. The time value of an option is greatest when the exercise price is close to the stock price. This is a direct consequence of Black-Scholes model.
3. The time value of a call is more the than the time value of a corresponding put. This comes out of Black-Scholes model as well. A common sense approach is that investors expect the stock price to rise. This is also true according to the capital asset pricing model. Thus they are willing to pay more for a call.

Real Options Valuation

A real option is a choice made available to the managers of a company with respect to business investment opportunities. It is referred to as "real" because it typically references projects involving a tangible asset instead of a financial instrument. Real options are choices a company's management makes to expand, change or curtail projects based on changing economic, technological or market conditions. Factoring in real options affects the valuation of potential investments, although commonly used valuations, such as net present value (NPV), fail to account for potential benefits provided by real options. Using real options value analysis (ROV), managers can estimate the opportunity cost of continuing or abandoning a project and make decisions accordingly.

Real options do not refer to a derivative financial instrument, but to actual choices or opportunities of which a business may take advantage or may realize. For example, investing in a new manufacturing facility may provide a company with real options of introducing new products, consolidating operations or making other adjustments to changing market conditions. In the course of making the decision to invest in the new facility, the company should consider the real option value the facility provides. Other examples of real options include possibilities for mergers and acquisitions (M&A) or joint ventures.

The precise value of real options can be difficult to establish or estimate. Real option value may be realized from a company undertaking socially responsible projects, such as building a community centre. By doing so, the company may realize a goodwill benefit that makes it easier to obtain necessary permits or approval for other projects. However, it's difficult to pin an exact financial value on such benefits. In dealing with such real options, a company's management team factors potential real option value into the decision-making process, even though the value is necessarily somewhat vague and uncertain.

Still, valuation techniques for real options do often appear similar to the pricing of financial options contracts, where the spot price refers to the current net-present value of a project, while the strike price corresponds to non-recoverable costs involved with the project. The most common method of valuing real options currently is a form of binomial tree following a latticed (flexible) model. Monte Carlo simulations are also often used in the evaluation of real options.

Real Option Valuation Methods

Different methods to valuation real options have been published over the last decades. Brach and Baecker list various approaches and discuss further details about the different calculation alternatives. The first approach to valuate real options was published by Black and Scholes and their so called Black-Scholes equation. However, not only Brach criticizes this approach by stating that „the Black Scholes formula, which is used to price financial options, may indeed not be the right formula to price many real options. Several of the basic assumptions and constraints that come along with the Black Scholes equation simply do not hold in the real word. This, however, does not imply that the use of real options analysis is impractical or incorrect. There are other methods to price real options that can be applied".

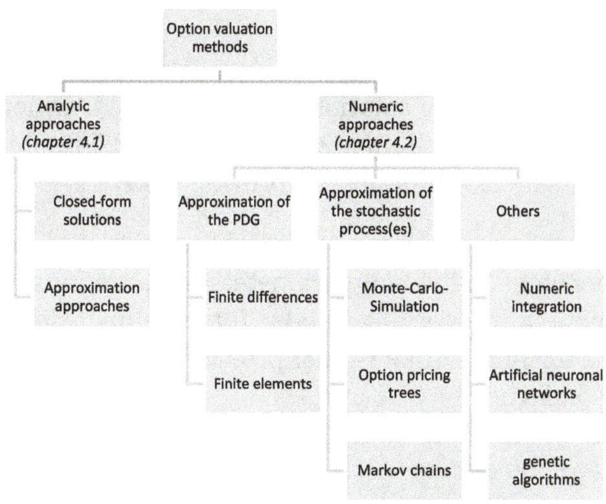

Fig.: Common option valuation methods

Nevertheless it is important to understand the basics of option prizing and its background in order to discuss and evaluate the already mentioned assumptions, constraints and results. Baecker provide an overview of methods to valuate options. In the following, we are going to present the most relevant approaches from our point of view and for the considered type of applications. For further understanding and implementation of the most common approaches Kodukula and Papudesu provide very descriptive explanations and examples.

Analytic Approaches

In the history of option valuation, a variety of analytic approaches have been published. In recent years, however, the only analytic approach with relevance for real option applications seems to be the Black-Scholes equation and modifications thereof. Therefore we will focus on this method in the following as it would go beyond the scope of this paper to discuss the whole range of available option valuation methods.

Black-Scholes equation:

One of the first and most recognized approaches to valuate real options was the closed-form analytic equation developed by Black and Scholes. Their partial differential equation (PDE) offers an analytic solution for a continuous time stochastic process (e.g. Brownian motion) under specific circumstances. The idea of the Black-Scholes equation is to valuate options based on only five parameters. The PDE can be noted as

$$\frac{\partial f}{\partial t} + rS\frac{\partial f}{\partial S} + \frac{1}{2}\sigma^2 S^2 \frac{\partial^2 f}{\partial S^2} = rf$$

with

f = price of a call option or other derivative contingent on S

S = stock price

t = time between 0 and T (maturity date)

r = risk free interest rate

σ = price volatility. (Hull)

For European call options, an analytic solution can be achieved. Other types of options can be considered as well but might require a numeric solution of the PDE. More details about the PDE, possible solutions and necessary assumptions are provided in Hull.

The possible closed-form solution makes it a comparably easy to use approach, lacking, however, transparency of the influence of individual parameters, assumptions and boundary conditions. (Uszczapowski) Furthermore, it is especially suitable for low-dimensional problems, which means in contrary, that solutions for multi-dimensional problems (such as many industrial investment decisions) are difficult to achieve.

Approximation Procedures

For applications that cannot be solved in an analytic way it may be possible to derive closed-form solutions for approximations of the original problem. To give an example, two or more correlated variables could be integrated in one variable in order to reduce the dimensions of the problem. Depending on the type of problem and the required accuracy of the results, such approximations might still deliver acceptable results. The advantage of this approach is the simplified use of the method, while the rising amount and impact of simplifications might falsify the results and disguise the influence of individual parameters.

Numeric Approaches

The scheme in figure divides the numeric approaches for option valuation in three subcategories. We will shortly introduce all of them, with an emphasis on the approximation of the stochastic processes, which we consider the most relevant for our type of applications.

Approximation of the PDG

In order to avoid the difficulties of solving a PDG, the price of an option can be assessed by using the discrete equivalent of the PDG. Typical methods are for example the finite differences and finite elements methods. Such approaches are frequently used in the fields of engineering and natural sciences. In economics and finance, however, there are some theoretical discussions (cf. Trigeorgis), but applications in the field of real options are scarce. Especially for multidimensional problems the complexity is very difficult to handle.

Approximation of the Stochastic Processes

Approximations of the stochastic processes exist in manifold forms. There are methodological differences between the approximation methods themselves and their application and implementation. We do not aim at providing a complete picture of all existing methods and combinations thereof but at outlining the general concepts, their applicability, advantages and disadvantages.

Option Pricing Trees (Binomial Pricing Model)

A frequently used option valuation method is the option pricing tree (also called lattice), often built on the binomial pricing model of Cox Its idea is not to use a PDG or estimates of volatility but probability distributions for certain state variables. In the easiest – the binomial – case, there are only two possible states of the asset value, it can either go up or down. In the following, the general structure of a binomial tree is indicated according to Brach and Hull.

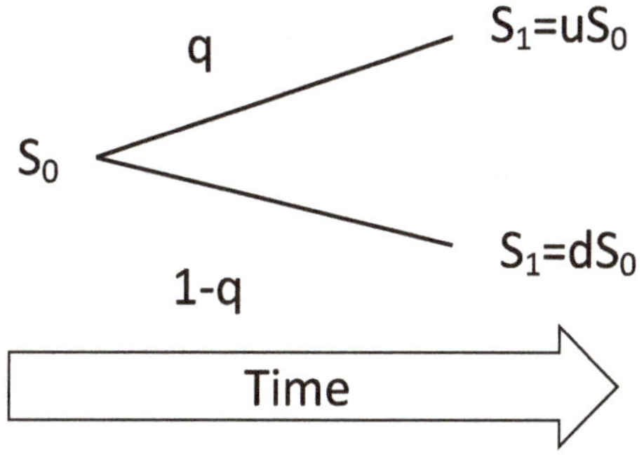

Value of the asset in t_1 :

$$S_0 = \frac{\left[q.uS_0 + (1-q) \times dS_0\right]}{(1+r)^t}$$

where

q= path probability

u= factor for path "up"

d= factor for path "down".

Pricing trees are based on a discrete time scheme which suites the needs of industrial investment decisions very well. Multidimensional problems, however, are difficult to implement as the calculation effort rises quickly with the number of nodes and branches to be considered. Furthermore, the dependency of the probability distributions, which are, in our context, hardly ever known in advance, is another disadvantage of this method. For other types of applications, however, there is a comparably large number of studies based on this approach, (e.g. Hundt; Lee and Shih,) so that its practical significance shall not be denied.

Monte-Carlo-Simulation

The idea of Monte-Carlo-Simulation is to calculate a large number of exemplary price paths following the rules of the underlying stochastic price process (often a Geometric Brownian Motion or a related stochastic process). The present value of the expected value of future payoffs can thus be calculated and considered as the risk neutral option value in a standard application.

According to Hull "the key advantage of Monte Carlo simulation is that it can be used when the payoff depends on the path followed by the underlying variable S as well as when it depends only on the final value of S. (For example, it can be used when payoffs depend on the average value of S between time 0 and time T.) Payoffs can occur at several times during the life of the derivative rather than all at the end. Any stochastic process for S can be accommodated. The procedure can also be extended to accommodate situations where the payoff from the derivative depends on several underlying market variables. The drawbacks of Monte Carlo simulation are that it is computationally very time consuming and cannot easily handle situations where there are early exercise opportunities."

Generally speaking, the Monte-Carlo-Simulation is a very flexible tool that can easily be adopted to the specific needs of the application, examples are provided by Laurikka and Koljonen and Muche. Especially in case of real option applications, where the circumstances to be considered do not fully comply with standard financial option characteristics, it is possible to adopt the simulation to the specific needs. In case of American options, however, the use of a standard Monte-Carlo-Simulation is more difficult. One approach, however, has been suggested for this specific situation and will be presented in the following.

Least Squares Monte-Carlo-Simulation

The LSM approach, published by Longstaff and Schwartz and discussed by Stentoft is an approach specifically suitable for multidimensional problems based on American options. Its aim is to approximate the value of American options by simulation, keeping the computational effort low in relation to the complexity of the problem while still achieving high quality results. The basic idea is to "regress the ex post realized payoffs from continuation on functions of the values of the state variables." (Longstaff and Schwartz,).

In general, various types of stochastic processes, such as geometric Brownian motions, but also jump diffusions or other more exotic processes can be handled. In case of multidimensional problems, however, the considered factors need to correlate to a certain extent. Otherwise a least-squares regression will not deliver reasonable results. Exemplary applications in the energy sector were published by Boomsma and Zhu and Fan.

Exercise Boundary Parameterization Approach

As a further extension of the LSM approach, the EBP aims at providing a defined stopping rule for each of the considered time steps. It is thus based on a discrete time consideration (as well as the LSM approach) and tries to maximize the expected value of the option at every time step, by calculating the values of the option according to the LSM approach for different simulated stopping or boundary values. This approach was developed by Gamba and a very descriptive explanation is provided in Hull.

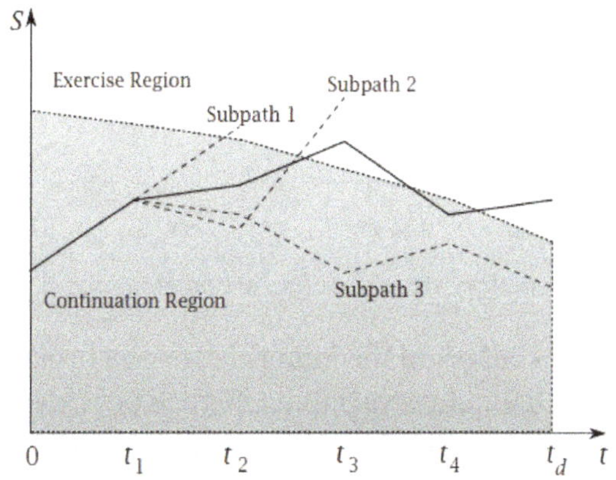

Figure: Visualization of EBP calculations

Figure visualizes the calculations performed by the EBP method. The subpaths are exemplary random paths generated by the Monte-Carlo-Simulation. If at time t, the value S_t of the subpath is in the exercise region, the option will be exercised for this path. If, however, the path is in the continuation region (such as all paths in this example are in t_1), the path will be followed without exercising the option. Once the option is exercised, there is no way back (irreversible option), so the value of this path is determined and it thus stops or, in a real option context, it continues with the cost/revenue parameters of the exercising option until the end of the considered lifetime T. The EBP identifies by simulation the threshold between the exercise and the continuation region at every time t_i that delivers the highest expected value $E(S_T)$.

A big advantage of this approach is that it is not necessary to predefine a certain, more or less arbitrary, stopping value but that the optimal stopping value is explicitly derived by the method itself. Furthermore the advantages and disadvantages of the LSM apply accordingly, as according to Hull the LSM can be considered as a part of the EBP.

An important disadvantage of both, LSM and EBP is the fact that they tend to underprice American options because of the assumption of suboptimal early exercise boundaries. (Hull,) In order to solve this issue, Andersen and Broadie proposed another extension of the EBP, introducing not only lower but also upper bounds to the price. We aim at giving a brief overview of methods, therefore we do not go deeper into the specifics of this extension as we consider it more important for a detailed quantitative analysis of a certain application than for the general understanding of the influence and applicability of real option valuation methods.

Others

Regarding the "other" methods, there is one method which we consider interesting in our context, the artificial neuronal network. As we do not aim at providing a full list of possible methods, we do not go deeper into other more specific approaches. Even though there might be successful applications for less popular methods we do not consider them appropriate in our context as we try to find an approach that does not only deliver good results but causes only reasonable implementation efforts and is as transparent and comprehensible as possible for people who might not be experts in finance and option valuation.

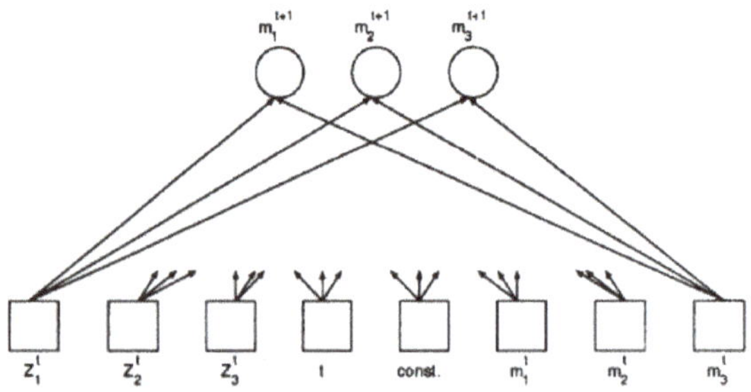

Figure: Exemplary structure of an artificial neuronal network

The neuronal network approach is based on the general idea of a broad set of input data and a significantly lower amount of output data or state variables. Figure provides an example where a company wants to deciding which product to produce in order to maximize the output. Based on various input parameters, the self-learning network teaches itself, which variables are most important and which thresholds they need to reach in order to switch the decision for the next period. Hahn and Taudes provide more specific information about the mathematical implementation of such a network.

In general, the most important disadvantage of this approach is the large amount of data that is necessary to set up and calibrate the network. In an industrial context – if data is available – it is usually historic data so that the approach assumes a forward projection not only of stochastic data (as other stochastic approaches do as well), but also of the influence and relevance of specific parameters. Depending on the context of the application, this is not necessarily the case. Furthermore, the determination of the major influencing factors and thus the methodology of decision making happens usually in a black box environment. Without detailed knowledge of the methodology itself and the underlying data, it will be hardly possible to understand the drivers and mechanisms of the evaluation process.

A brief literature survey showed that there are some theoretical studies and exemplary applications of the methodology, yet there are very few practical examples in real option valuation. This leads to the assumption that the disadvantages mentioned above (including the complexity of the method) are too severe compared to the specific advantages of the methodology that it is of large practical use.

Real Option Value Theory

Real option value (ROV) theory is a management (or investor) strategic planning tool that may be used to explain the "unreasonable" or "irrational" pricing that is observed in certain situations in the capital markets.

There have always been situations where investors have made investments at prices that cannot be justified by the intrinsic valuation of the subject investment. These investors are admired (particularly if they are successful) as risk takers who invest perhaps on a "hunch."

This discussion considers how ROV theory may explain some of that intuition. This discussion considers how investment risk takers can better handle uncertainty when they have the right—but not the obligation—to take some action in the future.

Discussion of Real Option Value Theory

ROV theory applies option pricing theory more broadly than does the typical application of financial option valuation (i.e., in the valuation of public company or private company stock options, warrants, grants, or rights). ROV theory is often used as an investment strategic tool.

Buyers of businesses or business ownership interests (including equity securities) may use ROV theory to justify their acquisition/investment pricing (or "overpricing") decisions.

The objective of this discussion is to introduce ROV theory and to prefer ROV theory as a possible explanation for certain capital market pricing phenomena.

When acquisition/investment prices cannot be rationally explained, it is not the generally accepted business valuation theory or approaches that should be challenged. The concept that is really under challenge is the definition of economic value. Investors who pay a price greater than intrinsic value—that is, the price that is can rationally be justified by the present value of expected future cash flow—may be paying what valuation analysts define as "investment value" rather than "fair market value".

That is, an "irrational" price may include components of the value that are brought to the subject investment by the particular investor/buyer. ROV theory has obvious implications to the valuation analyst or the transactional financial adviser:

1. When using empirical transactional pricing evidence as a guideline indicator of investment fair market value,
2. When advising buyers/investors in the development of potential acquisition candidates, and
3. When pricing and structuring proposed acquisition/investment transactions.

ROV theory also has obvious implications to the valuation, transactional fairness, and other investment analysis of:

1. Merger and acquisition transaction pricing;
2. Initial public offering pricing;
3. Capital budget investment decision making;
4. Capital market investment decision making; and
5. Lost profit analysis and other economic damages analysis related to securities fraud, lack of public disclosure, expropriations and condemnations, and other securities-related litigation claims.

Investment Value versus Fair Market Value

The various forms of the efficient market hypothesis essentially assume the following:

1. All appropriate information is available to investors.
2. Investors use that information when making their investment pricing decisions.

The price that an investor pays for any security investment incorporates the security holder's right to (1) invest, (2) wait, or (3) divest.

These are the "reactive" attributes of most financial instruments, including both publicly traded company and privately held company stock options.

However, ROV theory also involves "proactive" attributes of stock options, with which the security holder actually takes action to increase the value of the option itself. With regard to virtually any investment decision, investors have the following choices:

1. Invest now
2. Take preliminary steps to invest later
3. Divest now
4. Take preliminary steps to divest later
5. Do nothing

Each investment choice creates a set of economic payoffs linked to further choices at a later time. This is the premise behind the proposition that all management investment, financing, and dividend decisions can be analysed in terms of option pricing.

As one may expect, the Black-Scholes option pricing model is where ROV theory conceptually begins. Consideration of the Black- Scholes option pricing model helps to explain these otherwise inexplicable "irrational" investment pricing decisions.

There are direct parallels in the economic variables of ROV theory and the six economic variables encompassed in the Black- Scholes option pricing formula. These economic variable parallels are presented in table.

Table
Financial Option Pricing Models versus ROV Analyses
Parallels in the Component Economic Variables

Black-Scholes Option Pricing Model Economic Variables	Real Option Valuation Analysis Economic Variables
Time to expiration	Time to expiration
Risk-free interest rate	Risk-free interest rate
Exercise price	Present value of fixed costs
Stock price	Present value of expected cash flow
Uncertainty of stock price movements	Uncertainty of expected cash flow
Dividends	Value lost during decision period

ROV theorists refer to this phenomenon as "flexibility value." This is where the "investment value" standard of value—versus the "fair market value" standard of value—appears to come into play in ROV theory.

Investment value is often defined as "the value to a particular investor based on individual investment requirements and expectations".

ROV theory seems to fit certain situations that are characterized by:

1. High levels of investment research and
2. High levels of investment development, manufacturing, and/or marketing.

For example, an investor may pay today's "irrational" price for the investment—and then the option buyer may use his/her influence to improve the economic value of the subject investment.

Implications of Real Option Value Theory

ROV theory has at least three important implications for valuation analysts, for transactional participants, and for investors:

1. Guideline security purchase/business acquisition transactions that are used to estimate market value indications may have been consummated based on ROV theory valuations.

2. In the negotiation and pricing of acquisition or divestiture opportunities, it is appropriate to consider simultaneous, multistage investment analyses—where the buyer can influence the value at a later point in time. This perspective may allow the buyer to compete for the investment opportunity at higher bid prices.

3. The analysis of the pricing and structuring of acquisitive investment transactions may benefit from the consideration of real option variables, thereby:

   a. Giving the investors proprietary rights and
   b. Escalating financial obligations with expiration dates.

References

- Smith, B. Mark (2003), History of the Global Stock Market from Ancient Rome to Silicon Valley, University of Chicago Press, p. 20, ISBN 0-226-76404-4
- What-are-put-options, Investment-knowledge-Bank: kotaksecurities.com, Retrieved 29 June 2018
- Black, Fischer; Scholes, Myron (1973). "The Pricing of Options and Corporate Liabilities". Journal of Political Economy. 81 (3): 637–654. doi:10.1086/260062. JSTOR 1831029
- Strike-price, accounting-dictionary: myaccountingcourse.com, Retrieved 20 May 2018
- Cox JC, Ross SA and Rubinstein M. 1979. Options pricing: a simplified approach, Journal of Financial Economics, 7:229–263.
- Exercising-options, how-options-really-work: optionstrading.org, Retrieved 10 July 2018
- Hull, John C. (2005), Options, Futures and Other Derivatives (excerpt by Fan Zhang)(6th ed.), Pg 6: Prentice-Hall, ISBN 0-13-149908-4
- Valuation-of-options-ws-12790: investorguide.com, Retrieved 29 April 2018

5

Time Value of Money

The theory of the time value of money proposes that there is a preferential profit in receiving money at the moment of transaction rather than later. It is based on the economic concept of time preference. The fundamental concepts of time value of money such as present value, net present value, adjusted present value and future value have been elaborately discussed in this chapter.

Time Value of Money

Time value of money (TVM) is the idea that money that is available at the present time is worth more than the same amount in the future, due to its potential earning capacity. This core principle of finance holds that provided money can earn interest, any amount of money is worth more the sooner it is received. One of the most fundamental concepts in finance is that money has a time value attached to it. In simpler terms, it would be safe to say that a dollar was worth more yesterday than today and a dollar today is worth more than a dollar tomorrow.

There are five variables that you need to know:

1. Present value (PV) - This is your current starting amount. It is the money you have in your hand at the present time, your initial investment for your future.
2. Future value (FV) - This is your ending amount at a point in time in the future. It should be worth more than the present value, provided it is earning interest and growing over time.
3. The number of periods (N) - This is the timeline for your investment (or debts). It is usually measured in years, but it could be any scale of time such as quarterly, monthly, or even daily.
4. Interest rate (I) - This is the growth rate of your money over the lifetime of the investment. It is stated in a percentage value, such as 8% or .08.
5. Payment amount (PMT) - These are a series of equal, evenly-spaced cash flows.

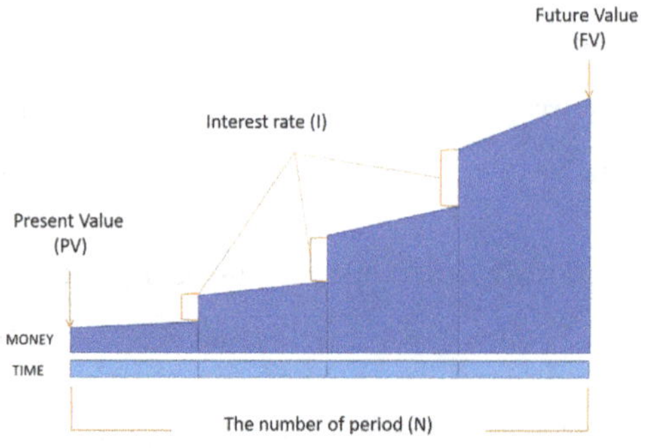

You can calculate the fifth variable if you are given any four of the five (all) variables listed above. A simple example of this would be: If you invest one dollar (PV) for one year (N) at 6% (I), you will receive $1.06 (FV). This would be the same as saying the present value of $1.06 you expect to receive in one year, is only $1.00 (PV).

Example of Time Value of Money

Suppose that a friend offers to pay you $1,000 today or $1,050 one year from today. This promise comes from someone that you trust very much, and thus you do not believe there is any risk that you will not be paid.

Offer that you Should Accept

It all depends on the return you can earn on your money. If you can earn 6% on your money, for instance, then you should accept the $1,000 today. If invested for one year, it would grow to $1,060, beating the option of receiving $1,050 one year from now.

However, if you can only earn a 4% return on your money, you should accept the offer of $1,050 paid one year from now. If you accept the $1,000 and invest it at a 4% return, it will only grow to $1,040 in one year, compared to receiving $1,050 after one year from your friend.

Using Time Value of Money

The underlying principles of time value of money are used in finance to value investments like stocks and bonds.

The basic formula for the time value of money is as follows:

$$PV = FV \div (1+I)^N,$$

where:

PV is the present value

FV is the future value

I is the required return

N is the number of time periods before receiving the money

But let's not get too far into the weeds just yet. With a simple example, we can better understand how the time value of money can be used to value investments.

Valuing a Stock with the Time Value of Money

Suppose you have the opportunity to invest in a stock. You believe that the business will improve over the next four years, and pay you four $2 annual dividends, after which you believe you'll be able to sell the stock for $40 per share. You want to achieve an annual return of at least 15% on your investment.

How much should you pay for this stock, assuming you need a 15% return?

Let's first lay out all the cash flows:

Time 0: Unknown investment

Year 1: $2 dividend

Year 2: $2 dividend

Year 3: $2 dividend

Year 4: $42 ($2 dividend plus sale of stock for $40 per share)

Now that we have this information, we can start valuing each cash flow.

We plug in the first cash flow ($2 dividend), discount rate (15% annual required return), and time (1 year) into the formula above to get the following:

PV = $2 ÷ (1+0.15)^1

We can further simplify and solve this equation, step by step:

PV = $2 ÷ (1.15)^1

PV = $2 ÷ (1.15)

PV = $1.74

After doing the math, we find that the first dividend is worth $1.74 in present dollars.

Now we have to calculate the present value of the second dividend. We plug in the second cash flow ($2 dividend), discount rate (15% annual required return), and time (2 years) into the formula above to get the following:

PV = $2 ÷ (1+0.15)^2

We can further simplify and solve this equation, step by step:

PV = $2 ÷ (1.15)^2

PV = $2 ÷ (1.3225)

PV = $1.51

We calculate that the present value of the second $2 dividend to be $1.51.

The second dividend is worth less ($1.51) than the first dividend ($1.74) in present dollars because it will come later in time. Cash flows in later periods have to be discounted by a greater amount to ensure we receive the required 15% annual return on our investment.

To complete this problem, we need to continue discounting all the remaining cash flows, then sum up the present values of all the cash flows. We'll skip the present value steps for the two remaining cash flows for brevity, but the answers are shown in the table below. See what you come up with and compare it to the table (if you're off by a penny or two, it's probably just due to rounding).

Time Period	Future Value	Present Value
Time 1	$2.00	$1.74
Time 2	$2.00	$1.51
Time 3	$2.00	$1.32
Time 4	$42.00	$24.01
Total	$48.00	$28.58

The final step is to sum up the present values of each cash flow to arrive at a value of $28.58 per share for this stock.

If our assumptions are correct about the dividend the stock will pay, and its value at the end of four years, we'll generate a 15% annual return on our investment in this stock provided that we do not pay a penny more than $28.58 per share.

Of course, the outputs generated by time value of money formulas are only as good as our inputs. If the company ceases to pay a dividend, or fails to trade for $40 per share in year 4, then $28.58 will prove to be a much too expensive price for the company's stock.

Present Value

Present value, also known as discounted value, is a financial calculation that measures the worth of a future amount of money or stream of payments in today's dollars adjusted for interest and inflation. In other words, it compares the buying power of one future dollar to purchasing power of one today.

It's an indication of whether the money an investor receives today can earn a return in the future. PV is widely used in finance in the stock valuation, bond pricing, and financial modeling.

Investors calculate the present value of a firm's expected cash flows to decide if the stock is worth investing in today. The firm's expected cash flows are discounted at a discount rate that is actually the expected return. The discount rate is inversely correlated to the future cash flows. The higher the discount rate, the lower the present value of the expected cash flows.

Example:

Karen wants to buy a flower shop near her home. First, she needs to estimate the future cash flows of the shop and then discount them to calculate their present value.

The flower shop costs $85,000 and Karen estimates that she will be able to earn $85,000 over the next 4 years. This sounds like a good deal right? Karen will make her money back in four years, right?

Well, technically she won't. The future streams of income are not equal to $85,000 in today's money. They are worth less. In order to find their real value, Karen should discount the earnings using a discount rate to calculate the PV.

Let's assume Karen's present value calculation shows that the $85,000 of future earnings actually equals $65,554 today. The PV of the future cash flows is $19,446 less than Karen's original investment, which means Karen might not want buy the flower shop.

Karen should buy the flower shop if the present value was positive, which means that the future cash flows of the shop should be higher than $85,000. However, as the flower shop has a value that is less than $85,000, Karen should step out of the deal.

$$PV = \frac{C_1}{(1+r)^n}$$

$$C_1 = Cash\ Flow\ at\ period$$

$$r = rate\ of\ return$$

$$n = number\ of\ periods$$

Use of Present Value Formula

The Present Value formula has a broad range of uses and may be applied to various areas of finance including corporate finance, banking finance, and investment finance. Apart from the various areas of finance that present value analysis is used, the formula is also used as a component of other financial formulas.

Example of Present Value Formula

An individual wishes to determine how much money she would need to put into her money market account to have $100 one year today if she is earning 5% interest on her account, simple interest.

The $100 she would like one year from present day denotes the C_1 portion of the formula, 5% would be r, and the number of periods would simply be 1.

Putting this into the formula, we would have

$$PV = \frac{\$100}{1.05}$$

When we solve for PV, she would need $95.24 today in order to reach $100 one year from now at a rate of 5% simple interest.

Alternative Formula

The Present Value formula may sometimes be shown as

$$PV = FV \frac{1}{(1+r)^n}$$

$$FV = Future\ Value$$

$$r = rate\ of\ return$$

$$n = number\ of\ periods$$

Net Present Value

Net present value (NPV) is the value of all future cash flows (positive and negative) over the entire life of an investment discounted to the present. NPV analysis is a form of intrinsic valuation and is used extensively across finance and accounting for determining the value of a business, investment security, capital project, new venture, cost reduction program, and anything that involves cash flow.

Calculating NPV

NPV tells you whether a certain project will generate cash flows according to your expectations or not. Using an assumed rate of return and investment horizon, it brings to light any adjustments required in your current investment to achieve a positive return.

NPV can be calculated by using the following formula:

NPV = [Cn/(1+r)^n], where n={0-N}

Where

Cn = difference of cash flows

r = discount rate

n = time in years

You need to follow selection criteria with regards to the usage of NPV. Calculation of NPV will result in three possible outcomes:

a. Positive NPV: In this situation, the present value of cash inflows is greater than the present value of cash outflows. This is an ideal situation for investment

b. Negative NPV: In this situation, the present value of cash inflows is less than the present value of cash outflows. This is not an ideal situation and any project with this NPV should not be accepted.

c. Zero NPV: In this situation, the present value of cash inflows equals the present value of cash outflows.

Usage of Net Present Value (NPV) Analysis

NPV analysis is used to help determine how much an investment, project, or any series of cash flows is worth. It is an all-encompassing metric, as it takes into account all revenues, expenses, and capital costs associated with an investment in its free cash flow (FCF).

In addition to factoring all revenues and costs, it also takes into the account the timing of each cash flow that can result in a large impact on the present value an investment. For example, it's better to have cash inflows sooner and cash outflows later, as opposed to the opposite of that.

Reason for Cash Flows being Discounted

The cash flows in net present value analysis are discounted for two main reasons, (1) to adjust for the risk of an investment opportunity, and (2) to account for the time value of money (TVM).

The first point (to adjust for risk) is necessary because not all businesses, projects, or investment opportunities have the same level of risk. Put another way, the probability of receiving cash flow a US Treasury bill is much higher than the probability of receiving cash flow from a young technology start-up.

To account for the risk, the discount rate is higher for riskier investments and lower for safer one. The US treasury example is considered to be the risk-free rate, and all other investments are measured by how much more risk they bear relative to that.

The second point (to account for the time value of money) is required because due to inflation, interest rates, and opportunity costs, money is more valuable the sooner it's received. For example, receiving $1 million today is much better than $1 million received five years from now. If the money is received today, it can be invested and earn interest, so it will be worth more than $1 million in five years' time.

Example

Let's look at an example of how to calculate the net present value of a series of cash flows. As you can see in the screenshot below, the assumption is that an investment will return $10,000 per year over a period of 10 years, and discount rate required is 10%.

Discount Rate 10.0%

Year	1	2	3	4	5	6	7	8	9	10
Discount Factor	0.91	0.83	0.75	0.68	0.62	0.56	0.51	0.47	0.42	0.39
Undiscounted Cash Flow	10,000	10,000	10,000	10,000	10,000	10,000	10,000	10,000	10,000	10,000
Present Value	9,091	8,264	7,513	6,830	6,209	5,645	5,132	4,665	4,241	3,855
Net Present Value	61,446									

The final result is that the value of this investment is worth $61,446 today. It means a rational investor would be willing to pay up to $61,466 today to receive $10,000 every year over 10 years. By paying this price, the investor would receive an internal rate of return (IRR) of 10%. By paying anything less than $61,000, the investor would earn an internal rate of return that's greater than 10%.

Drawbacks

NPV is a frequently used tool in the field of finance. But NPV doesn't tell you everything that you need to know.

It suffers from the following limitations:

a. NPV is based on a lot of assumptions and estimates. If any of the assumptions are wrong, the entire exercise of valuations will be rendered futile.

b. NPV doesn't take into account risks inherent in an investment. This may lead to overestimation of the cash flows which can mislead the investors.

c. NPV ignores the possibilities of any escalations in the project cost in future. Sudden unforeseen expenditure may disbalance the entire projections.

Difference between NPV and IRR

NPV is the difference between the present value of cash inflows and the present value of cash outflows. Internal rate of return (IRR) on the other hand is the discount rate which equates the present value of cash inflows with the present values of cash outflows. IRR is calculated by assuming that NPV equals to zero. It shows the breakeven point or the point where there's neither profit nor loss. Conversely, NPV shows the excess inflows over the outflows.

Adjusted Present Value

Adjusted present value is an investment appraisal technique similar to net present value method. However, instead of using weighted average cost of capital as the discount rate, ungeared cost of equity is used to discount the cash flows from a project and there is an adjustment for the tax shield provided by related debt capital.

Formula:

Adjusted Present Value =

PV of Cash Flows using Ungeared Cost of Equity + Present Value of Tax Shield

Where PV stands for 'present value' and ungeared cost of equity is the required rate of return for a firm that is financed by equity. It is calculated using the following formula:

Ungeared Cost of Equity = Risk Free Rate + Asset beta × (Market Return − Risk Free Return)

Since interest cost is allowable as tax deduction therefore, when calculating taxable income it provides tax savings (also called tax shield).

Tax Savings = Tax Rate × Interest Expense Related to the Project

Tax savings are discounted using gross cost of debt.

Example:

A project costing $50 million is expected to generate after tax cash flows of $10 million a year forever. Risk free rate is 3%, asset beta is 1.5, required return on market is 12%, cost of debt is 8%, annual interest costs related to project are $2 million and tax rate is 40%. Calculate the adjusted present value of the project.

Solution:

Adjusted Present Value = Present Value of Cash Flows + Present Value of Tax Savings

We need to find ungeared cost of equity which is 3% + 1.5*(12% – 3%) = 16.5%. Using this rate the present value of cash flows = $10 million/0.165 = $60.61 million. Initial investment is $50 million no net present value of future cash flows using ungeared cost of equity is $10.61 million ($60.61 million-$50 million).

Present value of tax savings = $2 million × 0.4 / 0.08 = $10 million

Adjusted present value = present value of cash flows + present value of tax savings = $10.61 million + $10 million = $20.61 million.

Decision Rule

The decision rule for adjusted present value is the same as net present value: accept positive APV projects and reject negative APV projects. The project discussed in the example has an APV of $20.61 which is positive hence the company should undertake the project.

Advantages of APV

Flexibility

APV is ideal for organizations whose ratio of debt to equity is in constant flux. Companies that go through many different projects that are capital-intensive would count, as would opportunities to carry out a leveraged buyout.

Transparency

While net present value (NPV) only looks at the more visible items contained in assets and liabilities, APV also looks at other real-world costs that will most certainly affect operations. This includes the implications of filing for bankruptcy, issuing bonds and writing off certain expenditures as tax deductions.

Compatible with Debt Repayments

Not all debt repayments appear in the figures that go into the calculation of net present value (NPV). On the other hand, any loan repayment schedules must be a part of calculated APV. If one company is pondering the acquisition of another, knowing those schedules would be crucial.

Increasing in Popularity

At the time of publication, only about 11 percent of firms in the United States use APV when considering the acquisition of other companies. It is a methodology that was born on a college campus and has been slow to spread in popularity. Its enhanced accuracy in providing a look at a company's actual worth, though, is gaining ground among CFO's across the country.

Disadvantages of NPV

The biggest disadvantage to the net present value method is that it requires some guesswork about the firm's cost of capital. Assuming a cost of capital that is too low will result in making suboptimal investments. Assuming a cost of capital that is too high will result in forgoing too many good investments.

In addition, the NPV method is not useful for comparing two projects of different size. Because the NPV method results in an answer in dollars, the size of the net present value output is determined mostly by the size of the input.

For example, a $1 million project will likely have a much higher NPV than a $1,000 project, even if the $1,000 project provides much higher returns in percentage terms. If capital is scarce -- and it usually is -- the NPV method is a poor method to use because projects of different size are not immediately comparable based on the output.

Future Value

Future value (FV) is the amount to which a current investment will grow over time when placed in an account that pays compound interest. In other words, it's the value of a dollar at some point in the future adjusted for interest.

FV is one of the most important concepts in finance, and it is based on the time value of money. Investors need to know what the FV of their investment will be after a certain period of time, calculated based on an assumed growth rate.

For instance, a $1,000 investment that pays a fixed interest rate of 5% will be $2,654 after 20 years, all things being equal. Therefore, the FV uses a single upfront investment and a constant rate of growth during the time horizon of the investment. On the downside, the FV is not adjusted for high inflation or changes in the interest rates, which are factors with a negative impact on any investment.

Formula

The formula to calculate the future value at the end of period N using simple interest is as follows:

$$FV_N = PV \times (1 + r)^N$$

Here PV is a present value, r represents an interest rate earned per period, and N is a number of periods.

Simple interest, however, is rarely used because it does not take into account the possibility that interest earned can be reinvested. In other words, there is no compounding in such a case.

The formula to calculate the future value at the end of period N using compound interest is as follows:

$$FV_N = PV + PV \times (1 + r) \times N$$

Here PV is a present value, r represents an interest rate earned per period, and N is a number of periods.

Compound Interest versus Simple Interest

As was mentioned above, simple interest is rarely used in financial calculations because it does not consider the impact of reinvesting interest earned. For example, if $1 is invested today at an annual rate of 12.5%, its future value after 15 years will amount to $2.88 using simple interest and $5.85 using compound interest.

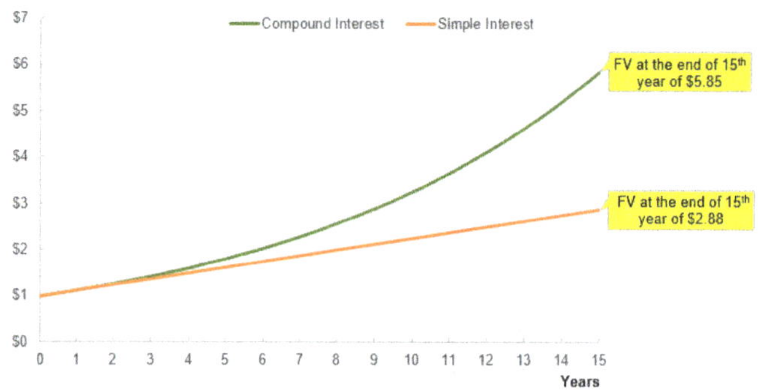

The difference of more than two times is the result of compounding. Actually, the worth of $1 increases linearly using simple interest and exponentially if compound interest is applied. The effect of exponential growth is graphically presented in the figure below.

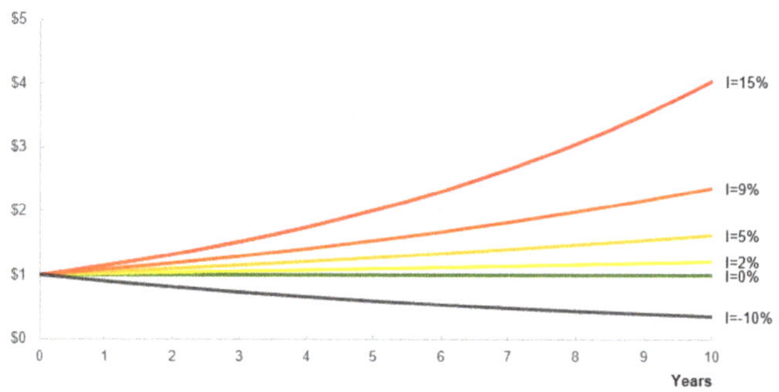

So, the greater the interest rate and the longer the investment, the faster the future value of $1 will grow.

Examples:

Let's assume that $100 is invested today for 5 years at an annual interest rate of 7.5%. The step-by-step compounding is shown in the figure below.

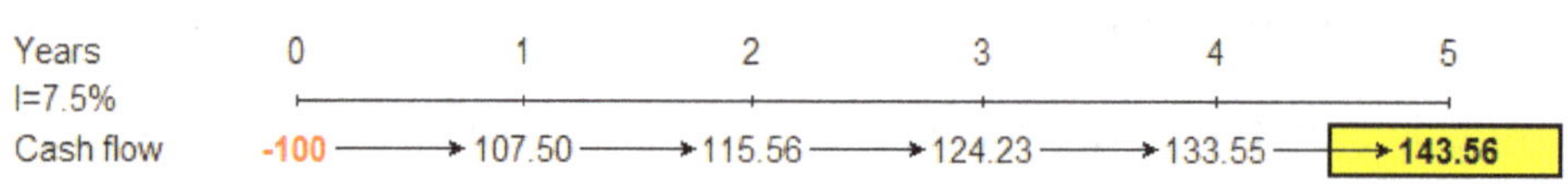

We start with $100 invested today and get $107.50 at the end of the first year. Now $107.50 is invested again and at the end of second year will amount to $115.56. This process continues the following years until the future value will grow to $143.56 at the end of the fifth year.

$FV_{\text{End of 1st year}} = \$100 \times (1 + 0.075) = \$107.50$

$FV_{\text{End of 2nd year}} = \$107.50 \times (1 + 0.075) = \$115.56$

$FV_{\text{End of 3rd year}} = \$115.56 \times (1 + 0.075) = \$124.23$

$FV_{\text{End of 4th year}} = \$124.23 \times (1 + 0.075) = \$133.55$

$FV_{\text{End of 5th year}} = \$133.55 \times (1 + 0.075) = \$143.56$

The compounding effect occurs after the first year when the interest of $7.50 is also reinvested at 7.5%. At the end of the second year, it will earn additional interest of $0.56 ($7.5 × 0.075) to the interest of $7.50 earned on the principal amount of $100. The process of compounding continues to the end of the investment life span.

We can also get the same result using the formula mentioned above.

$FV_{\text{End of 5th year}} = \$100 \times (1 + 0.075)5 = \$143.56$

If simple interest were applied, the future value of $100 would amount to $137.50.

$FV_{\text{End of 5th year}} = \$100 + \$100 \times 0.075 \times 5 = \$137.50.$

References

- Introduction-what-is-time-value-of-money-1806581: psu.instructure.com, Retrieved 21 June 2018
- Time-value-of-money, knowledge-center: fool.com, Retrieved 15 April 2018
- Present-value, accounting-dictionary: myaccountingcourse.com, Retrieved 16 July 2018
- Adjusted-present-value, capital-budgeting, managerial: accountingexplained.com, Retrieved 15 June 2018
- Advantages-and-disadvantages-of-net-present-value, knowledge-center: fool.com, Retrieved 25 March 2018
- Future-value, accounting-dictionary: myaccountingcourse.com, Retrieved 26 May 2018
- Future-value-of-money: financialmanagementpro.com, Retrieved 12 July 2018

6

Risks and Returns in Capital Budgeting and Investment

Capital budgeting involves allocating resources for capital, expenditures or investments. There is a certain degree of risk associated with investments. Any benefit accrued from an investment is known as a return. High risk investments generally have higher returns if successful. The topics elaborated in this chapter on financial risk, credit risk, liquidity risk, time-weighted return, holding period return, expected return, etc. will help in developing a better understanding of risks and returns in capital budgeting and Investment.

Financial Risk

Financial Risk as the term suggests is the risk that involves financial loss to firms. Financial risk generally arises due to instability and losses in the financial market caused by movements in stock prices, currencies, interest rates and more.

Financial Risk is one of the major concerns of every business across fields and geographies. This is the reason behind Financial Risk Manager FRM Exam gaining huge recognition among financial experts across the globe.

Types of Financial Risks

Financial risk is one of the high-priority risk types for every business. Financial risk is caused due to market movements and market movements can include host of factors. Based on this, financial risk can be classified into various types such as market risk, credit risk, liquidity risk, operational risk and legal risk.

- Market Risk:

This type of risk arises due to movement in prices of financial instrument. Market risk can be classified as Directional Risk and Non - Directional Risk. Directional risk is caused due to movement in stock price, interest rates and more. Non- Directional risk on the other hand can be volatility risks.

- Credit Risk:

This type of risk arises when one fails to fulfill their obligations towards their counter parties. Credit risk can be classified into sovereign risk and settlement risk. Sovereign risk usually arises due to difficult foreign exchange policies. Settlement risk on the other hand arises when one party makes the payment while the other party fails to fulfill the obligations.

- Liquidity Risk:

This type of risk arises out of inability to execute transactions. Liquidity risk can be classified into asset liquidity risk and funding liquidity risk. Asset liquidity risk arises either due to insufficient buyers or insufficient sellers against sell orders and buy orders respectively.

- Operational Risk:

This type of risk arises out of operational failures such as mismanagement or technical failures. Operational risk can be classified into fraud risk and model risk. Fraud risk arises due to lack of controls and Model risk arises due to incorrect model application.

- Legal Risk:

This type of financial risk arises out of legal constraints such as lawsuits. Whenever a company needs to face financial loses out of legal proceedings, it is legal risk.

Every small business faces financial risks. However, you can lower your risks and improve your chances of success when you become aware of several external and internal financial risk factors.

External Risks

- Economic Risks

Economic downturns or failures as well as economic changes within certain industries, geographies or demographic groups play a role in your business's success. Any of these changes can decrease income and increase expenses.

While you cannot eliminate or even control economic risks, you can prepare for them.

1. Strategize ways to combat economic downturns.
2. Boost savings during good economic seasons.
3. Diversify investments, products and your customer base.
4. Pay debts quickly.
5. Look for new financing options regularly.
6. Continue to innovate.

- Legal Risks

Safety regulation updates and tax law changes can happen at any time. You may find yourself facing a mandatory safety system upgrade, an unexpected property tax increase or a government ban on a product you produce.

Prepare for legal risks when you save a cash reserve. It can pay for unforeseen regulation or tax changes. Be sure you stay up-to-date on industry trends, too, so you are better prepared to shift your business model, focus or products based on legal changes.

Internal Risks

Receivables

Part of your business strategy may include extending credit to your customers. You give them the product and they have a set time to pay the invoice. Sometimes, though, those customers cannot or will not pay their bills on time. As a result, you will not be able to pay your expenses.

Consider requesting payment up-front or build a cash reserve that covers unpaid invoices and all your regular expenses. These steps allow you to continue paying your bills, and they protect your business.

Performance Risks

You have a great deal of control over performance risks even though they vary based on your specific business and its structure and products. Some typical performance risk factors that affect your bottom line include underperforming quarters, bad investments, new competition, planning errors, personnel challenges or quality issues.

These performance risks are often avoidable. Consider implementing several helpful suggestions.

- Save enough cash to cover a slow quarter.
- Decrease expenses and debt where possible.
- Maintain consistent high quality standards.
- Improve your hiring process then take measures to retain quality employees.
- Focus on doing the best job possible so you can confidently face competition.
- Evaluate performance regularly with a mentor and financial advisor.

Credit Risk

Credit risk is the risk of loss by a person or entity that has extended credit to another party. Credit risk is considered to be higher when the borrower does not have sufficient cash flows to pay the creditor, or it does not have sufficient assets to liquidate to repay the creditor. If the risk of non-payment is higher, the lender is more likely to demand compensation in the form of a higher interest rate.

The credit being extended is usually in the form of either a loan or an account receivable. In the case of an unpaid loan, credit risk can result in the loss of both interest on the debt and unpaid principal, whereas in the case of an unpaid account receivable, there is no loss of interest. In both cases, the party granting credit may also incur incremental collection costs. Further, the party to whom cash is owed may suffer some degree of disruption in its cash flows, which may require expensive debt or equity to cover.

Credit risk is a lesser issue where the selling party's gross profit on a sale is quite high, since it is really only running the risk of loss on the relatively small proportion of an account receivable that is comprised of its own cost. Conversely, if gross margins are small, credit risk becomes a substantial issue.

Credit risk is a particular problem when a large proportion of sales on credit are concentrated with a small number of customers, since the failure of any one of these customers could seriously impair the cash flows of the seller. A similar risk arises when there is a large proportion of sales on credit to customers within a particular country, and that country suffers disruptions that interfere with payments coming from that area.

There are several ways to mitigate credit risk. A company that is contemplating the extension of credit to a customer can reduce its credit risk most directly by obtaining credit insurance on any invoices issued to the customer (and may even be able to bill the customer for the cost of the insurance). Another alternative is to require very short payment terms, so that credit risk will be present for a minimal period of time. A third option is to offload the risk onto a distributor by referring the customer to the distributor. A fourth option is to require a personal guarantee by someone who has substantial personal resources.

A lender that wants to reduce its credit risk can do so by increasing the interest rate on any loans issued, requiring substantial collateral, or requiring a variety of debt covenants that allow it to call the loan if they are breached, and to force the customer to pay off the debt before it is allowed to spend funds on other activities (such as paying dividends).

Types of Credit Risk

There are, generally, three types of credit risk:

- Credit spread risk occurring due to volatility in the difference between investments' interest rates and the risk free return rate.
- Default risk arising when the borrower is not able to make contractual payments.
- Downgrade risk resulting from the downgrades in the risk rating of an issuer.

Calculating Credit Risk

Credit risk is calculated on the basis of the overall ability of the buyer to repay the loan. This calculation takes into account the borrowers' revenue-generating ability, collateral assets, and taxing authority (like government and municipal bonds).

The credit risk is calculated in the following manner:

- Estimate the FICO score of the consumer. The FICO score is a quantifying measure which helps in determining the creditworthiness of an individual as well as his repayment history. Where on one hand, the FICO score indicates the manner in which an individual repays his debt; on the other hand, it does not ensure the repayment in future.
- Calculate the debt-to-income ratio. This is determined by the monthly recurring debts of a company divided by the gross monthly income. Individuals with a debt-to-income ratio below 35% are considered as acceptable credit risks.

- Factor in the potential debt of the borrower. Potential debt refers to the debt which can be taken on by an individual on the basis of his credit card balances and general creditworthiness for obtaining new credit lines.

While the definition of credit risk may be straight forward, measuring it is not. Many factors can influence an issuer's credit risk and in varying degrees. Some examples are poor or falling cash flow from operations (which is often needed to make the interest and principal payments), rising interest rates (if the bonds are floating-rate notes, rising interest rates increase the required interest payments), or changes in the nature of the marketplace that adversely affect the issuer (such as a change in technology, an increase in competitors, or regulatory changes). The credit risk associated with foreign bonds also includes the home country's socio-political situation and the stability and regulatory practices of its government.

Ratings agencies like Moody's and Standard & Poor's analyse bond offerings in an effort to measure an issuer's credit risk on a particular security. Their results are published as ratings that investors can track and compare with other issuers.

S&P's ratings range from AAA (the most secure) to D, which means the issuer is already in default. Moody's ratings go from Aaa to C. Only bonds rated BBB or better are considered "investment grade." Bonds rated below BBB- or Baa3 are considered "junk."

Importance

Credit risk is one of the most fundamental types of risk. After all, it represents the chance the investor will lose his or her investment. All bonds, except for those issued by the U.S. government, carry some credit risk. This is one reason corporate bonds almost always have higher coupon payment amounts than government bonds.

Liquidity Risk

Liquidity of an asset is its ease of convertibility into cash or a cash equivalent asset. Liquidity risk arises from the difficulty of selling an asset quickly without incurring large losses. For a banking and financial firm "liquidity risk includes both the risk of being unable to fund [its] portfolio of assets at appropriate maturities and rates and the risk of being unable to liquidate a position in a timely manner at reasonable prices." Sometimes it is defined in terms of maturity mismatch between assets and liabilities while at others it is defined in terms of asynchronous timing of cash in flows and cash outflows from the business. The bank regulatory literature defines it as "risk to a bank's earnings and capital arising from its inability to timely meet obligations when they come due without incurring unacceptable losses.

Sources of Liquidity Risk

Liquidity risk emanates from the nature of banking business, from the macro factors that are exogenous to the bank, as well as from the financing and operational policies that are internal to the banking firm.

Banks provide maturity transformation. Taking deposits that are callable on demand or that on average has shorter maturity than the average maturity of the financing contracts they sell. While maturity transformation provides liquidity insurance to the depositors, which is valued by them, it exposes banks to liquidity risk themselves. Since banks specialize in maturity transformation they take pool deposits and take care to match their cash inflows and outflows in order to address the liquidity risk they face.

However, maturity mismatch at a given time is not the only source of liquidity risk. The risk of this kind can arrive from many directions and its pinch depends on various factors. In a nutshell its sources (i) on assets side depends on the degree of inability of bank to convert its assets into cash without loss at time of need, and (ii) on liabilities side it emanates from unanticipated recall of deposits. Using the categorization in Jameson and adding a few more we can break them into following behavioural and exogenous sources:

1. Incorrect judgment or complacent attitude of the bank towards timing of its cash in- and out-flows.
2. Unanticipated change in the cost of capital or availability of funding.
3. Abnormal behavior of financial markets under stress.
4. Range of assumptions used in predicting cash flows.
5. Risk activation by secondary sources such as:
   i. Business strategy failure
   ii. Corporate governance failure
   iii. Modeling assumptions
   iv. Merger and accusations policy
6. Breakdown in payments and settlement system.
7. Macroeconomic imbalances.

To the extent the timing of the cash flows can be predicted the liquidity risk can be controlled. But increasingly, the banks are getting involved in providing contingent credit and liquidity services to borrowers whose main source of funding lies elsewhere in the capital markets and who turn to banks only in contingencies. Thus the bank's judgment on cash out-flows can turn out to be incorrect, hence the first source of liquidity risk. Further, involvement of banks in the derivative products with collateral requirements increases the possibility of large amounts of contingent calls for cash or security.

The second source of liquidity risk listed above stems from the unanticipated difference in the realized and assumed availability of funding, marketability of its assets or their use as collateral in raising funds quickly, and the amount of haircut anticipated. This can happen due to causes general to the banking sector or specific to the bank. Sometimes a major bank (money centre), on whom the smaller banks rely, would experience a credit squeeze or a rating downgrade thus affecting the funds availability to the other banks.

The third factor, behavior of the capital markets in stressed condition, lies outside the control of a bank but it does have implications for liquidity of banks. First adverse movements in the capital markets change the availability of funds to the bank if it desires to raise it through them. Second, increasing reliance by the banks on whole sale markets rather than small depositors affects the composition of risk sensitive market savvy depositors in the depositor pool of the bank. These depositors are quick to move funds away form the bank at the first signs of trouble, thus increasing the probability of a 'run' on the bank or a liquidity problem.

The fourth factor is not a cause in itself but determines the preparedness of the bank to liquidity shocks. Larger the number of scenarios and range of assumptions for which a bank has stress tested its strategies against liquidity crisis greater is the likelihood of smooth management of the risk.

The fifth source is most difficult to envisage ex ante where " a potential exposure to a liquidity risk is activated by a secondary risk source". Current examples of such happenings include that of collapse of General American in 1999 and Long Term Capital Management (LTCM). The former closed down because it concentrated on short-term instruments for its funding needs and had heavily relied on a few market sensitive institutional investors (money market mutual funds) for its funding. All other things were very fine with General American. The financial problems started elsewhere in an outside company which was providing re-insurance facility to it. Responding to this, General American made a business move and recaptured the reinsurance portfolio thereby self-insuring all its obligations. As soon as the rating of General American was downgraded because of its self-insurance move, the institutional investors started recalling their funds creating a liquidity problem for it. General American was quickly assassinated within days.

Fragile and unreliable payments and settlement system is the sixth source of liquidity risk. Smooth operations of the banking sector and financial markets depend on sound operation of this system. A break down can trigger liquidity problems not only for a single bank but also for the entire banking and financial sector thus resulting in a generalized financial crisis.

Macroeconomic imbalances and sector wide shocks are another avenues giving rise to liquidity risk. These factors are particularly important in developing countries. Excessive government borrowing from domestic markets and banks increases cost of funding for the banks. In many restrictive environments it gives rise to financial repression where banks are required to finance government expenditures at less than the market price. In some cases the excessive government borrowing is accomplished by creating funding arbitrage leading to disintermediation – banks generating funds from cheaper sources and channelling them into short-term high return government securities. In all such circumstances liquidity risk of the banks increases substantially either involuntarily or voluntary by changing the composition of asset portfolio of the bank. Then, any shock to the system can create liquidity problems for individual banks and for the banking sector as a whole.

Fiscal imbalances are not the only macroeconomic source of liquidity risk. Persistent current or capital account imbalances, large savings and investment gap, high inflation all can lead to similar risks.

Types of Liquidity Risk

Asset liquidity – Due to the lack of liquidity in market an asset cannot be sold it is basically subset of market risk. This can be done by:

- Widening bid/offer spread
- Making explicit liquidity reserves
- Lengthening holding period for Vary calculations
- Funding liquidity – Risk that liability:
- Cannot be met when they fall due
- Can only be met at an uneconomic price
- Can be name-specific or systemic.

Causes of Liquidity Risk

There are many causes of liquidity risk liquidity risk actually arises when the one party wants to trading an asset cannot do it because in the market no one wants to trade that asset .The persons who are about to hold or currently hold the asset and want to trade that asset then liquidity risk become partial important to them as it affects their ability to do business.

From drop of price to zero is very different from that appearance of liquidity risk. In the case when the assets price drop to zero then market said that asset is valueless. On the other hand when one party found that the other party is not interested in buying and selling of an asset then it become a big problem for the participant of a market to find the other interested party. So we can say that in the emerging markets or low volume markets the risk of liquidity is higher.

Due to uncertain liquidity the liquidity risk is known as a financial risk.

When the credit rating falls the institution may lose its liquidity, in this way rapid unexpected cash outflows, or as a result of this happening the counterparties may avoid the business of buying and selling with or borrowing the loan to the institutions. A firm is also exposed to liquidity risk if markets on which it depends are subject to loss of liquidity. The firm is also seen to the risk of liquidity when the markets in they depend are under the liquidity loss.

Liquidity risks tend to compound other risks. If a trading organization has a position in an illiquid asset, its limited ability to liquidate that position at short notice will compound its market risk. Let us suppose a firm has a cash flows offsetting on a given day of with two different counter parties. If the counter party do not make the payment and become a payment defaults. In this way firm will have to make the cash from some other sources in order to make payment. Credit risk is the risk arises due to the liquidity.

A position can be hedged against market risk but still entail liquidity risk. This is true in the above credit risk example-the two payments are offsetting, so they entail credit risk but not market risk. Another example is the 1993 Metallgesellschaft debacle. Futures contracts were used to hedge an Over-the-counter finance OTC obligation. It is debatable whether the hedge was effective from a market risk standpoint, but it was the liquidity crisis caused by staggering margin calls on the futures that forced Metallgesellschaft to unwind the positions.

As compared to the risks like market, credit and other risks the liquidity risk is also has to be managed. It is impossible to isolate the liquidity risk because it has the tendency to compound the other risks overall the most simple circumstances. Liquidity risk does not exist in the comprehensive metrics. In order to assessed the liquidity risk the certain techniques of asset liability management can be applied on a day by day basis. A simple test is conducted for the liquidity risk in ordered to see the net cash flows. Any day which shows a sizeable negative cash flow is of concern.

Analyses such as these cannot easily take into account contingent cash flows, such as cash flows from derivatives or mortgage-backed securities. If an organization's cash flows are largely contingent, liquidity risk may be assessed using some form of scenario analysis. A general approach using scenario analysis might entail the following high-level steps:

- Construct multiple scenarios for market movements and defaults over a given period of time.
- Assess day-to-day cash flows under each scenario.
- Because balance sheets differ so significantly from one organization to the next, there is little standardization in how such analyses are implemented.
- Regulators are primarily concerned about systemic and implications of liquidity risk.

Liquidity Gap

The liquidity gap is the net liquid assets of a firm.

As a static measure of liquidity risk it gives no indication of how the gap would change with an increase in the firm's marginal funding cost.

Liquidity Risk Elasticity

Culp denotes the change of net of assets over funded liabilities that occur when the liquidity premium on the bank's marginal funding cost rises by a small amount as the liquidity risk elasticity. For banks this would be measured as a spread over libor, for nonfinancial the LRE would be measured as a spread over commercial paper rates.

Problems with the use of liquidity risk elasticity are that it assumes parallel changes in funding spread across all maturities and that it is only accurate for small changes in funding spreads.

Measures of Asset Liquidity

Following are the measures of asset liquidity.

Bid-offer spread:

The bid-offer spread is used by market participants as an asset liquidity measure. To compare different products the ratio of the spread to the product's mid-price can be used. The smaller the ratio the more liquid the asset is.

This spread is comprised of operational costs, administrative and processing costs as well as the compensation required for the possibility of trading with a more informed trader.

Market depth:

Hachmeister refers to market depth as the amount of an asset that can be bought and sold at various bid-ask spreads. Slippage is related to the concept of market depth. Knight and Satchell mention a flow trader needs to consider the effect of executing a large order on the market and to adjust the bid-ask spread accordingly. They calculate the liquidity cost as the difference of the execution price and the initial execution price.

Immediacy:

Immediacy refers to the time needed to successfully trade a certain amount of an asset at a prescribed cost.

Resilience:

Hachmeister identifies the fourth dimension of liquidity as the speed with which prices return to former levels after a large transaction. Unlike the other measures resilience can only be determined over a period of time.

Managing Liquidity Risk

- Liquidity-adjusted value at risk:

Liquidity-adjusted VAR incorporates exogenous liquidity risk into Value at Risk. It can be defined at VAR + ELC (Exogenous Liquidity Cost). The ELC is the worst expected half-spread at a particular confidence level.

Another adjustment is to consider VAR over the period of time needed to liquidate the portfolio. VAR can be calculated over this time period. The BIS mentions "a number of institutions are exploring the use of liquidity adjusted-VAR, in which the holding periods in the risk assessment are adjusted by the length of time required to unwind positions".

- Liquidity at risk:

Greenspan discusses management of foreign exchange reserves. The Liquidity at risk measure is suggested. A country's liquidity position under a range of possible outcomes for relevant financial variables (exchange rates, commodity prices, credit spreads, etc.) is considered. It might be possible to express a standard in terms of the probabilities of different outcomes. For example, an acceptable debt structure could have an average maturity averaged over estimated distributions for relevant financial variables in excess of a certain limit. In addition, countries could be expected to hold sufficient liquid reserves to ensure that they could avoid new borrowing for one year with certain ex ante probability, such as 95 percent of the time.

- Scenario analysis-based contingency plans:

The FDIC discuss liquidity risk management and write contingency funding plans should incorporate events that could rapidly affect an institution's liquidity, including a sudden inability to securitize assets, tightening of collateral requirements or other restrictive terms associated with secured borrowings, or the loss of a large depositor or counterparty. Greenspan's liquidity at risk concept is an example of scenario based liquidity risk management.

- Diversification of liquidity providers:

If several liquidity providers are on call then if any of those providers increases its costs of supplying liquidity, the impact of this is reduced. The American Academy of Actuaries wrote "While a company is in good financial shape, it may wish to establish durable, ever-green (i.e., always available) liquidity lines of credit. The credit issuer should have an appropriately high credit rating to increase the chances that the resources will be there when needed".

- Derivatives:

Withdrawal option: A put of the illiquid underlying at the market price.

Bermudan-style return put option: Right to put the option at a specified strike.

Return swap: Swap the underling's return for LIBOR paid periodically.

Return swaption: Option to enter into the return swap.

Liquidity option: "Knock-in" barrier option, where the barrier is liquidity metric.

Other

Funding sources are abundant and provide a competitive cost advantage.

Funding is widely diversified. There is little or no reliance on wholesale funding sources or credit-sensitive funds providers.

Market alternatives exceed demand for liquidity, with no adverse changes expected.

Capacity to augment liquidity through asset sales and/or securitization is strong and the Bank has an established record in accessing these markets.

The volume of wholesale liabilities with embedded options is low.

The Bank is not vulnerable to funding difficulties should a material adverse change occur in market perception.

Support provided by the parent company is strong.

Earnings and capital exposure from the liquidity risk profile is negligible.

Quantity of Liquidity Risk Indicators

In order to assess the quantity of liquidity risk the following indicator should be used. Every characteristic is not necessary to be demonstrated.

- Low

The sources of funding are abundant and provide an advantage of competitive cost.

Funding is generally expanded. There is little or no reliance on wholesale funding sources or other credit-sensitive funds providers. On the sources of wholesale funding or others providers of credit sensitive fund in it there is no trust.

The demand for liquidity goes above by the market alternatives and there are no any expected changes.

Capacity to augment liquidity through asset sales and/or securitization is strong and the Bank has an established record in accessing these markets.

The wholesale liabilities have a low volume with fixed options.

The bank is not weak to funding difficulties should a material adverse change occur in market perception.

The parent company provides the support which is strong.

Earnings and capital exposure from the liquidity risk profile is negligible.

- Moderate

The funding sources which are sufficient are available that provides a liquidity which is cost effective.

Funding is generally expanded, by a few providers that may share their common objectives and their economic influences, but no significant concentrations. The wholesale funding is clear and it has a modest reliance. The market alternatives that is available in order to meet the demand for liquidity on reasonable terms.

The Bank possesses the potential capacity to expand liquidity through asset sales and/or securitization. The bank has a modest experience in order to access these markets.

Some wholesale funds contain embedded options, but potential impact is not significant.

The Bank is not excessively vulnerable to funding difficulties should a material. The adequate support is provided by the parent company.

Earnings or capital exposure from the liquidity risk profile is manageable.

- High

Funding sources and liability structures suggest current or potential difficulty in maintaining long-term and cost-effective liquidity.

Borrowing sources may be concentrated in a few providers or providers with common investment objectives or economic influences. A significant reliance on wholesale funds is evident.

Liquidity needs are increasing, but sources of market alternatives at reasonable terms, costs, and tenors are declining.

The bank exhibits little capacity or potential to augment liquidity through asset sales or securitization. A lack of experience accessing these markets or unfavorable reputation may make this option questionable.

Material volumes of wholesale funds contain embedded options. The potential impact is significant.

The bank's liquidity profile makes it vulnerable to funding difficulties should a material adverse change occur.

Parent company provides a little or unknown support.

Potential exposure to loss of earnings or capital due to high liability costs or unplanned asset reduction may be substantial.

Liquidity Risk Management

Achieving best practice

Managing liquidity risk is often about applied common sense, like operational risk it requires a firm-wide approach and this places a high demand on the right processes and procedures.

Any management information system used to mitigate liquidity risk should be:

Accurate

The best way of encouraging accuracy is to keep reporting simple.

Communicative

Report and information should speak plainly.

Regular

Timely reporting allows managers to judge changes in the market and their organization's liquidity profile.

Comprehensive

Must reflect your organizational reality, such as different entities, jurisdictions and regulations.

Realistic

Scenario must be rigorous if risk is to be identified in real situations.

Quality of Liquidity Risk Management

The following indicators, as appropriate, should be used when assessing the quality of liquidity risk management.

- Strong

The polices are approved by the board and communicate guidelines effectively for the liquidity risk management and responsibilities are designated.

The liquidity risk management process is effective in identifying, measuring, monitoring, and controlling liquidity risk. The process of liquidity risk management is effective for identifying liquidity risk, for measuring, monitoring, and controlling the liquidity risk.

A sound culture reflects that has proven.

Liquidity risk is fully understood by the management in all the aspects.

Management anticipates and responds well to changing market conditions.

The contingency funding plan is well-developed, effective and useful. The plan incorporates reasonable assumptions, scenarios, and crisis management planning, and is tailored to the needs of the institution.

Management information systems focus on significant issues and produce timely, accurate, complete, and meaningful information to enable effective management of liquidity.

Internal audit is comprehensive and effective.

The scope and frequency are reasonable.

- Satisfactory

Polices are approved by the Board which communicate adequately guidance for liquidity risk management and responsibilities are assigned.

There may be a minor weakness present.

The liquidity risk management process is generally effective in identifying, measuring, monitoring, and controlling liquidity.

There may be minor weaknesses given the complexity of the risks undertaken, but these are easily corrected.

The key aspects of liquidity risk are reasonably understands by the management.

Management adequately responds to changes in market conditions when changes occur in the market conditions the management respond adequately.

The plan of contingency funding is adequate.

The plan is current, reasonably addresses most relevant issues, and contains an adequate level of detail including multiple scenario analysis.

The plan may require minor refinement.

Management information systems adequately capture concentrations and rollover risk, and are timely, accurate, and complete.

Recommendations are minor and do not impact effectiveness.

Internal audit is reasonable.

Any weaknesses are minor and do not impair effectiveness or reliance on audit findings.

- Weak

The Board has approved policies which are insufficient or incomplete.

In one or more material respects the policy is incomplete

The process of liquidity risk management is useless in identifying, monitoring and controlling the liquidity risk.

This may be true in one or more material respects, given the complexity of the risks undertaken. The liquidity risk does not fully understand by the management. In the conditions when the market changes the management does not take any timely or suitable actions and do not participate.

The contingency funding plan is inadequate or nonexistent.

The plan may not consider cost-effectiveness or availability of funds in a non-investment grade or CAMEL "3" environment.

The information systems of management are deficient. The plan may be there but they do not adopted by the institutions, it is not reasonable, or they are not implemented as it should be.

The information which is material may be a incomplete or lacking.

Due to one or more material deficiencies the internal auditor coverage is missing or useless.

Common Problems and Misconceptions

Liquidity risk is one of the least understood and most underestimated risks that financial markets participants are exposed to.

Reasons for this include:

- âUnder normal market conditions, liquidity problems are not observed
- Liquidity risk does not lend itself to readily usable measures
- Despite specific BIS recommendations, liquidity risk management is left out of capital adequacy calculations due to a lack of control and regulation
- 'Liquidity management' is often confused with 'liquidity risk management'
- Market and credit risk management focus on assets, while liquidity risk can stem from liabilities as well

Liquidity risk is also different in nature to market and credit risk and needs to be thought of differently;

â€¢ Normal markets analyses (expected or going-concern situations) are insufficient; liquidity risk can only be understood with scenario-based stress testing

â€¢ Historical measures of liquidity are irrelevant; prospective views are essential

â€¢ Liquidity risk cannot be readily hedged, and can only be militated against through rigorous monitoring and controls â€¢ The pricing of many instruments does not properly charge for liquidity.

Equity Risk

Investing cash in a company's stock is usually more risky than investing in so-called 'risk free' investments, such as government bonds. This is called equity risk.

We must have heard about equity risk in relation to equity risk premium – the larger return investors expect to receive for taking their money out of 'risk free' investments and taking on equity risk by investing in the stock market instead.

The risks of investing in equity include share price falls, receiving no dividends or receiving dividends lower in value than expected. They also include the risk that a company restructure may make it less profitable. Alternatively a company may fail. If this happens, you may be at the end of a long list of creditors and therefore risk not get the value of your investment back.

Equity risk premium is defined as "excess return that an individual stock or the overall stock market provides over a risk-free rate". This excess compensates investors for taking on the relatively higher risk of the equity market. The size of the premium can vary as the risk in the stock, or just the stock market in general, increases. For example, higher risks have a higher premium. The concept of this is to entice investors to take on riskier investments. A key component in this is the risk-free rate, which is quoted as "the rate on longer-term government bonds". These are considered risk free because there is a low chance that the government will default on its loans. However, the investment in stocks isn't guaranteed, because businesses often suffer downturns or go out of business.

To calculate the equity-risk premium, subtract the risk free rate from the return of a stock over a period of time. For example, if the return on a stock is 17% and the risk-free rate over the same period of time is 9%, then the equity-risk premium would be 8% for the stock over that period of time.

Risk Premium

A risk premium is the return in excess of the risk-free rate of return an investment is expected to yield; an asset's risk premium is a form of compensation for investors who tolerate the extra risk, compared to that of a risk-free asset, in a given investment. For example, high-quality corporate bonds issued by established corporations earning large profits typically have very little risk of default. Therefore, such bonds pay a lower interest rate, or yield, than bonds issued by less-established companies with uncertain profitability and relatively higher default risk.

Think of a risk premium as a form of hazard pay for your investments. Just as employees who have relatively dangerous jobs receive hazard pay as compensation for the risks they undertake, risky investments must provide an investor with the potential for larger returns to compensate for the risks of the investment.

Risk Compensation

Investors expect to be properly compensated for the amount of risk they undertake in the form of a risk premium, or additional returns above the rate of return on a risk-free investment such as U.S. government-issued securities. In other words, investors risk losing their money because of the uncertainty of a potential investment failure on the part of the borrower in exchange for receiving extra returns as a reward if the investment is profitable. Therefore, the prospect of earning a risk premium does not mean investors can actually get it because it is possible the borrower may default absent a successful investment outcome.

Earnings Reward

A risk premium can be a true earnings reward as some risky investments are inherently more profitable when and if they come through as an investment success. Investments with certainties and predictable outcomes are not likely to become business breakthroughs when already operating in well-penetrated markets. Only novel and risky business and investment initiatives could potentially offer above-average returns the borrower may then use as an earnings reward for investors. This is one underlying incentive that has encouraged some investors to seek riskier investments, knowing there could be potentially bigger payoffs.

Premium Cost

A risk premium can be costly for borrowers, especially when their investments are not potentially the most prosperous ones. The more risk premium they pay investors as risk compensation the more financial burden they may take on, which likely hurts the very success of their investments and increases the chance of a default. With this perspective in mind, it is in the best interest of investors themselves to reconsider the level of risk premium they demand, or else they must be prepared to fight over debt collections in the event of a default. In many borrowing-laden bankruptcies, for example, investors only receive back cents on the dollar on their investment, despite prior promises of a risk premium.

Formula

$$Risk\ Premium = r_a - r_f$$

$$r_a = asset\ or\ investment\ return$$

$$r_f = risk\ free\ return$$

The formula for risk premium, sometimes referred to as default risk premium, is the return on an investment minus the return that would be earned on a risk free investment. The risk premium is the amount that an investor would like to earn for the risk involved with a particular investment.

For example, in the US treasury bill (T-bill) is generally used as the risk free rate for calculations in the US, however in finance theory the risk free rate is any investment that involves no risk.

Risk Premium of the Market

The risk premium of the market is the average return on the market minus the risk free rate. The term the market in respect to stocks can be connoted as an entire index of stocks such as the S&P 500 or the Dow. The market risk premium can be shown as:

$$Market\ Risk\ Premium = R_m - R_f$$

The risk of the market is referred to as systematic risk. In contrast, unsystematic risk is the amount of risk associated with one particular investment and is not related to the market. As an investor diversifies their investment portfolio, the amount of risk approaches that of the market. Systematic and unsystematic risk and their relation to returns is where the many clichés about diversifying your investment portfolio is derived.

Risk Premium on a Stock using CAPM

The risk premium of a particular investment using the capital asset pricing model is beta times the difference between the return on the market and the return on a risk free investment.

$$Expected\ Return = r_f + \underbrace{\beta\left(r_m - r_f\right)}_{risk\ premium}$$

The return on the market minus the return on a risk free investment is called the market risk premium. From here, the capital asset pricing model can be rewritten as

$$Expected\ Return = r_f + \underbrace{\beta\left(Market\ Risk\right)}_{risk\ premium}$$

Risk-adjusted Return on Capital

As its name suggests, risk-adjusted return on capital analysis (RAROC) is a method for factoring risk into the computation and evaluation of financial returns. It may be applied to individual assets such as loans or trading positions, to complete portfolios, to business units, and even to entire lines of business. Properly performed, it ensures that all units are charged the same cost of capital rates, effectively levelling the playing field for managers and traders whose decisions are being evaluated. This topic illustrates how institutions can apply RAROC methodology to derivatives (in case, a simple interest rate swap) to ensure that products are providing acceptable returns on a risk-adjusted basis.

The basic premise underlying the RAROC method is that riskier products and ventures create greater potential for loss than less risky ventures. Losses that actually occur will ultimately reduce the capital available to the business. Riskier ventures should therefore generate higher profits to compensate for the greater risks they create. RAROC adjusts for higher risk by allocating higher amounts of capital to riskier projects. The riskier venture must therefore earn more absolute profit to achieve the same rate of return on capital as a less risky venture.

With RAROC, the amount of capital assigned to a product or unit is generally set equal to the highest loss that the unit is likely to realize over a given period. In the case of an individual instrument, this amount does not represent the full face or notional value, but the change in market value that would result from the most adverse change in interest rates, currency exchange values, or credit default rates that can reasonably be expected to take place.

This largest foreseeable change is usually estimated from historical data. Analysts might see, for example, that in the past five years interest rate fluctuations have averaged ± n basis points per year. About 68% of all outcomes will fall within one standard deviation (*) of this historical mean, and 99% will fall within three standard deviations.

Determining the largest probable exposure is a matter of judgment and experience. A company experienced in managing a certain type of risk might feel comfortable estimating its largest foreseeable exposure as n + 1*, while a conservative firm might want to increase its estimate to n + 3*. An even more conservative firm might adopt a worst case scenario, such as setting the largest foreseeable loss equal to the maximum change seen over a period.

A Fixed/Floating Interest Rate Swap

Interest rate swaps are commonly used to hedge rate exposures. The following example will illustrate the RAROC analysis for a simple swap:

Suppose a manufacturing firm with a sub-investment grade credit rating (Ba1) wants to obtain fixed-rate funds for five years for plant expansion, but does not want to pay the high rate required by the bond market. A multinational bank with a higher credit rating (Aa) wants floating rate funds to match short-term assets, or may simply want to earn the swap fee income.

The fact that differences in short-term borrowing rates between the Ba1 and Aa borrowers are significantly less than differences in their long-term borrowing rates provides the economic rationale for the swap. The manufacturer must pay more for corresponding short-term funds than the bank, but these higher short-term borrowing rates are still less than the cost savings obtained in the long-term market.

Both parties can therefore benefit from a fixed/floating swap in which the bank pays the manufacturer a floating rate while the manufacturer pays the bank a fixed rate over a given period, e.g., five years.

Suppose the notional value of the swap is USD10,000,000 with quarterly payments over a five-year term. While the fixed and floating rates are different, the swap will be structured such that interest rate projections make the swap have a current net present value of zero.

As the counterparty that will receive fixed rate payments and pay out floating rate payments, the bank faces two separate risk scenarios:

- Interest rate risk when interest rates rise. Rising rates reduce the NPV of the fixed payments the bank receives and increase the floating rate it pays. (Note that in this situation the bank does not incur credit risk. If the counterparty defaults on payments, the bank will be better off.)
- Credit risk when interest rates fall. Declining rates increase the NPV of the fixed rate payments the bank receives and decrease the floating rate payments it makes. The swap

becomes an income-producing asset; the only risk to the bank is that its counterparty will default on the agreement.

Formula

The formula for RAROC is:

RAROC = (Revenue – Expenses – Expected Loss + Income from Capital) / Capital

In this formula, expected loss equals the average loss expected over a period of time.

As an example, assume Project A needs $500,000 in capital. Revenue from the project is expected to be $125,000 and expenses total $40,000. The industry average expected loss on a project of this type is $25,000, and the income from the capital in the project equals $10,000. Project B is a very different type of project. It has capital requirements of $100,000; revenue and expenses are expected to be $15,000 and $5,000 respectively. The expected loss is $2,000, and the income from the capital is $0. Based on these numbers, the RAROCs are:

> Project A: ($125,000 – $40,000 – $25,000 + $10,000) / $500,000 = $70,000 / $500,000 = 14%
>
> Project B: ($15,000 – $5,000 – $2,000 + $0) / $100,000 = $8,000 / $100,000 = 8%

The RAROC calculations show that Project A is the better investment. RAROC is an easy formula that can help any business owner, analyst, or accountant quickly gain insights into how different types of projects perform after adjusting for the projects' inherent risks.

Risk Reward Ratio

Risk-reward ratio is a formula used to measure the expected gains of a given investment against the risk of loss.

Risk-reward ratio is typically expressed as a figure for the assessed risk separated by a colon from the figure for the prospective reward. While the acceptable ratio can vary, trade advisers and other professionals often recommend a ratio between 2:1 and 3:1 to determine a worthy investment. Typically, the ratio quantifies the relationship between the potential dollars lost, should the investment or action fail, versus the dollars realized if all goes as planned.

Investors use the risk-reward ratio to determine the viability or worthiness of a given investment. They sometimes limit risk by issuing stop-loss orders, which trigger automatic sales of stock or other securities when they hit a specific value. Without such a mechanism in place, risk is potentially unlimited, which renders the risk-reward ratio incalculable.

Calculating the RRR

Let's say the distance between your entry and stop loss is 50 points and the distance between the entry and your take profit is 100 points.

Then the reward risk ratio is 2:1 because 100/2 = 2.

Reward Risk Ratio Formula:

RRR = (Take Profit – Entry) / (Entry – Stop loss)

and vice versa for a sell trade

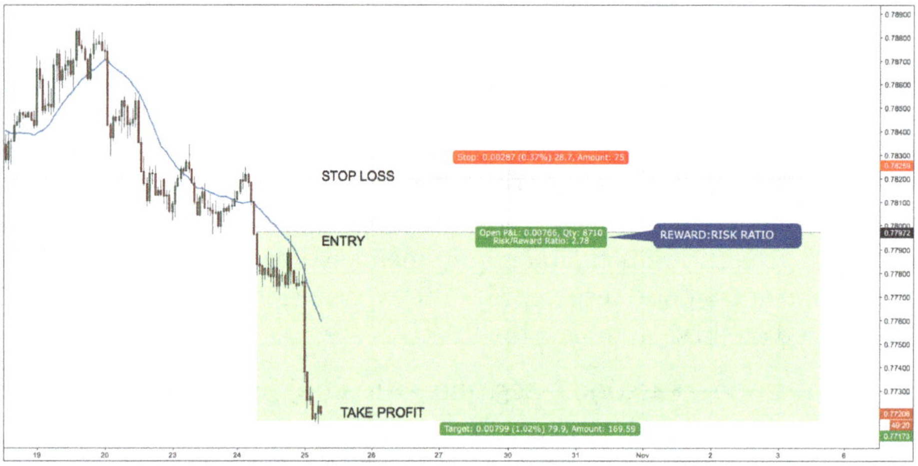

Rate of Return

Required rate of return is the minimum acceptable return on investment sought by individuals or companies considering an investment opportunity.

Investors across the world use the required rate of return to calculate the minimum return they would accept on an investment, after taking into consideration all available options. When calculating the required rate of return, investors look at overall market returns, risk-free rate of return, volatility of the stock and overall project cost. The required rate of return drives the type of investments that can be made. For instance, someone requiring a higher rate of return would necessarily have to look at riskier investments. Finance professionals routinely calculate the required rate of return for purchasing new equipment, new product rollouts and potential mergers. For example: an investor who can earn 10 per cent every year by investing in US Bonds, would set a required rate of return of 12 per cent for a riskier investment before considering it.

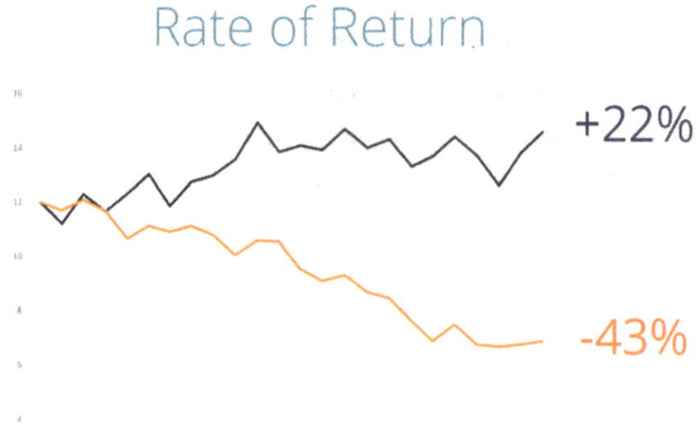

Formula for Rate of Return

The standard formula for calculating ROR is as follows:

$$\text{Rate of Return} = \frac{\text{Ending value of investment - Begining value of investment}}{\text{Beginning value of investment}} \times 100$$

Keep in mind that any gains made during the holding period of the investment should be included in the formula. For example, if a share costs $10 and its current price is $15 with a dividend of $1 paid during the period, the dividend should be included in the ROR formula. It would be calculated as follows:

(($15 + $1 – $10) / $10) x 100 = 60%

Rate of Return Calculation Example

Adam is a retail investor and decides to purchase 10 shares of Company A at a per unit price of $20. Adam holds onto shares of Company A for 2 years. In that time frame, Company A paid yearly dividends of $1 per share. After holding them for 2 years, Adam decides to sell all 10 shares of Company A at an ex-dividend price of $25. Adam would like to determine the rate of return during the two years he owned the shares.

To determine the rate of return, first calculate the amount of dividends he received over the two-year period:

10 shares x ($1 annual dividend x 2) = $20 in dividends from 10 shares

Next, calculate how much he sold the shares for:

10 shares x $25 = $250 (Gain from selling 10 shares)

Lastly, determine how much it cost Adam to purchase 10 shares of Company A:

10 shares x $20 = $200 (Cost of purchasing 10 shares)

Plug all the numbers into the rate of return formula:

= (($250 + $20 – $200) / $200) x 100 = 35%

Therefore, Adam realized a 35% return on his shares over the two-year period.

Annualized Rate of Return

Note that the regular rate of return describes the gain or loss, expressed in a percentage, of an investment over an arbitrary time period. The annualized ROR, also known as the Compound Annual Growth Rate (CAGR), is the return of an investment over each year.

Formula for Annualized ROR

The formula of annualized ROR is as follows:

$$\text{Annualized Rate of Return} = \left(\frac{\text{Ending value of investment}}{\text{Beginning value of investment}} \right)^{\frac{1}{\#\text{ of year}}} - 1$$

Similar to the simple rate of return, any gains made during the holding period of this investment should be included in the formula.

Example of Annualized Rate of Return

Let us revisit the example above and determine the annualized ROR. Recall that Adam purchased 10 shares at a per unit price of $20, received $1 in dividends per share each year, and sold the shares at a price of $25 after 2 years. The annualized ROR would be as follows:

$$((\$250 + \$20) / \$200)^{1/2} - 1 = 16.1895\%$$

Therefore, Adam made an annualized return of 16.1895% on his investment.

Alternative Measures of Return

Return can mean different things to different people, and it's important to know the context of the situation to understand what they mean. In addition to the above methods for measuring returns, there several other types of formulas.

Common alternative types of returns include:

- Internal Rate of Return (IRR)
- Return on Equity (ROE)
- Return on Assets (ROA)
- Return on Investment (ROI)
- Return on Invested Capital (ROIC)

Internal Rate of Return

The internal rate of return is a discounting cash flow technique which gives a rate of return that is earned by a project. We can define the internal rate of return as the discounting rate which makes a total of initial cash outlay and discounted cash inflows equal to zero. In other words, it is that discounting rate at which the net present value is equal to zero.

IRR is a prominent technique for evaluation of big projects and investment proposals widely used by management of the company, banks, financial institution etc. for their various purposes. The calculation of an IRR is little tricky. It is advantageous in terms of its simplicity and it has certain disadvantages in the form of limitations under certain special conditions.

Example of Internal Rate Return (IRR)

Explanation of internal rate of return with an example would probably create a better and correct picture in mind.

Suppose a company is investing in a simple project which will fetch five thousand dollars in the next three years and the initial investment in the Definition of Internal Rate of Return (IRR) and its Explanation with Example, Calculation, Interpretation, Advantages and Disadvantages project is say ten thousand dollars. The internal rate of return is 23.38%. It makes the decision making very simple. We just need to compare these percentage returns to the one which we can get by investing somewhere.

Calculation of Internal Rate of Return

We have stated the IRR of 23.38% above in our example. We will understand the calculation using the same example and find out the stated IRR. Formula / Equation of IRR is stated below:

Initial Cash Outlay + Present Value of all Future Cash Inflows = 0

- -10,000 + 5000 / (1 + IRR)1 + 5000 / (1 + IRR)2 + 5000 / (1 + IRR)3 = 0

Finding out the IRR from above equation is not a simple equation solving exercise. We need to use either trial and error method or interpolation method to find out the required IRR which makes equation equal to zero. Trial and error is a method in which you keep trying arbitrary values to equate the equation whereas interpolation method is more scientific. We find two extreme values which give value of equation greater than zero and less than zero.

Year	Cash Flows	At 18%	At 25%
0	-10000	-10000	-10000
1	5000	4237.29	4000
2	5000	3590.92	3200
3	5000	3043.15	2560
Total		871.36	-240

At 25% calculation is nearer to 0. To find a percentage of IRR which makes it zero we will do the following calculation.

IRR = 25 – (25-18) * 240 / (871.36 + 240) Or,

IRR = 18 + (25-18) * 871.36 / (871.36 + 240)

The will give an answer of 23.49% which almost same as 23.38%. We can find quite exact percentage by using a formula in Microsoft Excel. The formula used is "IRR".

Interpretation of IRR and Project Acceptance Criterion

IRR makes the decision making very simple. We just need to compare the IRR percentage to the one which we can get by investing somewhere or some other benchmarks which are decided by the management of evaluator. A project that is not able to get its investment back, this method will give a negative percentage. This is commonly called as Negative IRR.

Advantages of internal rate of return

The various advantages of internal rate of return method of evaluating investment projects are as follows:

- Time value of money

The first and the most important thing is that it considers the time value of money in evaluating a project which is a big lacking in accounting rate of return.

- Simplicity

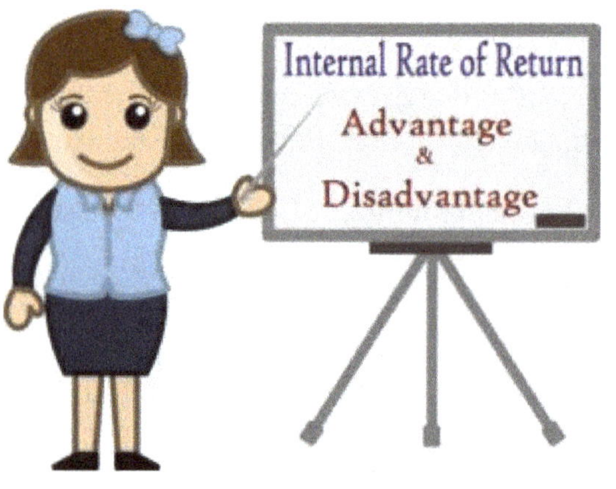

The most attractive thing about this method is that it is very simple to interpret after the IRR is calculated. It is very easy to visualize for managers and that is why this is preferred till the time they come across certain occasional situations such as mutually exclusive projects etc.

- Hurdle rate/required rate of return has not required

The hurdle rate is a difficult and subjective thing to decide. In IRR, the hurdle rate or the required rate of return is not required for finding out IRR. It is not dependent on the hurdle rate and hence the risk of a wrong determination of hurdle rate is mitigated.

- Required rate of return is a rough estimate

A required rate of return is a rough estimate being made by the managers and the method of IRR is not completely based on required rate of return. Once IRR is found out, we can compare it with the hurdle rate. If the IRR is far away from the estimated required rate of return, the manager can safely take the decision on either side and also keep a room for estimation errors.

Disadvantages of Internal Rate of Return

The method of internal rate of return does not prove very fruitful under certain special type of conditions which are discussed below:

- Economies of scale ignored

One pitfall in the use of IRR method is that it ignores the actual dollar value of benefits. A project value of $1000000 with 18% rate of return should always be preferred over a project value of $10000 with 50% rate of return. No need of analysis, we can apparently see that the dollar benefit of the former project is $180000 whereas the latter one is only $5000. Absolutely No Comparison. IRR method will rank the latter project, with very less dollar benefit, first simply because the IRR of 50% is higher than 18%.

- Impractical implicit assumption of reinvestment rate

While analysing a project with IRR method, it implicitly assumes that the positive future cash flows are reinvested at IRR. If a project has low IRR, it will assume reinvestment at a low rate of return and on the contrary if the other project has very high IRR, it will assume reinvestment rate at the very high rate of return. This situation is practically not valid. At the time you receive those cash flows, having the same level of investment opportunity is rarely possible.

- Dependent or contingent projects

Many times, finance managers come across a situation when the project under evaluation creates a compulsion of investing in other projects. For example, if you invest in a big transporting vehicle, you would need to arrange a place for parking that also. Such projects are called dependent or contingent projects which have to be considered by the manager. IRR may permit buying of the vehicle but if the total proposed benefits are wiped off in arranging the parking space, there is no point investing.

- Mutually exclusive projects

Sometimes investors come across mutually exclusive projects which mean if one is accepted other cannot be accepted. Building a hotel or a commercial complex on a particular plot of land is an example of mutually exclusive projects. In such situations, knowing whether they are worth investing is not enough. The challenge is to know which one is the best. IRR will give a percentage interpretation value which is not enough.

- Different terms of projects

Consider two projects with different project duration. One ends after 2 years and the other ends after 5 years. The first project has an additional point of reinvesting the money which is unlocked at the end of the 2nd year for another 3 years till the other project ends. This point is not considered by IRR method.

- A mix of positive and negative future cash flows

When a project has some negative cash flow in between other positive cash flow, the equation of IRR is satisfied with more than one rate of return i.e. it reaches the trap of Multiple IRR.

Modified Internal Rate of Return

Modified internal rate of return, shortly referred to as MIRR, is the internal rate of return of an investment that is modified to account for the difference between re-investment rate and investment return.

Formula:

$$Modified\ Internal\ Rate\ of\ Return = \sqrt[n]{\frac{Terminal\ Value\ of\ Cash\ Inflows}{Present\ Value\ of\ Cash\ Outflows}} - 1$$

Where:

n	=	The number of years of investment.
Terminal Value	=	Future value of the net cash inflows from investment assumed to be re-invested at the rate of cost of capital *(or a specified re-investment rate where relevant)* over the investment period.

Example

A 3 year investment has cash inflows of $100,000 each year. Cost of capital is 10%.

Solution

$100,000 x 1.1² = 121,000 *(Year 1 inflows re-invested for 2 years)*

$100,000 x 1.1 = 110,000 *(Year 2 inflows re-invested for 1 years)*

$100,000 x 1.0 = 100,000 *(Year 3 inflows cannot be re-invested)*

Terminal Value 331,000

Present Value	=	Present value of the net cash outflows incurred during the investment period discounted at the cost of capital.

Example:

A project requires an initial investment of $100,000 and shall incur net cash outflows of $50,000 annually in years 1 and 2 on account of trading losses. Cost of capital is 10%.

Solution:

$100,000 ÷ 1.0 = 100,000 (initial investment)

$50,000 ÷ 1.1 = 45,455 (Year 1 cash outflows)

$50,000 ÷ 1.1² = 41,322 (Year 2 cash outflows)

Terminal Value 186,777

Explanation:

The calculation of IRR implicitly assumes that the positive cash flows earned during the life of a project are re-invested at the rate of the IRR until the end of the investment period. This could cause the IRR to be overly optimistic. MIRR was developed to counter this assumption.

MIRR calculates the return on investment based on the more prudent assumption that the cash inflows from a project shall be re-invested at the rate of the cost of capital. As a result, MIRR usually tends to be lower than IRR.

The decision rule for MIRR is very similar to IRR, i.e. an investment should be accepted if the MIRR is greater than the cost of capital. However, when evaluating multiple investments that are mutually exclusive (i.e. where selection of one investment would result in the abandonment of another investment), it is preferable to select investments with the highest NPV rather than the highest MIRR because NPV analysis offers a better measure of the impact of an investment on the wealth of the investor. Like IRR, MIRR should still be used to assess the sensitivity of the proposed investments in such cases.

Example:

Mr. A is considering an investment of $250,000 in a start up.

The cost of capital for the investment is 13%.

Following cash flows are expected:

Year	$
0	(250,000)
1	50,000
2	100,000
3	200,000

Calculate MIRR for the proposed investment and interpret your answer.

Solution:

Step 1: Calculate the Terminal value of Inflows:

Cash Inflow	Duration	Rate	Working	Terminal Value
50,000	2 years	13%	$(50{,}000 \times 1.13^2)$	63,845
100,000	1 years	13%	(100,000 x 1.13)	113,000
200,000	0 years	13%	-	200,000
				376,845

Step 2: Calculate the Present value of Outflows:

Cash Inflow	Duration	Rate	Working	Terminal Value
250,000	0 year	-		**250,000**

Step 3: Calculate MIRR

$$MIRR = \sqrt[n]{\frac{\text{Terminal Value of cash inflows}}{\text{Present Value of cash outflows}}} - 1$$

$$= \sqrt[n]{\frac{376,845}{250,000}} - 1$$

$$= 1.1466 - 1$$

$$= 0.1466$$

$$= 14.66\%$$

Step 4: Interpret

The investment should be accepted by Mr. A because the cost of capital (i.e. 13%) is lower than the MIRR (i.e. 14.66%).

The cost of capital will need to increase by more than 12.8%* before the investment becomes financially unviable.

$$\frac{^{*}14.66\% - 13\%}{13\%} = 12.8\%$$

Advantages

- MIRR overcomes 2 major drawbacks of IRR including the elimination of multiple IRRs in case of investments with unusual timing of cash flows and secondly the re-investment problem discussed earlier.
- Helps in the measurement of sensitivity of an investment towards variation in the cost of capital.

Limitations

- As with IRR, MIRR may lead to sub-optimal decision making when multiple investment options are being considered. As MIRR does not quantify the impact of different investments on the wealth of investors in absolute terms, NPV provides a more effective theoretical basis for selecting investments that are mutually exclusive (i.e. where the selection of one investment results in the abandonment of another investment, e.g. due to shortage of funds).
- MIRR can be hard to understand for people belonging from a non-financial background. The theoretical basis for MIRR is also disputed among academics.

Risk-Free Rate of Return

The risk-free rate of return is the theoretical rate of return of an investment with zero risk. The risk-free rate represents the interest an investor would expect from an absolutely risk-free investment over a specified period of time.

In theory, the risk-free rate is the minimum return an investor expects for any investment because he will not accept additional risk unless the potential rate of return is greater than the risk-free rate.

In practice, however, the risk-free rate does not exist because even the safest investments carry a very small amount of risk. Thus, the interest rate on a three-month U.S. Treasury bill is often used as the risk-free rate for U.S.-based investors.

Determination of a proxy for the risk-free rate of return for a given situation must consider the investor's home market, while negative interest rates can complicate the issue.

Currency Risk

The three-month U.S. Treasury bill is a useful proxy because the market considers there to be virtually no chance of the government defaulting on its obligations. The large size and deep liquidity of the market contribute to the perception of safety. However, a foreign investor whose assets are not denominated in dollars incurs currency risk when investing in U.S. Treasury bills. The risk can be hedged via currency forwards and options but affects the rate of return.

The short-term government bills of other highly rated countries, such as Germany and Switzerland, offer a risk-free rate proxy for investors with assets in euros or Swiss francs. Investors based in less highly rated countries that are within the eurozone, such as Portugal and Greece, are able to invest in German bonds without incurring currency risk. By contrast, an investor with assets in Russian rubles cannot invest in a highly rated government bond without incurring currency risk.

Negative Interest Rates

Flight to quality and away from high-yield instruments amid the long-running European debt crisis has pushed interest rates into negative territory in the countries considered safest, such as Germany and Switzerland. In the United States, partisan battles in Congress over the need to raise the debt ceiling have sometimes sharply limited bill issuance, with the lack of supply driving prices sharply lower. The lowest permitted yield at a Treasury auction is zero, but bills sometimes trade with negative yields in the secondary market. And in Japan, stubborn deflation has led the Bank of Japan to pursue a policy of ultra-low, and sometimes negative, interest rates to stimulate the economy. Negative interest rates essentially push the concept of risk-free return to the extreme; investors are willing to pay to place their money in an asset they consider safe.

Price Return

The price return is the rate of return on an investment portfolio, where the return measure takes into account only the capital appreciation of the portfolio, while the income generated by the assets in the portfolio, in the form of interest and dividends, is ignored. This contrasts with the total return, which does take into account the income generated in the portfolio.

Often, when the return of a stock market index is quoted in the press, the quoted returns concern price returns, rather than the total returns. Examples are the S&P 500 and the MSCI EAFE, which are typically quoted in terms of price return. This is clearly misleading, since, economically speaking, it is the total return that is the only thing that matters. Whether that return is generated in the form of cash income or in capital appreciation is irrelevant as long as one can always liquidate the investment to realise the capital appreciation into cash.

For the same reason, it is inappropriate to evaluate the skill of a portfolio manager by comparing the total return on the portfolio to the price return of an index. After all, the total return on the index will always exceed the price return on the same index, so the portfolio manager could simply outperform the price return of the index by investing in the index. Even so, the use of price indices is still quite common in the investment industry.

Accounting Rate of Return

Accounting rate of return (also known as simple rate of return) is the ratio of estimated accounting profit of a project to the average investment made in the project. ARR is used in investment appraisal.

Formula:

Accounting Rate of Return is calculated using the following formula:

$$\text{ARR} = \frac{\text{Average Accounting Profit}}{\text{Average Investment}}$$

Average accounting profit is the arithmetic mean of accounting income expected to be earned during each year of the project's life time. Average investment may be calculated as the sum of the beginning and ending book value of the project divided by 2. Another variation of ARR formula uses initial investment instead of average investment.

Decision Rule

Accept the project only if its ARR is equal to or greater than the required accounting rate of return. In case of mutually exclusive projects, accept the one with highest ARR.

Example: An initial investment of \$130,000 is expected to generate annual cash inflow of \$32,000 for 6 years. Depreciation is allowed on the straight line basis. It is estimated that the project will generate scrap value of \$10,500 at end of the 6th year. Calculate its accounting rate of return assuming that there are no other expenses on the project.

Solution:

Annual Depreciation = (Initial Investment − Scrap Value) ÷ Useful Life in Years

Annual Depreciation = (\$130,000 − \$10,500) ÷ 6 ≈ \$19,917

Average Accounting Income = \$32,000 − \$19,917 = \$12,083

Accounting Rate of Return = \$12,083 ÷ \$130,000 ≈ 9.3%

Example: Compare the following two mutually exclusive projects on the basis of ARR. Cash flows and salvage values are in thousands of dollars. Use the straight line depreciation method.

Project A:

Year	0	1	2	3
Cash Outflow	-220			
Cash Inflow		91	130	105
Salvage Value				10

Project B:

Year	0	1	2	3
Cash Outflow	-198			
Cash Inflow		87	110	84
Salvage Value				18

Solution

Project A:

Step 1: Annual Depreciation = (220 – 10) / 3 = 70

Step 2:

Year	1	2	3
Cash Inflow	91	130	105
Salvage Value			10
Depreciation*	-70	-70	-70
Accounting Income	21	60	45

Step 3: Average Accounting Income = (21 + 60 + 45) / 3

= 42

Step 4: Accounting Rate of Return = 42 / 220 = 19.1%

Project B:

Step 1: Annual Depreciation = (198 – 18) / 3 = 60

Step 2:

Year	1	2	3
Cash Inflow	87	110	84
Salvage Value			18
Depreciation*	-60	-60	-60
Accounting Income	27	50	42

Step 3: Average Accounting Income = (27 + 50 + 42) / 3

= 39.666

Step 4: Accounting Rate of Return = 39.666 / 198 ≈ 20.0%

Since the ARR of the project B is higher, it is more favorable than the project A.

Advantages

1. Like payback period, this method of investment appraisal is easy to calculate.
2. It recognizes the profitability factor of investment.

Disadvantages

1. It ignores time value of money. Suppose, if we use ARR to compare two projects having equal initial investments. The project which has higher annual income in the latter years of its useful life may rank higher than the one having higher annual income in the beginning years, even if the present value of the income generated by the latter project is higher.
2. It can be calculated in different ways. Thus there is problem of consistency.
3. It uses accounting income rather than cash flow information. Thus it is not suitable for projects which having high maintenance costs because their viability also depends upon timely cash inflows.

Average Accounting Return

The average accounting return method of evaluating business investments is based on using the accounting rate of return for a specified number of years to arrive at an average rate of return for the period. Typically, the average accounting return method is used as a tool for comparing potential profitability of two or more investment opportunities. Like most analytical tools, using this comparison method comes with its share of pros and cons.

Accounting Rate of Return

The accounting rate of return is calculated by subtracting depreciation from the total cash flow, then dividing the result of that calculation by the initial investment. The result is the percentage of the initial investment you can expect to earn for the period. The result is used to arrive at the average accounting return rate; the accounting rate of return for each year is added together then divided by the number of years included in the calculation.

Uses

While the average accounting return rate can be used as a tool for evaluating the purchase of new companies or stocks, the tool is typically used as a quick method of deciding on internal business investments. For example, if the budget allows for the purchase of a new piece of machinery that would increase productivity, the average accounting return rate would be used to determine how long it would take for the increased productivity from the machinery to pay off the initial investment.

Pros

Calculating the average rate of return is easy. Managers can quickly see whether an investment opportunity may be lucrative enough to justify doing further evaluation. Return to the example of purchasing new machinery to increase productivity. If the initial calculation shows the purchase will only garner a 2 percent increase in profits but investing in trucks to deliver products to the customers will reduce the shipping costs by 10 percent, then management should decide the reduced shipping costs is a better investment.

Cons

The biggest drawback in using the average accounting return method is it does not take into account the time value of money. This is the concept that money is worth a known amount today, but there is no certainty what the same amount of money will be worth in the future. In other words, you know what you can buy today with a given amount of money. You do not know what you can buy for the same amount of money tomorrow, and the longer it takes you to earn back your investment, the greater the risk involved with sustaining the purchasing power of that future money value.

Time-weighted Return

The time-weighted return (TWR) or time weighted rate of return (TWRR) of an investment is the buy-and-hold return that and investors will earn when they have bought the fund and held it passively over time. It differs from the dollar-weighted or money-weighted return, where we also take into consideration investors withdrawals and deposits over the life of the investment.

Time-weighted returns do not take into account the timing of inflows into and outflows out of the portfolio. Since fund managers, in general, do not have any control over the flows in and out of a portfolio, time-weighted rate of returns are an appropriate measure for performance in the context of mutual funds and other types of funds. They provide a measure of performance that is not influenced by the decisions made by investors (i.e. adding and withdrawing money). Now, let's go over to how to calculate time weighted returns.

Formula:

The time-weighted rate of return is fairly simple and is very similar to calculating the compounded rate of return. The time-weighted rate of return formula is the following

$$r_{twr} = (1+r_1)\cdot(1+r_2)\cdot(1+r_3)\cdot\ldots\cdot(1+r_T)-1$$

Example:

Let's consider a simple example that applies the above formula to a set of returns. Suppose we have a mutual fund manager that reports the following set of annual returns over the past 5 years; -5%, 7%, 3% – 2%, and 10%. Now we want to know what an investment at the start of this 5-year period would have yielded. To do this, we apply the above formula

$$r_{twr} = (1-0.05)\cdot(1+0.07)\cdot(1+0.03)\cdot(1-0.02)\cdot(1+0.1)-1$$

which equals 12.87%. This means that over a 5-year period, an investor will have earned a cumulative return of 12.87%. When we annualize this return, we find that the investor earned 2.5% per year, on average.

Time-weighted returns are very useful when analysing the buy-and-hold return that an investor would have earned.

Example:

Matthew invested $300,000 in December 2016. In October 2017, his portfolio value was $292,897 and he made a contribution of $18,555. In December 2017, the portfolio value was $298,984. How can Matthew calculate the time-weighted rate of return of his portfolio for the period January 1 to December 31, 2017?

Matthew needs to calculate first the portfolio return of the first sub-period from December 2016 to October 2017 during which no external cash flow (contribution or withdrawal) occurred.

TWRR1 = (V1 – V0) / V0 = ($341,897 – $300,000) / $300,000 = 0.1397

Then, Matthew needs to calculate the portfolio return of the second sub-period from October 2016 to December 2017 during which external cash flows occurred.

TWRR2 = (V1 – V0) / V0 = (($298,984 – ($292,897 + $18,555)) / ($292,897 + $18,555) = ($298,984 – $311,542) / $311,542 = -0.040

Now that the returns of both sub-periods are calculated, Matthew can calculate the time-weighted rate of return of his portfolio over the entire period January 1 to December 31, 2017 by linking the sub-period returns.

TWWR = (1+TWRR1) x (1+TWWR2) – 1 = ((1+0.1397) x (1-0.040)) – 1 = (1.1397 x 0.960) – 1 = 1.094 – 1 = 0.094 = 9.4%

Holding Period Return

Holding period return is the total return earned on an investment over its whole holding period expressed as a percentage of the initial value of the investment. It is calculated as the sum of total return (i.e. capital gain (i.e. ending value of investment minus opening value of investment) and any interest or dividends) divided by the opening value of investment.

There are two sources of return for any bond, common stock, real estate, etc.: (a) capital gain and (b) income. The capital gain or loss results from the movement in bond or stock or real estate price/value from the date of purchase to the date on which the holding period return is calculated. The income results from coupon payments, dividends, rents, etc.

Holding period return is not a standardized measure of return. A given holding period return might be for a single day or a 5-year period and we won't know. Comparison between holding period return on different investments directly is not appropriate. We need to find out the total time over which the return is calculated and then convert it to annualized holding period return.

Holding period returns for multiple periods can be connected using the time-weighted rate of return or money-weighted rate of return.

Formula:

Holding period return refers to total returns over the period for which an investment was held, usually expressed in percentage of initial investment, and is widely used for comparing returns from various investments held for different periods of time. It also captures any additional income from the investment apart from helping calculate the growth or decline in value over multiple periods.

$$\text{Holding Period Return (HPR)} = \text{Income} + \frac{(\text{End of period value- Initial value})}{\text{Intitial value}}$$

Here's the formula of Holding Period Return an alternative version of the formula can be used for calculating return over multiple periods from an investment. It is useful for calculating returns over regular intervals which could include annualized or quarterly returns. Here, t = number of years

$$Annualized\ HPR = \left\{ \frac{\left[\left(Income + End\ of\ period\ value - Initial\ value \right) \right]}{Initial\ value + 1/t_{-1}} \right\}$$

Alternatively, returns for regular time intervals can be calculated thus:

$$(1+\text{HPR}) = (1+r_1)\times(1+r_2)\times(1+r_3)\times(1+r_4)$$

Here, r_1, r_2, r_3, r_4 are periodic returns.

It can also be represented thus:

$$\text{HPR} = \left[(1+r_1)\times(1+r_2)\times(1+r_3)\times\ldots(1+r_n)\right]-1$$

Here, r = return per period

n = number of periods

Examples of formula:

Suppose if an individual bought a stock which paid dividends of $50 and its price reached $170 from the initial price of $140 at which it was bought a year ago.

Now, we can calculate the HPR as follows:

- HPR = [$50 + ($170 – $140)] / $140 = 57.14%

Now, we would try to calculate the annualized returns for the same stock over a period of 3 years. Let us suppose the stock paid dividends worth $50 each year and returns varied with 21% growth for the first year, followed by 30% returns for the second year and -15% returns for the third year.

Now, we would calculate the annualized HPR as below:

- HPR = [(1 + 0.21) x (1 + 0.30) x (1 – 0.15)] – 1
- = [(1.21) x (1.30) x (0.85)] -1 = 33.70%
- The result would be HPR of 33.71 for all 3 years.

The advantage of using this method is that it would help take into account effect of compounding over the years which would lead to a realistic outcome.

Explanation of holding period return formula

HPR can be used to calculate total returns for an investment for a single or multiple periods, including various forms of returns, which might be added improperly otherwise when calculating total returns. For instance, if someone holds a stock for a certain amount of time, and it pays dividends periodically, these dividends also need to be taken into account along with changes in stock prices. It would also require keeping in mind that rise in the value of investment during multiple periods of return lead to compounding effect, which might be left out in simpler calculations.

For instance, if an investment grew by 10% annually, it would be erroneous to assume that in two years the growth on initial value would be 20%. It has to be calculated taking into account 10% growth for the first year and then calculating 10% growth over 'this' amount for the 2nd year, leading to a total return of 21.1% in two years, instead of 20%.

Relevance and use of HPR Formula

One of the key applications of holding period return formula is in accurately calculating the effect of compounding while estimating total returns on an investment for multiple periods. Apart from that, it has great utility in comparing various investments held for different time intervals in terms of their total returns over these periods.

Expected Return

The expected return on an investment is the expected value of the probability distribution of possible returns it can provide to investors. The return on the investment is an unknown variable that has different values associated with different probabilities. Expected return is calculated by multiplying potential outcomes (returns) by the chances of each outcome occurring, and then calculating the sum of those results.

In the short term, the return on an investment can be considered a random variable that can take any values within a given range, with some distinct probabilities. The expected return is based on historical data, which may or may not provide reliable forecasting of future returns. Hence, the outcome is not guaranteed. Expected return is simply a measure of probabilities intended to show the likelihood that a given investment will, on average, generate a positive return, and what the likely return will be.

Expected Return

$$= R_1P_1 + R_2P_2 + \ldots + R_nP_n$$

Where;
R = Return expectation in a given scenario
P = Probability of the return being achieved in the scenario
n = Scenario number

The purpose of calculating the expected return on an investment is to provide an investor with an idea of the probable return on an investment that carries some level of risk, such as a stock or mutual fund. This gives the investor a basis for comparison with the risk-free rate of return, as well as with the eventual actual return that the investor receives. The interest rate on 3-month U.S. Treasury bills is often used to represent the risk-free rate of return.

Basics of Probability Distribution

For a given random variable, its probability distribution is a function that shows all the possible values it can take. It is confined to a certain range that is derived from the statistically possible maximum and minimum values of the given variable. Distributions can be of two types: discrete and continuous. Discrete distributions take only specific values within a given range, whereas a random variable following a continuous distribution can take any value within the given range. Tossing a coin has two possible outcomes and is thus an example of a discrete distribution. A distribution of the height of adult males, which can take any possible value within a stated range, is a continuous probability distribution.

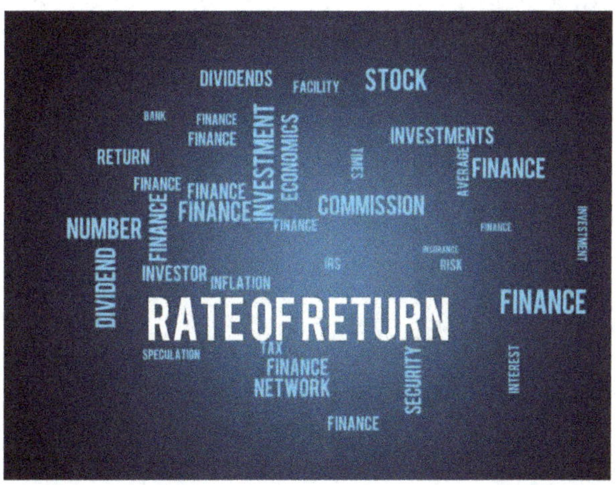

Calculating Expected Return for a Single Investment

Let us take an investment A, which has a 20% probability of giving a 15% return on investment, a

50% probability of generating a 10% return, and a 30% probability of resulting in a 5% loss. This is an example of calculating a discrete probability distribution for potential returns.

The probabilities of each potential return outcome are derived from studying historical data on previous annual returns on investment by the investment asset being evaluated. So, for example, the probabilities stated in this case might be derived from studying the performance of the asset over the previous 10 years and finding that it generated a 15% return on investment during two of those 10 years, a 10% return for five of the 10 years, and suffered a 5% loss for three of the 10 years.

The expected return on investment A would then be calculated as follows:

Expected Return of A = 0.2(15%) + 0.5(10%) + 0.3(-5%)

(That is, a 20%, or .2, probability times a 15%, or .15, return; plus a 50%, or .5, probability times a 10%, or .1, return; plus a 30%, or .3, probability of a return of negative 5%, or -.5)

= 3% + 5% – 1.5%

= 6.5%

Therefore, the probable long-term average return for Investment A is 6.5%.

Calculating Expected Return of a Portfolio

Calculating expected return is not limited to calculations for a single investment. Expected return can also be calculated for a portfolio. The expected return for an investment portfolio is the weighted average of the expected return of each of its components.(weighted by the percentage of the portfolio's total value that each component of the portfolio accounts for). Examining the weighted average of various portfolio assets can also help investors assess the diversification of their investment portfolio.

To illustrate the expected return for an investment portfolio, let's assume the portfolio is comprised of investments in three assets – X, Y, and Z – and that $2,000 is invested in X, $5,000 invested in Y, and $3,000 is invested in Z. Assume that the expected returns for X, Y, and Z have been calculated and found to be 15%, 10%, and 20%, respectively. Based on the respective investments of $2,000, $5,000, and $3,000 in each component asset, then the portfolio's expected return can be calculated as follows:

Expected Return of Portfolio = 0.2(15%) + 0.5(10%) + 0.3(20%)

= 3% + 5% + 6%

= 14%

Thus, the expected return of the portfolio is 14%.

Note that although the simple average of the expected return of the portfolio's components is 15% (the average of 10%, 15%, and 20%), the portfolio's expected return of 14% is slightly below that simple average figure, due to the fact that half of the investor's capital is invested in the asset with the lowest (10%) expected return rate.

Analysing Investment Risk

In addition to calculating expected return, investors also need to consider the risk characteristics of investment assets before making any buying decisions, in order to determine whether the portfolio's components are properly aligned with the investor's risk tolerance and investment goals.

For example, assume that two portfolio components have shown the following returns, respectively, over the past five years:

Portfolio Component A: 12%, 2%, 25%, -9%, 10%

Portfolio Component B: 7%, 6%, 9%, 12%, 6%

Calculating the expected return for both portfolio components yields the same figure: an expected return of 8%. However, when each component is examined for risk, based on year-to-year deviations from the average expected returns, you find that Portfolio Component A carries five times more risk than Portfolio Component B (A has a standard deviation of 12.6%, while B's standard deviation is only 2.6%). Standard deviation represents the level of variance that occurs from the average.

Role of Risk Tolerance and other Factors

The concept of expected return is part of the overall process of evaluating a potential investment for inclusion in one's portfolio. Although market analysts have come up with straightforward mathematical formulas for calculating expected return, individual investors will consider additional factors when putting together an investment portfolio that matches up well with their personal investment goals and level of risk tolerance.

For example, an investor might consider the specific existing economic or investment climate or conditions that are prevalent when they are making stock selections. During times of extreme uncertainty, investors will likely be inclined to lean toward generally safer investments and those with lower volatility, even if the investor is ordinarily more risk-tolerant. Thus, an investor might shy away from stocks with high standard deviations from their average return, even if their calculations show the investment to offer an excellent average expected return.

It's also important to keep in mind that expected return is calculated based on a stock's past performance. However, if an investor has knowledge about a company that leads them to believe that, going forward, it will substantially outperform as compared to its historical norms, they might choose to invest in a stock that doesn't appear all that promising based solely on expected return calculations. A helpful financial metric to consider in addition to expected return is the return on investment ratio (ROI), a profitability ratio that directly compares the value of increased profits a company has generated through capital investment in its business.

Although not a guaranteed predictor of stock performance, the expected return formula has proven to be an excellent analytical tool that helps investors forecast probable investment returns and assess portfolio risk and diversification.

References

- Pros-cons-average-accounting-return-method-34428: smallbusiness.chron.com, Retrieved 11 April 2018
- Time-weighted-return, finance-basics, finance-topics: breakingdownfinance.com, Retrieved 11 June 2018
- Time-weighted-rate-of-return, accounting-dictionary: myaccountingcourse.com, Retrieved 29 March 2018
- Holding-period-return-670669: xplaind.com, Retrieved 12 May 2018
- Holding-period-return-formula-hpr: wallstreetmojo.com, Retrieved 25 June 2018

Permissions

All chapters in this book are published with permission under the Creative Commons Attribution Share Alike License or equivalent. Every chapter published in this book has been scrutinized by our experts. Their significance has been extensively debated. The topics covered herein carry significant information for a comprehensive understanding. They may even be implemented as practical applications or may be referred to as a beginning point for further studies.

We would like to thank the editorial team for lending their expertise to make the book truly unique. They have played a crucial role in the development of this book. Without their invaluable contributions this book wouldn't have been possible. They have made vital efforts to compile up to date information on the varied aspects of this subject to make this book a valuable addition to the collection of many professionals and students.

This book was conceptualized with the vision of imparting up-to-date and integrated information in this field. To ensure the same, a matchless editorial board was set up. Every individual on the board went through rigorous rounds of assessment to prove their worth. After which they invested a large part of their time researching and compiling the most relevant data for our readers.

The editorial board has been involved in producing this book since its inception. They have spent rigorous hours researching and exploring the diverse topics which have resulted in the successful publishing of this book. They have passed on their knowledge of decades through this book. To expedite this challenging task, the publisher supported the team at every step. A small team of assistant editors was also appointed to further simplify the editing procedure and attain best results for the readers.

Apart from the editorial board, the designing team has also invested a significant amount of their time in understanding the subject and creating the most relevant covers. They scrutinized every image to scout for the most suitable representation of the subject and create an appropriate cover for the book.

The publishing team has been an ardent support to the editorial, designing and production team. Their endless efforts to recruit the best for this project, has resulted in the accomplishment of this book. They are a veteran in the field of academics and their pool of knowledge is as vast as their experience in printing. Their expertise and guidance has proved useful at every step. Their uncompromising quality standards have made this book an exceptional effort. Their encouragement from time to time has been an inspiration for everyone.

The publisher and the editorial board hope that this book will prove to be a valuable piece of knowledge for students, practitioners and scholars across the globe.

Index

CPSIA information can be obtained
at www.ICGtesting.com
Printed in the USA
LVHW061323050721
691470LV00021B/691

9 781641 720953